GREAT TREASURY
OF MERIT

Also by Geshe Kelsang Gyatso

Meaningful to Behold
Clear Light of Bliss
Buddhism in the Tibetan Tradition
Heart of Wisdom
Universal Compassion
A Meditation Handbook
Joyful Path of Good Fortune
Guide to Dakini Land
The Bodhisattva Vow
Heart Jewel

GREAT TREASURY OF MERIT

A COMMENTARY TO THE PRACTICE OF
OFFERING TO THE SPIRITUAL GUIDE

Geshe Kelsang Gyatso

Tharpa Publications
London

First published in 1992

Tharpa Publications
15 Bendemeer Road
London SW15 1JX

Cover painting of Lama Losang Tubwang Dorjechang
by the Tibetan artist Chating Jamyang Lama
Frontispiece of the Field of Merit
by the Tibetan artist Jampa Tseten
Cover photo of Geshe Kelsang Gyatso by Robin Bath
Line illustrations by Ani Kelsang Wangmo

British Library Cataloguing in Publication Data
Gyatso, Geshe Kelsang 1932-
Great Treasury of Merit:
A Commentary to the Practice of
Offering to the Spiritual Guide
1. Mahayana Buddhism
I. Title
294.3422

ISBN 0 948006 16 1 – papercase
ISBN 0 948006 22 6 – paperback

Set in Palatino by Tharpa Publications
Printed on acid-free 250-year longlife paper
and bound in Great Britain by Biddles Ltd., Guildford

Contents

Illustrations

Acknowledgements

This book, *Great Treasury of Merit*, is an extensive commentary to the profound traditional Guru yoga practice, *Offering to the Spiritual Guide*, the gateway through which we can accumulate the merit necessary for successful Tantric practice. The book is based upon detailed and authoritative oral commentaries given by Venerable Geshe Kelsang Gyatso during courses held first at Manjushri Institute through the winter of 1979-80, and then at Madhyamaka Centre in 1986 and 1990. From the depths of our hearts we thank the author for his immeasurably great kindness in preparing this book, which will make these very precious and important teachings available throughout the English-speaking world.

Tapes of the respective original teachings were faithfully transcribed by Sylvie Shaw, Lucy James, and others, and initial editing of the transcript from Manjushri Institute was carried out by Michael Garside, whose draft was then typed onto disc by James Belither.

The full draft was passed on to Gen Thubten Gyatso for final editing, and checked closely by the author. It was then prepared for publication by Lucy James, Kelsang Zöpa, Bobby Goodman, Alexandra Roberts, and others in the Tharpa Editorial Office. Our thanks go to all of these dedicated students of the author for their excellent work.

May this book help all living beings to accumulate great merit, and thereby attain great happiness.

Roy Tyson, Director,
Manjushri Institute,
January 1991

Vajradhara

Introduction

Offering to the Spiritual Guide, or *Lama Chöpa* in Tibetan, is a special Guru yoga of Je Tsongkhapa that is related to Highest Yoga Tantra. It was compiled by the first Panchen Lama, Losang Chökyi Gyaltsän, as a preliminary practice for Vajrayana Mahamudra. Although the main practice is reliance upon the Spiritual Guide, it also includes all the essential practices of the stages of the path (Lamrim) and training the mind (Lojong), as well as both the generation stage and completion stage of Highest Yoga Tantra.

Guru yoga, or lamai näljor in Tibetan, is a special method for receiving the blessings of our Spiritual Guide. Here, the term 'Guru' does not imply that our Spiritual Guide should be Indian, nor does the term 'Lama' imply that our Spiritual Guide should be Tibetan. Our Spiritual Guide is any spiritual Teacher who sincerely leads us into spiritual paths by giving correct instructions. Thus our Spiritual Guide can be oriental or western, lay or ordained, male or female. These days, for example, it is quite possible to meet a Spiritual Guide who is a western lay female. The term 'yoga' in this context indicates a special way of viewing our Spiritual Guide.

All schools of Buddhism agree that the practice of Guru yoga, or relying upon a Spiritual Guide, is the root of the spiritual path and the foundation of all spiritual attainments. We can understand this from our ordinary experiences. For example, if we want to acquire special skills, become proficient at a particular sport, or learn to play a musical instrument well, we naturally seek a qualified teacher to instruct us. By following our teacher's example and sincerely applying his or her instructions, eventually we accomplish our aim and become just like our teacher. If reliance upon a qualified teacher is necessary for mundane achievements such as these, how much more necessary is it for spiritual attainments such as liberation or enlightenment?

There are two main streams within Buddhism: the Hinayana, or Lesser Vehicle, and the Mahayana, or Great Vehicle; and the practice of relying upon a Spiritual Guide is fundamental to both. According to the Hinayana, we should regard our Spiritual Guide as being *like* a Buddha and, with a mind of faith and devotion, offer gifts and service to him and repay his kindness by following his advice and practising his instructions. According to the Mahayana, however, we should regard our Spiritual Guide as an *actual* Buddha and, with a mind of faith, rely upon him sincerely in both thought and deed.

The ultimate goal of a Hinayana practitioner is the attainment of liberation. This depends upon practising the three higher trainings, and this in turn depends upon first developing the motivation of renunciation. All these attainments depend upon the kindness of a qualified Spiritual Guide. For example, the motivation of renunciation does not arise automatically in our mind but has to be cultivated using special methods. First we have to understand the unsatisfactory nature of samsara and develop a wish to escape from it. This depends upon having a clear understanding of impermanence, rebirth, karma, refuge, and the four noble truths. Without a Spiritual Guide to instruct us in these practices and to encourage us to train in them we will never gain these experiences.

Once we have developed renunciation we engage in the three higher trainings: training in higher moral discipline, training in higher concentration, and training in higher wisdom. To practise higher moral discipline we first need to receive vows from a qualified Spiritual Guide who then helps us to practise pure moral discipline by teaching us what is to be practised and what is to be avoided; and by setting an immaculate example for us to follow.

On the basis of our training in higher moral discipline we practise higher concentration by training in tranquil abiding. This entails overcoming the five obstacles by applying the eight antidotes. Without receiving instructions from a qualified Spiritual Guide we do not even know what these obstacles and antidotes are, let alone what to do about them. Thus it is only by relying upon a Spiritual Guide who gives instructions and guidance based on his own experience that we are able to progress through the nine mental abidings and eventually attain tranquil abiding.

Once we have attained tranquil abiding, if we then train in higher wisdom by placing our mind in single-pointed concentration on emptiness we will soon attain superior seeing, and with this we will eventually be able to eradicate our self-grasping and attain liberation from samsara. However, emptiness is a profound object, and it is impossible to gain a realization of it without the skilled instructions and guidance of a qualified Spiritual Guide. Therefore, all the stages of the Hinayana path to liberation, from initially generating renunciation through to the abandonment of self-grasping and the attainment of liberation, are accomplished only through the kindness of a qualified Spiritual Guide.

Just as reliance upon a qualified Spiritual Guide is essential for completing the Hinayana path, it is also essential for training on the Mahayana path. All the stages of the Mahayana path, from generating equanimity and great compassion through to the final attainment of Buddhahood, are accomplished only through the guidance and blessings of a Mahayana Spiritual Guide. To enter into the Mahayana path we must first generate the motivation of bodhichitta. Like renunciation, this motivation does not arise naturally but has to be cultivated using special methods such as the sevenfold cause and effect and equalizing and exchanging self with others. Without receiving instructions and guidance from a Mahayana Spiritual Guide we could never gain these precious realizations. Once we generate bodhichitta we need to receive

Bodhisattva vows from a Mahayana Spiritual Guide, who then instructs us in the practice of the six perfections and guides us on the five Mahayana paths and the ten Bodhisattva grounds until we attain the Mahayana Path of No More Learning, or Buddhahood. Without the inspiration of our Spiritual Guide's pure example, his unmistaken instructions, and his constant blessings, we would never complete this training.

If training in the Sutra stages of the path is impossible without relying upon a Spiritual Guide, it is completely unthinkable to enter into Tantric practices without relying upon a Tantric Master. Buddha's Tantric teachings are very difficult to understand and they are scattered throughout many scriptures without any clear indication as to the correct sequence in which they are to be practised. If we try to practise Tantra without relying upon a qualified Tantric Master we will only increase our confusion. In the scriptures it says that no matter how long we churn water we will never produce butter and, in the same way, no matter how long we try to practise Tantra without relying upon a qualified Spiritual Guide, we will never attain Tantric realizations. If, on the other hand, we find a fully-qualified Tantric Spiritual Guide, receive empowerments from him, rely upon him with deep faith, keep our vows and commitments purely, and practise sincerely the instructions on generation stage and completion stage, we can easily attain enlightenment within one short human life.

We can see therefore that all spiritual training, whether Hinayana or Mahayana, Sutra or Tantra, depends upon the guidance and blessings of a qualified Spiritual Guide. In the *Blue Scripture* Geshe Potawa says:

> The crown of all instructions gathered together
> Is not to forsake the holy Spiritual Guide.
> It is the treasury of all,
> The source of all good qualities such as faith
> and bodhichitta.

Also, in the *Condensed Meaning of the Stages of the Path* Je Tsongkhapa says:

The root of all that is good and auspicious,
And of all excellence now and in the future,
Is striving to rely properly in thought and deed
Upon the holy Spiritual Guide who reveals the path.
Seeing this you should please him by offering a
    dutiful practice,
Never forsaking him even at the cost of your life.
I who am a Yogi practised in this way,
You who seek liberation, please do the same.

He also says:

The kind Teacher is the source of all good qualities
Of virtue and excellence, both mundane and
    supramundane.

Also, the *Condensed Perfection of Wisdom Sutra* says:

Good disciples who respect their Spiritual Guides
Should always rely upon their wise Spiritual Guides.
If you ask why, qualities of wisdom arise from them;
They reveal the perfection of wisdom.
The Conqueror who possesses all supreme good
    qualities says
'The qualities of a Buddha depend upon the
    Spiritual Guide.'

There is never a time when we do not need to rely upon a Spiritual Guide. Even after we have attained enlightenment we still need to rely sincerely upon our Spiritual Guide so as to show a good example to others. For example, Avalokiteshvara's crown is adorned by Amitabha to show how he relies upon his Spiritual Guide. Similarly, Maitreya's crown is adorned by a stupa, symbolizing his reliance upon his Spiritual Guide, Buddha Shakyamuni.

A pure Spiritual Guide must have authentic spiritual attainments, hold a pure lineage, cherish the Buddhadharma, and with love and compassion give unmistaken teachings to his or her disciples. If we meet such a Spiritual Guide we should consider ourself to be very fortunate. We

Manjushri

should develop faith in him and rely upon him sincerely by practising purely what he teaches. Geshe Potawa says that if a pure disciple meets a pure Spiritual Guide it is not difficult for him or her to reach enlightenment.

Our mind is like a field, our Spiritual Guide's instructions are like seeds sown in that field, and our faith in our Spiritual Guide is like water that germinates these seeds. If these three come together we will quickly and easily harvest a rich crop of Dharma realizations. If we do not have these conditions at the moment we should pray that we will find them in the future.

Once we have met a qualified Spiritual Guide, the way to rely upon him is basically very simple. All we have to do is to develop faith in him and put his instructions into practice to the best of our ability. If we do this, our Dharma realizations will naturally increase and we will quickly attain enlightenment. We develop faith in our Spiritual Guide by regarding him as a living Buddha, the synthesis of all objects of refuge. Even though our Spiritual Guide may appear to us in an ordinary aspect we should avoid seeing faults in him and learn to see him as a Buddha instead. We need to develop deep faith in our Spiritual Guide and always keep a pure view of him. We should try to feel close to him, maintaining a happy and affectionate mind towards him at all times. We should regard our Spiritual Guide as our mother who cares for us and cherishes us, as our father who provides us with all we need and protects us from danger, as the moon that cools the heat of the delusions in our mental continuum, as the sun that dispels the darkness of ignorance in our mind, and as a kind benefactor who gives us the priceless gift of Dharma.

To meet a fully-qualified Spiritual Guide is infinitely more meaningful than to possess external wealth. Our Spiritual Guide is our real benefactor. He gives us the inner wealth of moral discipline, concentration, and wisdom, and eventually leads us to the supreme bliss of full enlightenment. Even if we have vast material wealth, if we lack these internal realizations, in reality we are impoverished. On the other hand, if through relying upon a Spiritual Guide we develop the realizations of the stages of the path to enlightenment within our mental continuum, we shall be truly rich, even if we have no material possessions. Therefore, we should not be preoccupied with external wealth and development but should put all our energy into relying sincerely upon a fully-qualified Spiritual Guide.

Putting our Spiritual Guide's instructions into practice is the supreme offering. According to Je Tsongkhapa's tradition, a qualified Spiritual Guide will be more pleased with his disciples' Dharma practice than with receiving material offerings. Even if we make prostrations all day long, or regularly give presents to our Spiritual Guide, such practices will have little power if we are not following the spiritual path he has taught us. On the other hand, if we practise our Spiritual Guide's instructions purely and with deep faith, even if we are unable to make physical prostrations or material offerings, we shall be continuously making offerings that delight our Spiritual Guide.

By practising Guru yoga sincerely, even someone who was formerly very evil can become enlightened; but without relying sincerely upon a Spiritual Guide even the most intelligent person will never become a Buddha. To begin with, Milarepa was very evil. Using black magic he killed thirty-six people before he met his Guru, Marpa. Later, by relying sincerely upon Marpa he was able to purify his mind completely, accumulate merit and wisdom, and finally attain enlightenment in that same life.

Our Spiritual Guide is a powerful field for accumulating merit, purifying negative karma, and receiving blessings. We need to accumulate merit to meet with success in our spiritual training. In the Sutras Buddha says that those who possess merit have no difficulty in fulfilling their wishes whereas those who lack merit find it hard, no matter how virtuous their wishes may be. Similarly, if we do not purify our previously accumulated negative karma it will function as an obstacle to pure Dharma realizations. Just as plants cannot grow in polluted soil, so Dharma realizations cannot grow in an impure mind. The practices of accumulating merit and purifying negativity, therefore, are essential preliminaries to successful Dharma practice. In general, all the Buddhas and holy beings are powerful objects before whom we can accumulate merit and purify our minds, but the supreme object is our own Spiritual Guide.

Similarly, all Buddhas are very kind because they bless the minds of sentient beings and reveal the Dharma, but our Spiritual Guide is kinder than all the Buddhas because he or she gives us blessings and Dharma instructions directly. Thus, in *Heruka Tantra* it says:

> He is the self-arisen Blessed One,
> Foremost amongst the Highest Yoga Tantra Deities;
> But the Vajra Master is superior to him
> Because he gives instructions.

Realizing this, we should seek a fully-qualified Spiritual Guide and rely upon him sincerely in both thought and deed.

In the *Perfection of Wisdom Sutra in Eight Thousand Lines* the story is told of a great Bodhisattva called Sadaprarudita who relied sincerely upon his Spiritual Guide, Dharmodgata, regarding him as more precious than his own life, and more important than all the Buddhas.

Even though he was a highly-realized meditator, Sadaprarudita longed to meet a Teacher who would explain the *Perfection of Wisdom Sutra* to him, for he realized that it was impossible to attain either liberation or enlightenment without realizing the meaning of this Sutra. Even though he had a strong wish to meet a qualified Spiritual Guide, and even though he wandered the length and breadth of the land in search of one, he was unable to find a Teacher who could give him the instructions he desired. So saddened was he by his failure to find a Spiritual Guide that he wept constantly. Others who knew him called him 'Sadaprarudita', which means, 'He who is constantly weeping'.

One day, while deep in meditation, Sadaprarudita received an extraordinary vision in which many Buddhas appeared directly before him. They told him that he had a close connection with a Bodhisattva called Dharmodgata and that he should seek him out and follow his instructions. Rising from meditation, Sadaprarudita set off in search of Dharmodgata. He travelled great distances and experienced many hardships, but his mind remained happy because he now knew that there was a Spiritual Guide who could give him the help he needed. Finally he discovered the whereabouts of Dharmodgata.

Sadaprarudita wanted to take some offerings to present to Dharmodgata, but he had no possessions at all. To raise some money with which to make offerings, he went to a nearby town and announced that he would sell his flesh to anyone who wanted it. The townsfolk assumed that he was crazy and ignored him, but the god Indra, seeing Sadaprarudita from the heavens, decided to test the sincerity of his intentions. Manifesting as an old man, he approached Sadaprarudita saying that he would buy some of his flesh. Sadaprarudita was delighted and immediately cut a piece of flesh from his thigh and gave it to him. The old man then said that he would also like some bone marrow. Sadaprarudita was even more delighted. Just as he was about to break his shin bone to extract some marrow, a young woman, the daughter of a local merchant, appeared on the scene and asked Sadaprarudita what he was doing. Sadaprarudita replied that he was selling his flesh and marrow so that he could make offerings to his Spiritual Guide. The woman asked how anyone could be so important that he would be prepared to go to such lengths to make offerings to him. Sadaprarudita explained that Dharmodgata would give him precious teachings on the perfection of wisdom and that by practising these instructions he would be able to attain enlightenment for the benefit of all living beings. Hearing this, the young woman developed great faith in Buddha and his teachings. She persuaded Sadaprarudita not to mutilate himself further, saying that she would ask her parents to donate the money he needed to make offerings.

At this point, Indra threw off his disguise and asked Sadaprarudita why the money was so important. Sadaprarudita replied that it was not the money that he needed but instructions on the path to enlightenment. Indra, seeing that Sadaprarudita's intention was genuine, offered to provide him with all the riches he required, but Sadaprarudita declined his offer, saying that he would now receive from the young woman's parents enough money to make offerings to Dharmodgata. He then set off with the young woman and many of her servants to meet Dharmodgata. They made offerings and received precious teachings on the perfection of wisdom, and by practising Dharmodgata's instructions they later attained full enlightenment.

If we think deeply about this story, we will see that there is nothing more precious than a qualified Spiritual Guide who can give us correct instructions on the path to enlightenment. If a great meditator such as Sadaprarudita, who was able to receive instructions directly from Buddhas, still needed to rely upon a Spiritual Guide, it goes without saying that we must find a qualified Spiritual Guide and rely upon him or her sincerely.

Je Tsongkhapa

The Pre-eminent Qualities of
Je Tsongkhapa and his Doctrine

The essence of Guru yoga is to develop strong conviction
that our Spiritual Guide is a Buddha, to make prostrations,
offerings, and sincere requests to him, and then to receive
his profound blessings. According to the Guru yoga of
Offering to the Spiritual Guide, we develop conviction that
our Spiritual Guide is the same nature as Je Tsongkhapa,
who is an emanation of the Wisdom Buddha Manjushri.
The commentary to this practice is presented under the
following two headings:

1 The pre-eminent qualities of Je Tsongkhapa and
  his doctrine
2 The Guru yoga of Je Tsongkhapa

THE PRE-EMINENT QUALITIES OF JE TSONGKHAPA
AND HIS DOCTRINE

One day, when Buddha Shakyamuni was giving teachings to his disciples, delivering the *King of Giving Instructions Sutra* (Tib. dam ngak pob pai gyal wo), a young boy,
who in reality was an emanation of Manjushri, appeared
before him. He offered Buddha a crystal rosary with the
prayer 'May I become the holder of the lineage of pure view
and pure deeds.' Buddha then prophesied that in the future
that boy would appear as a monk called Losang Dragpa at
a place called Ganden near Drikhung, and that he would
become the holder of the lineage of pure view and pure
deeds. Just as Buddha predicted, Je Tsongkhapa, whose
ordained name was Losang Dragpa, appeared in Tibet in
the fourteenth century and founded his first monastery,
called Ganden, near a place called Drikhung.

Although Je Tsongkhapa was an emanation of Manjushri who possessed clairvoyance and miracle powers, he did not appear as a special, exalted being, but manifested as an ordinary, humble practitioner. In this aspect he showed an immaculate example to others, gave pure teachings, and led thousands of people into correct spiritual paths. He spread a very pure Buddhadharma throughout Tibet, showing how to combine the practices of Sutra and Tantra, and in particular how to practise the Vinaya and Highest Yoga Tantra together.

Je Tsongkhapa was like a mother teaching her children. A mother patiently teaches her children everything they need to know, from how to eat and how to walk, through to how to read and how to write. In the same way, Je Tsongkhapa patiently taught the Tibetans everything they needed for their spiritual development, from the initial step of entering into a spiritual practice through to the ultimate attainment of Buddhahood. Clearly and unmistakenly, he taught how to practise step by step – how to take the initial step of entering into the Buddhadharma, how then to enter into the Mahayana, and finally how to enter into the Vajrayana and attain full enlightenment; and he also showed special methods to accomplish these results swiftly. The incomparable kindness of Je Tsongkhapa was celebrated by the first Dalai Lama, Je Gendundrub, in his *Song of the Eastern Snow Mountain*, in which he says:

For the fortunate people of Tibet, the Land of the
    Snows, your kindness, O Protector, is inconceivable.
Especially for myself, Gendundrub, a holder of nyomlä,
The fact that my mind is directed towards Dharma
Is due solely to your kindness, O Venerable Father
    and Sons.

From now until I attain enlightenment
I shall seek no refuge other than you.
O, Venerable Father and Sons
Please care for me with your compassion.

14

Although I cannot repay your kindness, O Protector,
I pray that, with my mind free from the influence of
   attachment and hatred,
I may strive to maintain your doctrine and cause it
   to flourish
Without ever giving up this endeavour.

Before Je Tsongkhapa appeared in Tibet there were many
other high beings practising Dharma, but most of them
revealed their spiritual attainments to others by displaying
clairvoyance, miracle powers, and so forth. Je Tsongkhapa
regarded such displays as of little value because they did
not help living beings to overcome their ignorance, which
is the principal cause of their suffering. If a Teacher displays
clairvoyance or miracle powers to his or her disciples, by
levitating in front of them for example, how does that help
them? Rather than helping, it may even cause hindrances.
The disciples may become suspicious or develop doubts,
and some may even feel uncomfortable in the knowledge
that their Teacher has the power to read their minds and
discover their innermost secrets. Such worries only cause
obstacles, both for the disciples and for the Teacher. In the
past, practitioners who have revealed their miracle powers
to others have been accused of practising black magic and
some have even found themselves in danger of their lives.
It was for these reasons that the Kadampa Geshes and Je
Tsongkhapa made a rule forbidding their followers to display their miracle powers. In the monasteries of Je Tsongkhapa's tradition any monk who made a public show of his
miracle powers would be asked to leave.
   Other traditions regard the display of miracle powers as
a sign of great attainment, but according to Je Tsongkhapa's tradition such demonstrations have little meaning.
After all, birds can fly in the sky and mice can travel
beneath the ground, but they remain as deluded as before,
and are no nearer to liberation or enlightenment as a result.
Moreover, during our countless former lives each one of us
has possessed miracle powers many times, but our minds

remain clouded in ignorance and we continue to take uncontrolled rebirths in states of suffering.

As a manifestation of the Wisdom Buddha Manjushri, Je Tsongkhapa realized that the best way to help living beings to overcome their ignorance was to set a good example and to give clear and profound teachings. Like a mother caring for her children, Je Tsongkhapa devoted his whole life to helping others eliminate their ignorance through his clear and profound teachings.

Je Tsongkhapa's teachings are like keys that unlock the meaning of Buddha's Sutras and Tantras. Without Je Tsongkhapa's works, simply by reading the scriptures we would find it impossible to discover Buddha's intention. These days we are able to practise the stages of the path to enlightenment, Lamrim, only because of the kindness of Je Tsongkhapa. The Lamrim teachings originated from Buddha himself, but they were arranged in their systematic form by Atisha, the great Indian Buddhist Master who was invited to Tibet by the king, Jangchub Ö. Everyone regards Atisha as very kind because he founded the pure tradition known as the Kadampa Tradition and because he wrote the original Lamrim text, *Lamp for the Path*, but if we look at this text we shall see that it is only a few pages long and that the complex meaning of all the stages of the path to enlightenment is condensed into very few words. Without explanation and commentary it is impossible for us to understand these teachings and put them into practice. It was Je Tsongkhapa who provided the essential explanations that enable us to practise Atisha's precious instructions. In his *Great, Middling,* and *Condensed Expositions of the Stages of the Path,* Je Tsongkhapa provides a completely clear and unmistaken guide to each of the essential practices of the path to enlightenment.

Je Tsongkhapa gave an especially clear and unmistaken explanation of profound emptiness according to the view of Protector Nagarjuna. Prior to Je Tsongkhapa's appearance in Tibet many practitioners had developed misunderstandings with respect to Buddha's teachings on emptiness.

Unable to distinguish the precise object of negation, they fell into the extremes of permanence and nothingness. Many Tibetans felt that if phenomena were completely empty of inherent existence it would be impossible to establish the infallibility of cause and effect, and so there would be no basis for practising moral discipline or other method practices such as compassion or bodhichitta. On the other hand, they felt that if there were a basis for the method practices, phenomena would exist from their own side, and consequently emptiness would be impossible. Je Tsongkhapa showed the errors in this way of thinking and clearly established that there is no contradiction between emptiness, the lack of inherent existence of all phenomena, and non-deceptive cause and effect. In this way he was able to establish the correct view of the middle way according to Nagarjuna's intention and thereby protect his followers from falling into the two extremes.

Besides Lamrim, Dharma practitioners today are also able to practise the special methods of training the mind, or Lojong. These practices, which are extracted from Lamrim and given particular emphasis, are powerful methods for generating a special bodhichitta through the practice of equalizing and exchanging self with others combined with the practice of taking and giving. As with Lamrim, the original instructions on Lojong are very brief and difficult for us to understand. For example, Geshe Chekhawa's root text, *Training the Mind in Seven Points*, is only two pages long. If we were to try to practise Lojong by relying upon this text alone we would find it very difficult to make progress. Je Tsongkhapa's commentaries unlock the hidden meaning of the texts on training the mind and enable us to put them into practice. We are able to practise the instructions on training the mind today only through the kindness of Je Tsongkhapa.

Je Tsongkhapa's works are also indispensable for the practice of Secret Mantra. If we were to try to practise Secret Mantra by relying upon the Tantras alone we would find the scriptures indecipherable. Without Je Tsongkhapa's commentaries to unlock their meaning, scriptures such as Vajradhara's *Root Tantra of Guhyasamaja*, or his *Heruka Root Tantra*, which also includes the instructions on *Vajrayogini Tantra*, would be like sealed treasure chests to which we could not gain access. In his Tantric teachings, Je Tsong-khapa explains the essential practices of all Tantric Deities. These days, for example, many people are able to practise the special yogas of Heruka and Vajrayogini only through the kindness of Je Tsongkhapa. Following Je Tsongkhapa's explanations, later Teachers wrote the exceptional sadhanas and commentaries of Heruka and Vajrayogini that are practised today.

From his profound wisdom Je Tsongkhapa presented a very special arrangement of Sutra and Tantra practices which, if followed sincerely, can lead to full enlightenment in one short human life. According to this arrangement we begin by practising Lamrim, the stages of the path, then we progress to Lojong, training the mind, and finally we advance to Vajrayana Mahamudra, which is the actual quick path to enlightenment. There is a Tibetan saying, 'chö ma nor chag lam lo sum', which means 'The unmistaken Dharma is Lamrim, Lojong, and Mahamudra.' Je Tsong-khapa taught how to incorporate all Dharma practices into this sequence. The first two, Lamrim and Lojong, are pre-liminary practices and Vajrayana Mahamudra is the actual practice. Many of Je Tsongkhapa's faithful followers have reached enlightenment in three years by practising the Vajrayana Mahamudra of the Gelugpa Tradition.

Before Je Tsongkhapa appeared in Tibet there were many misunderstandings and wrong practices with respect to Buddha's Tantric teachings. Many Tibetans felt that the practices of Tantra were incompatible with keeping pure Vinaya vows, and as a consequence they either abandoned Tantra for the sake of practising the Vinaya or they aban-doned the Vinaya for the sake of practising Tantra. Je Tsongkhapa refuted these wrong views and showed how all Buddha's teachings can be practised purely without contradiction. Externally he showed how to practise the pure moral discipline of the Vinaya by keeping all two hundred and fifty three vows of a fully-ordained monk immaculately; internally he showed how to engage in the vast practices of the Bodhisattva's deeds by maintaining pristine Bodhisattva vows; and secretly he showed how to practise the two stages of Secret Mantra, that culminate in the supreme union of bliss and emptiness, by cherishing his Tantric vows and commitments more dearly than his life. These remarkable qualities of Je Tsongkhapa are praised in a special dedication verse that is often recited in Dharma Centres:

> May I meet the doctrine of Conqueror Losang
>   Dragpa
> Who has a pure practice of stainless moral discipline,
> The courageous practice of the extensive deeds of a
>   Bodhisattva,
> And the yogas of the two stages to supreme bliss
>   and emptiness.

Although Je Tsongkhapa never made a public display of his miracle powers while he was alive, there were occasions when he revealed them privately. For example, at one time when he was residing in central Tibet he received many messages from his mother, who was a long way away in eastern Tibet, saying that she missed him very much and wanted him to return home. Because he was so busy helping others Je Tsongkhapa felt that he could not interrupt his work to make such a long journey and so to console his mother he drew a portrait of himself on a piece of paper and sent it to her through a messenger. When Je Tsongkhapa's mother received the portrait it spoke to her saying 'Don't worry, dear Mother, I am here.' Later the portrait was taken to Kumbum Monastery where it became a holy object of offering and prostration for thousands of monks.

When Je Tsongkhapa passed away, the whole country was overwhelmed with sorrow at the loss of their precious Teacher. Not only could they no longer see him directly but, since there were very few representations of him, most people were unable to see even his likeness. Consequently, many craftsmen set about making statues and painting thangkhas of him. Although Je Tsongkhapa had not publicly displayed his miracle powers while he was alive, after he passed away he performed many miracles through these statues and thangkhas. Eight statues in particular have since become very famous. They are known as:

1 Je she par ma (The Venerable One who Disappeared with a Smile)
2 Je nga dra ma (The Venerable One who is a Better Likeness)
3 Je shen pän ma (The Venerable One who is More Beneficial to Others)
4 Je ku thim ma (The Venerable One who Dissolved into the Body)
5 Je nam pur ma (The Venerable One who Rose into Space)
6 Je tsong pön gelek ma (The Venerable Chief Merchant Gelek)
7 Je tsö dog ma (The Venerable One who Pacifies Conflicts)
8 Je ling pur ma (The Venerable One Gone to Another Land)

The story of the first statue is as follows. At one time a humble practitioner tried to find a statue of Je Tsongkhapa for his retreat but was unsuccessful, so during his retreat he made a small statue and placed it on his shrine. For him this statue was like the living Je Tsongkhapa, and every day before beginning his meditation he made offerings and prostrations in front it. One day as he rose from meditation he noticed that the statue was gradually melting into light. As he watched, the statue suddenly smiled and, rising into space, completely disappeared. The meditator was astonished and could hardly believe what he had seen. After reflecting for a long time he decided to go to his Teacher to tell him what had happened. His Teacher was delighted and told him to make another statue exactly like the previous one. This he did, and it is this statue that subsequently became known as The Venerable One who Disappeared with a Smile.

The second and third statues were made by two craftsmen who were engaged in a friendly contest to see who was the more skilled at making statues. They took the two statues to a high Lama to adjudicate. As the Lama was examining them with a faithful mind, one statue spoke saying 'I am a better likeness.' Then the other statue retorted 'But I am more beneficial to others.' This is how these two famous statues received their names.

The fourth statue is named after one that belonged to a practitioner called Nyungnä Lama, whose main practice was the Guru yoga of Je Tsongkhapa. He used to keep a statue of Je Tsongkhapa on his shrine, and he regarded this statue as the living Je Tsongkhapa. Each day he would practise Guru yoga from going for refuge up to dissolving Guru Tsongkhapa into his heart. Because he practised so sincerely he developed a very pure heart and attained a special experience of concentration. One day, while visualizing Je Tsongkhapa dissolving into his heart, he experienced his statue actually dissolving into him, and when he rose from meditation the statue on his shrine had completely disappeared. After this he quickly attained many high realizations. News of this event spread and the craftsman who had made the statue became very famous. Later he made another statue of Je Tsongkhapa to which he gave the name, The Venerable One who Dissolved into the Body.

The fifth statue belonged to a monastery where it was often seen by one particularly sincere practitioner to rise into space and then return to its place on the shrine. Because of this, the statue became known as The Venerable One who Rose into Space.

The sixth statue was made by a government minister who was a faithful disciple of Je Tsongkhapa, and Je Tsongkhapa himself had blessed it. One day however an evil person out of jealousy stole the statue and, taking it a long way away, threw it into a large river. Some time later an important merchant called Gelek was travelling on horseback in that area when he noticed a brightly-coloured rainbow standing vertically in space, apparently emerging from the bed of a river. Thinking that this was an unusual sign, he decided to spend the night nearby. The next morning the rainbow was still there and so he decided to investigate further. Although the local people could see nothing in the river, Gelek was not convinced. Securing himself with ropes he waded into the icy river and dived to the bottom. There he found the statue of Je Tsongkhapa radiating brightly-coloured rainbow lights. When he came to the surface the onlookers were astonished to see that he had not drowned, and even more astonished to see the precious statue that he was holding. Since it was the chief merchant Gelek who retrieved the statue, it subsequently became known as The Venerable Chief Merchant Gelek.

The seventh statue comes from a part of eastern Tibet where at one time there was prolonged civil war. The local people longed for the fighting to stop and so they went to a nearby Lama who was renowned as a great meditator and asked him what they should do. He told them to construct a large statue of Je Tsongkhapa in their town and make offerings and requests in front of it. This they did and soon afterwards the fighting stopped and peace prevailed throughout the region. This statue later became known as The Venerable One who Pacifies Conflicts.

The eighth statue is named after a much revered statue of Je Tsongkhapa that mysteriously disappeared from Tibet. Pure practitioners with clairvoyance realized that the statue had gone to another land far away where the ground was strewn with diamonds and where the language and customs were completely different. They also realized that the statue was benefiting the people of that land, and so they decided to make another one similar to it and named it The Venerable One Gone to Another Land.

Miracles such as these are not confined to ancient times. Even today there are many statues and other representations of Je Tsongkhapa that possess special qualities.

For example, there was one Geshe called Geshe Jatse whom I knew well when I was at Sera Monastery in Tibet. When he had completed his Geshe training he withdrew to a mountain cave to do retreat and remained there, living just like Milarepa, for the rest of his life. When he died his many disciples, together with a large number of onlookers, went to the cave to pay their respects and, to their astonishment, saw that Geshe Jatse's statue of Je Tsongkhapa had grown teeth and hair. I heard this account directly from these disciples, some of whom I knew well.

My first Teacher in philosophy at Ngamring Jampaling Monastery was called Geshe Palden. At one time he did a long close retreat on Je Tsongkhapa counting *Migtsema* prayers. At the end of his retreat an image of Je Tsongkhapa appeared on one of the beads of his mala. He showed this to me and I saw it very clearly.

There are many other stories such as these which show that, even in these impure times, faithful practitioners can receive unceasing blessings from Je Tsongkhapa. If we keep a painting or statue of Je Tsongkhapa on our shrine and, with deep faith, regard that representation as the living Je Tsongkhapa and make offerings, prostrations, and requests in front of it, our lifespan and Dharma realizations will definitely increase. In particular, it is said that if a statue of Je Tsongkhapa is kept in a house the members of that household will not experience problems of poverty and their wisdom will naturally increase.

Togdän Jampäl Gyatso

Why We Need to Practise the Guru Yoga of Je Tsongkhapa

THE GURU YOGA OF JE TSONGKHAPA

The Guru yoga of Je Tsongkhapa will now be explained under three headings:

1 Why we need to practise the Guru yoga of Je Tsongkhapa
2 The origin and lineage of these instructions
3 The actual instructions

WHY WE NEED TO PRACTISE THE GURU YOGA OF JE TSONGKHAPA

Because we are so attached to worldly activities we usually have little desire to practise Dharma at all, let alone the Guru yoga of Je Tsongkhapa. This is our main obstacle. To overcome it we need to reflect on the reasons why it is necessary to practise this special Guru yoga.

There are two main Guru yogas related to Je Tsong-khapa: *Offering to the Spiritual Guide*, or *Lama Chöpa*, which is practised in conjunction with Highest Yoga Tantra, and *The Hundreds of Deities of the Joyful Land*, or *Ganden Lhagyäma*, which is a more general yoga that can be practised in association with either Sutra or Tantra. This second practice is very famous and all followers of Je Tsongkhapa memorize it and practise it regularly. Contained within this practice is a special prayer called the *Migtsema* prayer. If we understand this prayer we will realize why it is so important to practise the Guru yoga of Je Tsongkhapa. The prayer is as follows:

Tsongkhapa, crown ornament of the scholars of the
  Land of the Snows,
You are Avalokiteshvara, the treasury of unobservable
  compassion,
Manjushri, the supreme stainless wisdom,
And Vajrapani, the destroyer of the hosts of maras;
O Losang Dragpa I request you, please grant your
  blessings.

mig me tse wai ter chen chän rä zig
dri me khyen pai wang po jam päl yang
dü pung ma lü jom dzä sang wai dag
gang chän khä pai tsug gyän tsong kha pa
lo zang drag pai zhab la söl wa deb

This prayer is very blessed because it was originally
uttered by Manjushri. It comes from Manjushri's *Emanation
Scripture*, which he transmitted directly to Je Tsongkhapa.
When Je Tsongkhapa received this prayer he changed two
of the lines and offered it to his Spiritual Guide, Rendapa,
but Rendapa returned it to Je Tsongkhapa in its original
form saying that it was more suitable for him.

Many of Je Tsongkhapa's followers have attained very
high realizations through the practice of *Migtsema* combined with the Guru yoga of Je Tsongkhapa. Those who
have completed an action retreat on Je Tsongkhapa can do
a hundred and eight ritual practices associated with *Migtsema*, which were composed by later Lamas. These include
rituals for healing mental and physical illnesses; for overcoming various obstacles; for averting inauspicious signs
and bad dreams; for making or stopping rain; and for
increasing lifespan, merit, and Dharma realizations. Above
all, the *Migtsema* practice is the best method for increasing
our faith in Je Tsongkhapa and his doctrine. If we have
faith and practise Je Tsongkhapa's teachings on Mahamudra sincerely we can attain enlightenment in three short
years. Our main problem is lack of faith.

The *Migtsema* prayer indicates that Je Tsongkhapa is an
emanation of Avalokiteshvara, Manjushri, and Vajrapani.

As an emanation of Avalokiteshvara he is the embodiment of the compassion of all the Buddhas; as an emanation of Manjushri he is the embodiment of the wisdom of all the Buddhas; and as an emanation of Vajrapani he is the embodiment of the power of all the Buddhas. Because Je Tsongkhapa is an emanation of Avalokiteshvara, Manjushri, and Vajrapani, when we make prostrations to him we make prostrations to all the Buddhas, when we make offerings to him we make offerings to all the Buddhas, when we make requests to him we make requests to all the Buddhas, and when we receive his blessings we receive the blessings of all the Buddhas. Therefore we definitely need to practise the Guru yoga of Je Tsongkhapa.

By relying upon Je Tsongkhapa our compassion, wisdom, and spiritual power naturally increase. In particular, because Je Tsongkhapa is an emanation of the Wisdom Buddha Manjushri, his faithful followers never experience difficulty in increasing their wisdom. Wherever there is a community of faithful followers sincerely practising Je Tsongkhapa's teachings, their inner wisdom naturally increases. Wisdom is very important. The more wisdom we have, the less ignorance we have; and the less ignorance we have, the less suffering we experience. If we have wisdom there is no basis for experiencing problems.

What is wisdom? Ordinary intelligence is not wisdom. For example, some people are very clever when it comes to making weapons, poisonous chemicals, or other destructive or harmful substances. Others have great expertise in business or politics. Similarly, some animals are very clever. Cats, for example, are very skilled at catching mice, and mice are very skilled at stealing food. However, these are not examples of wisdom. Wisdom never causes suffering or non-virtue.

Wisdom is a virtuous, intelligent mind that understands its object unmistakenly and functions to dispel deluded doubt. Because it is a virtuous mind, wisdom always causes happiness; it never causes suffering or problems. Moreover, because it understands its object unmistakenly, wisdom always leads to correct paths and correct actions; it never deceives living beings. If we always engage in correct actions there is no basis for problems to arise and so we always experience good results. Moreover, wisdom dispels deluded doubts which obstruct the development of faith and impede our spiritual progress.

If our wisdom is weak we experience obstacles, but if our wisdom is strong we have no problems. Wisdom teaches us what to do and what not to do; it is like an inner Teacher that we carry in our hearts, and like a Protector that protects us from engaging in wrong actions and having to experience their unpleasant results. When we are discouraged, disappointed, or depressed, wisdom lifts our mind and makes us happy; and when we are over-excited or distracted, wisdom calms our mind and reduces our distractions. With wisdom our mind is always balanced and comfortable.

In the *Perfection of Wisdom Sutra* Buddha says that if we lack wisdom we are like a blind person, but if we possess wisdom we can see everything. Wisdom is the supreme eye that enables us to see all the different types of path. Ordinary eyes can see only external paths that lead from one external place to another, but wisdom eyes can also see internal paths. There are many different types of internal path. Some lead to rebirth in lower realms, some lead to rebirth in higher realms, and some lead to rebirth in Pure Lands. Some internal paths lead to liberation, others lead to enlightenment. Wisdom eyes can see all these different paths. Moreover, wisdom guides us to make correct decisions about which internal paths to follow. Without wisdom it is very easy to follow wrong paths. Because of our lack of wisdom, we have been following wrong paths since beginningless time. Although we have always sought happiness and contentment, hitherto our actions have resulted largely in suffering and dissatisfaction. This shows that we have been following wrong internal paths.

There are many different types of wisdom, such as wisdom arising from listening, wisdom arising from contemplation, wisdom arising from meditation, wisdom that realizes conventional truths, and wisdom that realizes ultimate truth. Each of these has many levels. If we want to be completely free from suffering and attain lasting happiness we definitely need to develop these different types of wisdom. Therefore we need to practise the Guru yoga of Je Tsongkhapa.

Wishing to eliminate our ignorance and increase our wisdom while ignoring or rejecting the Guru yoga of Je Tsongkhapa is a contradiction because Je Tsongkhapa is the Wisdom Buddha. Whereas most of the Tibetan Lamas prior to Je Tsongkhapa emphasized the attainment and display of miracle powers, Je Tsongkhapa saw his main responsibility as helping sentient beings to eliminate their ignorance through improving their wisdom. He understood very clearly that the development of wisdom is the only certain path that leads to freedom from suffering. Therefore, instead of revealing miracle powers, Je Tsongkhapa spent his whole life giving teachings, revealing clearly and unmistakenly the path to liberation. If we reject the practice of Je Tsongkhapa we shall only increase our ignorance.

Just as we need to improve our wisdom, so we also need to improve our compassion and spiritual power. Since Je Tsongkhapa is an emanation of Avalokiteshvara, the Buddha of compassion, and of Vajrapani, the Buddha of spiritual power, if we practise the Guru yoga of Je Tsongkhapa our compassion and spiritual power will naturally increase. Wishing to increase our compassion and spiritual power while ignoring or rejecting the Guru yoga of Je Tsongkhapa is also a contradiction. More detail on the practices of *Migtsema* and *Ganden Lhagyäma* can be found in the commentary entitled *Heart Jewel*.

From the point of view of Highest Yoga Tantra, the Lord of the compassion lineage is Heruka, the Lord of the wisdom lineage is Yamantaka, and the Lord of the lineage of spiritual power is Guhyasamaja. To attain enlightenment swiftly, we must receive the blessings of these three Deities. When we practise the Guru yoga of *Offering to the Spiritual*

Guide, the principal object of refuge and Field for Accumulating Merit is Je Tsongkhapa who, as an emanation of the Wisdom Buddha, is the same nature as Yamantaka. Within his body we visualize the thirty-two Deities of Guhyasamaja, and at the same time we generate ourself as Heruka. In this way we are able receive the blessings of all three Deities and engage in all the essential practices of Highest Yoga Tantra within one session.

As already mentioned, the sequence for attaining enlightenment in one short human life is first to gain some experience of Lamrim, then to practise Lojong, and then to engage in Vajrayana Mahamudra. The Guru yoga of *Offering to the Spiritual Guide* includes all these practices. Because it contains all the instructions on the stages of the path to enlightenment, it possesses all the pre-eminent qualities of the Lamrim texts. Thus, by relying upon this practice we will understand that there are no contradictions within Buddha's teachings, we will take all Buddha's teachings as personal advice and put them into practice, we will easily realize Buddha's ultimate intention, and we will naturally become free from the great fault and all other faults. Moreover, because this Guru yoga contains all the instructions on training the mind, it also possesses the pre-eminent qualities of the Lojong texts. Thus, as Geshe Chekawa says in *Training the Mind in Seven Points* 'It is like a diamond, like the sun, and like a medicinal tree.' More detail on the pre-eminent qualities of Lamrim and Lojong can be found in *Joyful Path of Good Fortune* and *Universal Compassion.*

Offering to the Spiritual Guide is also a preliminary practice for Vajrayana Mahamudra and includes all the stages of the generation stage and completion stage of Highest Yoga Tantra. If we engage in this practice regularly and sincerely we will receive special blessings so that when we finally engage in a three year retreat on Vajrayana Mahamudra we will find it very easy to gain realizations. Many of Je Tsongkhapa's followers such as Mahasiddha Dharmavajra, Gyalwa Ensäpa, and Khädrub Sangye Yeshe have attained enlightenment in three years through relying upon this special Guru yoga. Unlike Milarepa, who did not have access to this practice, they did not have to undergo great hardships to gain realizations but were able to progress smoothly and swiftly through the stages of Vajrayana Mahamudra by relying upon this Guru yoga. This is the uncommon quality of Je Tsongkhapa's Guru yoga. Therefore, if we want to attain enlightenment swiftly and easily we definitely need to develop faith in Je Tsongkhapa and practise his Guru yoga sincerely.

The extent to which we receive the benefits of this Guru yoga depends upon our faith in Je Tsongkhapa. To increase our faith we need to contemplate again and again why we need to practise the Guru yoga of Je Tsongkhapa. Then, if we follow Je Tsongkhapa's tradition purely without mixing with other traditions, and rely upon his Dharma Protector, Dorje Shugdän, our faith in Je Tsongkhapa, and therewith our realizations, will naturally increase. If we follow this advice – to develop deep, unchanging faith in Je Tsongkhapa, to follow his tradition purely without mixing, and to rely sincerely upon the Dharma Protector Dorje Shugdän – we will definitely receive great benefits. If a Teacher encourages us to do these things it is we who experience the benefits, not the Teacher. There is nothing partisan about this advice; it is given only for our benefit. Experience shows that realizations come from deep, unchanging faith, and that this faith comes as a result of following one tradition purely – relying upon one Teacher, practising only his teachings, and following his Dharma Protector. If we mix traditions many obstacles arise and it takes a long time for us to attain realizations.

Baso Chökyi Gyaltsän

Tharpa Publications
15 Bendemeer Road
London SW15 1JX
England

Tharpa Publications

MAILING LIST

Tharpa Publications are publishers of Buddhist books and visual Dharma reproductions. If you would like to be placed on our mailing list and receive further details of our books, prints, posters and cards, as well as future publications, then please complete this card and mail it to us. We look forward to hearing from you.

TP1/91

Name _____

Address _____

_____ Country _____

We are always interested to receive your comments and suggestions for future publications _____

_____

_____

_____

The Origin and Lineage of these Instructions

The lineage of this instruction, known as the 'Uncommon Whispered Lineage', was transmitted from Buddha Vajradhara to Manjushri and from Manjushri directly to Je Tsongkhapa. From Je Tsongkhapa it has been passed down to the present Teachers through exactly the same lineage as the Mahamudra of the Virtuous Tradition. It has already been explained that there are two main Guru yogas related to Je Tsongkhapa: *The Hundreds of Deities of the Joyful Land*, or *Ganden Lhagyäma*, and *Offering to the Spiritual Guide*, or *Lama Chöpa*. Both of these were transmitted by Buddha Manjushri to Je Tsongkhapa in a special scripture which is known as the *Kadam Emanation Scripture*. This scripture also includes instructions on Vajrayana Mahamudra, as well as six sadhanas of Manjushri: *Accomplishing Outer Manjushri*, *Accomplishing Inner Manjushri*, *Accomplishing Secret Manjushri*, *Accomplishing Manjushri's Body Mandala*, *Accomplishing Wheel of Dharma Manjushri*, and *Accomplishing Solitary Manjushri*.

The Hundreds of Deities of the Joyful Land was passed by Je Tsongkhapa to his disciple, Je Sherab Senge. This great Lama lived and practised at a place called Se in Tibet, and he and his two principal disciples later became known as the 'Segyupa Father and Sons'. The lineage of the practice of *The Hundreds of Deities of the Joyful Land* is known as the 'Segyu Lineage'. More information on this lineage can be found in *Heart Jewel*.

The lineage of *Offering to the Spiritual Guide* developed as follows. After Je Tsongkhapa passed away, his tradition was preserved and promoted by his two principal disciples, Khädrubje and Togdän Jampäl Gyatso. Khädrubje,

who was an emanation of Vajrapani, became Je Tsongkhapa's successor at Ganden Monastery. While he
remained there, he gave extensive teachings to large num-
bers of disciples, just as his Spiritual Guide, Je Tsongkhapa,
had done. He was particularly skilled at logic and debate
and was able to answer all questions regarding Je
Tsongkhapa's teachings and to resolve misunderstandings
concerning them. So sharp was his wisdom, and so incisive
his reasoning, that he was compared to the great Indian
Buddhist Master Dharmakirti, an emanation of Manjushri
who revealed the essential instructions on logic and
reasoning.

Je Tsongkhapa transmitted all the essential instructions
on Vajrayana Mahamudra to Khädrubje, who practised
them sincerely. Because he was charged with the great
responsibility of ensuring that Je Tsongkhapa's precious
teachings continued to flourish, Khädrubje would often
make requests for guidance and inspiration to Je Tsongkhapa after he had passed away. On five separate occasions
Je Tsongkhapa appeared directly to Khädrubje, each time
in a different form. On one occasion, when he was reflecting on the extraordinary kindness of Je Tsongkhapa,
Khädrubje was so overcome with sadness at the loss of his
Spiritual Guide that he began to weep. With his eyes filled
with tears, he started to compose a praise to Je Tsongkhapa
in which he expressed his deep yearning to see him again.
As soon as he had finished composing the praise, Je
Tsongkhapa appeared before him riding on an elephant,
surrounded by an aura of light. Je Tsongkhapa asked
Khädrubje why he was crying and Khädrubje replied that
it was because he was thinking of Je Tsongkhapa's kindness. He asked Je Tsongkhapa where he had been since he
passed away and Je Tsongkhapa replied that he was abiding in a Pure Land in the north-east. They continued to talk
for a long time before the vision of Je Tsongkhapa finally
absorbed. At other times Je Tsongkhapa appeared to
Khädrubje in other manifestations, such as Manjushri
riding on a lion, and a Yogi riding on a tiger.

Whereas Khädrubje remained at Ganden emphasizing Je Tsongkhapa's tradition of giving clear and unmistaken teachings, Togdän Jampäl Gyatso spent most of his life in isolated forests and mountain caves emphasizing Je Tsongkhapa's tradition of meditation retreat. By practising sincerely the instructions on Vajrayana Mahamudra, he attained great enlightenment in three years. Although both Khädrubje and Togdän Jampäl Gyatso received the lineage of the *Emanation Scripture* from Je Tsongkhapa, it was Togdän Jampäl Gyatso who passed it on to others, and so it is he who is regarded as the next lineage Guru after Je Tsongkhapa.

Togdän Jampäl Gyatso passed the lineage of these instructions to Khädrubje's younger brother, Baso Chökyi Gyaltsän. Baso Chökyi Gyaltsän spent his entire life practising these instructions and realized them fully. He transmitted them to Mahasiddha Dharmavajra, a great meditator who spent his whole life in retreat in mountain caves. At one time Mahasiddha Dharmavajra was in retreat in a cave high up on a mountain called Chumo Lhari, which is near Tashi Lhunpo Monastery in western Tibet. During one of his sessions Je Tsongkhapa appeared to him as a unification of three holy beings. His outer aspect was as Je Tsongkhapa wearing the three robes of a monk and a yellow Pandit's hat, with his right hand in the mudra of expounding Dharma and his left hand in the mudra of meditative equipoise holding a jewelled bowl filled with nectars. At his heart was Buddha Shakyamuni, and at his heart was Conqueror Vajradhara. This aspect of Je Tsongkhapa is known in Tibetan as 'je sempa sum tseg', which means 'Je Tsongkhapa, the Unification of Three Holy Beings'. He is also known as 'Lama Losang Tubwang Dorjechang'. Here, 'Lama' means 'Guru', indicating that Je Tsongkhapa is our Spiritual Guide, 'Losang' is short for 'Losang Dragpa', which is Je Tsongkhapa's ordained name, 'Tubwang' is short for 'Shakya Tubwang', which is the Tibetan name for Buddha Shakyamuni, and 'Dorjechang' is Tibetan for Vajradhara.

While appearing in this form, Je Tsongkhapa transmitted to Mahasiddha Dharmavajra the instructions on *Offering to the Spiritual Guide*, together with the instructions on Vajrayana Mahamudra and all the other essential instructions from the *Emanation Scripture*. By relying upon these precious instructions, Mahasiddha Dharmavajra attained enlightenment in three years. Later, when Mahasiddha Dharmavajra's ordinary form passed away, many local people saw five-coloured rainbow lights pouring out of his cave and illuminating the whole mountain. When they went to his cave it was completely empty. Mahasiddha Dharmavajra had attained a rainbow body and his ordinary form had totally disappeared.

Since the time when Manjushri transmitted the *Emanation Scripture* to Je Tsongkhapa, thousands of practitioners within the Gelugpa Tradition have attained enlightenment by practising these instructions. Moreover, because these instructions have the uncommon close lineage they are extremely blessed, and those who practise them sincerely are able to attain enlightenment in three years with considerable ease, without having to undergo the kinds of hardship experienced by Milarepa.

Before he passed away, Mahasiddha Dharmavajra checked with his clairvoyance to see to whom he should pass on the lineage of these precious instructions. He saw that a Yogi called Losang Döndrub, who was in retreat hundreds of miles away at a place called Ensa, had a very special connection with Je Tsongkhapa, and that he was a suitable recipient for this lineage. Using his miracle powers he travelled in an instant the great distance to Losang Döndrub's cave and manifested outside it in the aspect of an old beggar monk. In those days, a beggar would wait outside reciting scriptures, indicating that he was in need of charity. Accordingly, Mahasiddha Dharmavajra began to recite Je Tsongkhapa's *Praise to Dependent Relationship*.

At that time Losang Döndrub was ill, but when he heard the beggar reciting this text by Je Tsongkhapa his mind became very happy and, despite his illness, he dragged himself to the door of his cave. Immediately on seeing the beggar his mind was filled with devotion and he felt sure that he must be a holy being. He invited the beggar into his cave and offered him tea. Upon questioning the beggar, he soon realized that he was indeed a great Yogi. He fell at Mahasiddha Dharmavajra's feet and requested him to take him into his care and give him Dharma instructions. Mahasiddha Dharmavajra replied that to receive these instructions Losang Döndrub would have to travel to his own cave at Chumo Lhari, and then he disappeared. Losang Döndrub underwent great hardship in finding Mahasiddha Dharmavajra's cave, but when he eventually arrived he immediately made tsog offerings and requested teachings. Mahasiddha Dharmavajra transmitted to him the full lineage of the instructions of the *Emanation Scripture*, including the instructions on *Offering to the Spiritual Guide*. Losang Döndrub then returned to his cave at Ensa and put these instructions into practice, finally attaining enlightenment in three years as his Teacher had done. After he attained enlightenment he wrote in one of his many songs:

My only good qualities are that first I made single-pointed requests to my Spiritual Guide, then I practised my sadhanas as soon as I received them, and finally I attained enlightenment in three years and three months.

Losang Döndrub later became known as Gyalwa Ensäpa, named after the cave where he meditated. Although he was never officially given the title, Gyalwa Ensäpa is considered to be the first Panchen Lama because Losang Chökyi Gyaltsän, who is recognized as the first Panchen Lama, was in fact an emanation of Gyalwa Ensäpa.

When he was a young boy Gyalwa Ensäpa received many visions of Buddha Shakyamuni. He also possessed natural clairvoyance and was able to know that people were about to visit his family even when they were still many days' journey away. Later, when he ordained as a monk, he was able to recite the entire *Perfection of Wisdom Sutra in Eight*

Thousand Lines from memory, both in Tibetan and in Sanskrit. His fellow monks, who had never heard Sanskrit spoken, thought that he was possessed by spirits!

Since his Spiritual Guide, Mahasiddha Dharmavajra, spent his entire life in retreat, it fell to Gyalwa Ensäpa to pass the lineage of the *Emanation Scripture* to others. He passed the lineage to Khädrub Sangye Yeshe, the root Guru of Losang Chökyi Gyaltsän, the first Panchen Lama, and it was from Khädrub Sangye Yeshe that the first Panchen Lama received this precious lineage. Since Mahasiddha Dharmavajra and his two principal disciples, Gyalwa Ensäpa and Khädrub Sangye Yeshe, became known as 'Ensäpa Father and Sons', this lineage is called the 'Ensa Lineage'. Later Kachen Yeshe Gyaltsän wrote a book containing biographies of all these lineage Gurus. Their stories are very inspiring and I hope that one day they will be translated from Tibetan for the benefit of western practitioners.

The first Panchen Lama, Losang Chökyi Gyaltsän, was a very wise and skilful protector of Je Tsongkhapa's doctrine. Later he became the root Guru of the fifth Dalai Lama. Because of the ambitions of a local baron at that time, the fifth Dalai Lama was not recognized immediately and he spent the first twenty-five years of his life appearing as an ordinary peasant labouring in the fields. To convert the baron to Dharma and persuade him to recognize the fifth Dalai Lama, the first Panchen Lama performed a special wrathful ritual called 'The practice of the wheel'. As a result the baron temporarily fell sick and no one was able to cure him. One night, through the power of his concentration, the Panchen Lama caused the baron to dream of a man who urged him to invite the Panchen Lama to come from Tsang to cure him. The next day, the baron sent for the Panchen Lama who accepted the invitation. When he arrived he performed many pujas and other rituals, and as a result the baron was completely cured. Out of gratitude the baron offered the Panchen Lama extensive riches but he refused them. When the baron asked him how he could repay his kindness, the Panchen Lama replied that he should recognize the fifth Dalai Lama. When the baron asked where he was, the Panchen Lama pointed to a young man labouring in a nearby field. Accordingly the fifth Dalai Lama was officially recognized and he went to study at Drepung Monastery. Later he became one of the most influential of all the Dalai Lamas.

Until the time of the first Panchen Lama, the lineage of the *Emanation Scripture* had been passed directly from Teacher to disciple without being written down, and only those with great good fortune even knew of its existence, let alone had the opportunity to practise the instructions. For this reason it became known as the 'Ensa Whispered Lineage'. However, because times were becoming more and more impure, and because sentient beings had less and less merit, the Panchen Lama worried that this precious lineage might soon be lost altogether, and so to preserve it for future generations he decided to write it down. Accordingly, he wrote a text entitled *The Main Path of the Conquerors, the Root Text of the Mahamudra*. This contains all the essential instructions on Mahamudra from the *Emanation Scripture*.

To practise Mahamudra successfully it is first necessary to complete four preliminary practices, which are known as 'the four great preliminary guides'. These are:

1 The great guide of going for refuge and
   generating bodhichitta, the gateway to the
   Buddhadharma and the Mahayana
2 The great guide of mandala offerings, the
   gateway to accumulating a collection of merit
3 The great guide of meditation and recitation of
   Vajrasattva, the gateway to purifying negativities
   and downfalls
4 The great guide of Guru yoga, the gateway to
   receiving blessings

So that faithful disciples could practise the fourth great guide as a preliminary to the actual Mahamudra, the first

Panchen Lama also compiled *Offering to the Spiritual Guide* based on the instructions from the *Emanation Scripture.* Since then, this practice has flourished in Tibet, Mongolia, China, and India; and now it is beginning to spread in the west. We should remember the great kindness of the first Panchen Lama in compiling this sadhana and try to practise it purely and sincerely.

Although *Offering to the Spiritual Guide* was compiled by the first Panchen Lama, it was not invented by him. In fact all the practices contained within the sadhana were taught by Buddha in his Sutra and Tantra teachings. So as to make this clear the first Panchen Lama wrote at the beginning of the sadhana:

> I shall prepare a throat ornament, a beautiful
> garland of flowers,
> Taken from the lotus garden of holy instructions
> of Sutra and Tantra,
> The sole supreme method for fortunate disciples
> To accomplish every benefit and happiness.

The full title of the sadhana in Tibetan is *Lama Chöpai Choga*, which means *The Ritual for Offering to the Spiritual Guide.* Even though it was first composed in Tibetan, the first Panchen Lama also gave the title in Sanskrit – *Guru puja sä kalpa* – at the head of the text. This was the practice that was usually adopted when a text was translated from Sanskrit into Tibetan to show that the text had not been invented by the Tibetans but was an authentic scripture from India. It is not usual to give a Sanskrit title for a text originally composed in Tibetan. Thus, Je Tsongkhapa's *Great Exposition of the Stages of the Path*, for example, has no Sanskrit title but is known in Tibetan simply as *Lamrim Chenmo.* Why then did the first Panchen Lama give a Sanskrit title to *Offering to the Spiritual Guide*? His purpose was to indicate that, even though he had compiled the sadhana, the practices contained within it originate from the Sutras and Tantras, and in particular from the Tantric teachings of Conqueror Vajradhara.

It is the tradition of both Atisha and Je Tsongkhapa to base all their teachings on the word of Buddha and never to teach anything that contradicts Buddha's teachings. According to these two great Teachers, unless an instruction is referred to in either the Sutras or the Tantras it cannot be regarded as an authentic Buddhist teaching, even if it is a so-called 'terma', or 'hidden treasure text'. Whenever they gave teachings or composed texts, both Atisha and Je Tsongkhapa quoted liberally from both the Sutras and the Tantras. In this way they showed their great respect for Buddha's original teachings and emphasized the importance of being able to trace instructions back to them.

In *Ornament for Mahayana Sutras*, Maitreya says that throughout the entire universe there is no one wiser than Buddha. Buddha understands directly and simultaneously all objects of knowledge and realizes the true nature of all phenomena. If we have faith in Buddha we should practise only those instructions that do not contradict his teachings. If we follow instructions that contradict Buddha we will make no spiritual progress and our practice will cause the degeneration of the Buddhadharma in this world. Similarly, if we claim to be a Buddhist Teacher but give teachings that contradict Buddha we will be destroying Buddha's doctrine. Therefore if we consider ourselves to be Buddhists we should take great care to practise only those teachings that originally come from Buddha. We should be careful not to be influenced simply by the reputation of a particular Teacher or book, but should check to see whether or not they are authentic. Even if we are told that by hearing a particular teaching or by reading a particular book we will attain enlightenment quickly, we should still be cautious and examine its authenticity first.

If, as the first Panchen Lama says, all the instructions contained within *Offering to the Spiritual Guide* had already been taught by Buddha, why did he compile the sadhana at all? Why did he not simply refer us to Buddha's original teachings? There are two reasons. First, Buddha's Tantric teachings are very difficult to understand, and second, they are scattered throughout various texts with no clear indication as to the sequence in which they are to be practised. If we were to try to practise these instructions by relying upon the Sutras and Tantras alone we would soon become discouraged and might even give up our Dharma practice altogether.

In compiling *Offering to the Spiritual Guide*, the first Panchen Lama has presented all the essential instructions in a way that is easy to understand, and he has arranged them in the sequence in which they are to be practised. He has included in one practice not only the great preliminary guide of Guru yoga combined with all the essential practices of generation stage and completion stage of Highest Yoga Tantra, but also the essential practices of Lamrim and Lojong. By practising *Offering to the Spiritual Guide*, therefore, we are able to practise all the stages of the path of Sutra and Tantra in one session.

In his autocommentary, the first Panchen Lama says that the various practices contained within *Offering to the Spiritual Guide* are like precious jewels that have been retrieved from an ocean bed. Even if we knew of the existence of jewels at the bottom of a vast ocean, without the help of a skilled navigator and a diver we would never be able to gain access to them. If we were to try to retrieve them on our own we would definitely find ourself in great danger. In the same way, without the first Panchen Lama's help in gathering up and presenting these precious jewel-like instructions, if we were to try to find them amongst the vast ocean of the Sutras and Tantras and put them into practice on our own, we would soon find ourself in difficulty.

Since the first Panchen Lama compiled this precious sadhana it has been transmitted, together with the uncommon Vajrayana Mahamudra of the Virtuous Tradition and all the other essential practices of the *Emanation Scripture*, through an unbroken lineage to our present Teachers. From Panchen Chökyi Gyaltsän the lineage passed through Drubchen Gendun Gyaltsän and Drungpa Tsöndru Gyaltsän to Könchog Gyaltsän, who transmitted it to the second

Panchen Lama, Losang Yeshe. From him it passed through various Lamas such as Losang Namgyal and Kachen Yeshe Gyaltsän down to Kyabje Trijang Rinpoche, who passed it on to our present Teachers. The entire close lineage of these instructions is given in the *Prayers of Request to the Mahamudra Lineage Gurus*, which can be found in Appendix II. If we read this prayer we will see that there is a completely pure and unbroken lineage from Conqueror Vajradhara down to our present root Guru.

By contemplating the special qualities of *Offering to the Spiritual Guide* and the purity of the lineage of these instructions we should come to feel extremely fortunate at having met such a precious practice. We should think:

This practice of Offering to the Spiritual Guide *contains all the essential practices of Sutra and Tantra, and the blessings of this lineage are still complete. If I now practise this Guru yoga sincerely I will be able to attain enlightenment in this very life, and become just like Gyalwa Ensäpa. How lucky I am!*

Drubchen Dharmavajra

The Preliminary Practices

The actual instructions on *Offering to the Spiritual Guide* are presented under two main headings:

1 How to practise during the meditation session
2 How to practise during the meditation break

How to practise during the meditation session is presented in three parts:

1 The preliminary practices
2 The actual practice
3 The concluding stages

THE PRELIMINARY PRACTICES

There are four preliminary practices:

1 Going for refuge and generating bodhichitta
2 Self-generation as the Deity
3 Purifying the environment and its inhabitants
4 Blessing the offerings

Going for refuge and generating bodhichitta has two parts:

1 Going for refuge
2 Generating bodhichitta

GOING FOR REFUGE

Before sitting down to begin the sadhana, we should clean the room and set up a shrine consisting of representations

45

of Buddha's body, speech, and mind. In particular we should set up images of our Spiritual Guide, Conqueror Vajradhara, Buddha Shakyamuni, and Je Tsongkhapa. In front of these we should set out at least one row of offerings including four waters. These will be explained below. We should then sit in a comfortable posture, either on a meditation cushion or on a chair, and begin the sadhana.

At the very beginning we should make sure that our mind is calm, peaceful, and free from conceptual distractions. Je Tsongkhapa once composed a text in which he asked a number of questions of Tibetan meditators. Later the first Panchen Lama wrote answers to these questions. One of Je Tsongkhapa's questions was 'What is the most important thing to do at the beginning of a meditation session?' The Panchen Lama replied that we should begin by examining our mind. Sometimes the mere act of examining the mind, if it is done conscientiously, will pacify our distractions. At the beginning our mind is very much orientated towards external phenomena and we are preoccupied with worldly affairs, but by bringing our attention inwards to examine the mind it is possible that these conceptual distractions will cease.

We should sit quietly for a few moments, watching to see what kinds of mind are arising. If they are pure, virtuous minds we can proceed immediately with the sadhana. If on the other hand they are non-virtuous or worldly minds we should first practise breathing meditation to eliminate them. All minds depend upon inner winds. Pure minds depend upon pure winds and impure minds depend upon impure winds. If we eliminate our impure winds we will naturally pacify our impure conceptual minds, and if we then generate pure inner winds we will naturally generate pure minds. Therefore we begin by imagining that all our impure minds and impure winds assume the form of dark, black smoke within us. With a strong wish to eliminate these we exhale gently through the nostrils. As we do so, we imagine that all this black smoke rises from the bottom of our lungs, leaves through our nostrils, and disappears into space. We feel completely clean within. Then as we slowly breathe in, we imagine that we are inhaling all the blessings of the Buddhas and Bodhisattvas in the form of pure, white light. This white light fills our body and mind and we feel completely pure. We repeat this two, three, or more times until our mind is completely pacified of all conceptual distractions and has become pure, happy, and single-pointed.

We practise breathing meditation at the beginning of a sadhana to eliminate impure minds and bring the mind to a neutral state. From that neutral state we can then easily generate a virtuous state of mind. If we do not first pacify our impure conceptual minds we will find it very difficult to generate pure minds. For example, if we wish to dye a piece of cloth that is already coloured, we will find it very difficult to achieve the colour we want without first bleaching the cloth. Pacifying the mind with breathing meditation is like bleaching cloth. If we use breathing meditation in this way, as a preliminary to more practical types of meditation, it is very helpful; but if we adopt breathing meditation as our main practice we will not attain any lasting results. We may temporarily pacify our mind and achieve a degree of inner peace, but unless we subsequently engage in practical meditations on the stages of the path – such as meditations on renunciation, compassion, bodhichitta, or emptiness – we will never bring about any lasting changes in our mind but will remain ordinary beings constantly prone to suffering.

Once we have brought our mind to a calm and neutral state we then need to generate an especially virtuous state of mind. This is done in association with the first verse of the sadhana:

> With a perfectly pure mind of great virtue,
> I and all mother sentient beings as extensive as space,
> From now until we attain the essence of enlightenment,
> Go for refuge to the Guru and Three Precious Jewels.

This verse reveals the causes of going for refuge, the way to go for refuge, and the objects of refuge. The causes of going for refuge are revealed by the first line. In general these are renunciation, great compassion, and faith in the Guru and Three Jewels. Because *Offering to the Spiritual Guide* is a Highest Yoga Tantra practice, it is particularly important to emphasize the second cause, great compassion.

We begin by briefly generating a mind of renunciation through recalling the faults of samsara. We need to be firmly convinced that the so-called pleasures of samsara are thoroughly deceptive and finally lead only to more suffering. If we find this difficult we should briefly contemplate death. No matter how many transient pleasures we may enjoy in this life, sooner or later we will have to die. At that time all the pleasures of this life will amount to nothing; they will just be vague memories, like a pleasant dream that has passed. All that remains at death are the results of our own actions, and all we can take with us are these karmic imprints. If we have used this life to create virtuous karma we will experience happiness in the next life, but if we have created negative karma we will have to experience suffering by taking rebirth in one of the lower realms. Moreover, if we do not attain liberation in this life we shall have to continue taking uncontrolled rebirths in samsara where there is no real happiness but only suffering and dissatisfaction. Thinking like this, we should try to generate fear of the sufferings of samsara in general and of the lower realms in particular. In this way we generate a mind of renunciation.

We generate renunciation by contemplating our own suffering. If on the basis of this we then turn our attention to others' suffering, we will naturally develop compassion. We should think:

> *I am only one but others are countless. All these countless living beings have been my kind mother in previous lives. They are all trapped within this vicious cycle of uncontrolled death and rebirth, experiencing suffering in life after life.*

We contemplate in this way until we find the suffering of others unbearable, and then we firmly resolve to do whatever needs to be done to free them from their suffering. This is the mind of great compassion.

Without losing this motivation, we then consider how we can free mother sentient beings from their suffering. We realize that only the Guru and the Three Jewels have the power to protect us. In this way we generate a mind of faith, the third cause of going for refuge.

In the root text it says 'With a perfectly pure mind of great virtue'. Here, 'mind of great virtue' refers primarily to the motivation of great compassion combined with faith in the Guru and Three Jewels. The words, 'perfectly pure' indicate that this motivation is free from self-grasping and self-cherishing. All virtuous minds and virtuous actions are pure to some extent, but they are only perfectly pure if they are completely free from contamination by self-grasping and self-cherishing. Buddha said that if we engage in virtue with a mind polluted by self-grasping or self-cherishing it is like eating delicious food that has been laced with poison. If we were to eat such food our initial experience would be one of pleasure, but this would soon give way to suffering as the poison took effect. In the same way, the effect of contaminated virtue is rebirth in one of the higher realms of samsara as a human or god, but, although the initial effect is good fortune, the long-term effect is all the suffering and misery of another rebirth in samsara. This point is explained by Chandrakirti in the second chapter of *Guide to the Middle Way*.

The next two lines of the root text reveal the way to go for refuge. We go for refuge not merely to seek protection for ourself, but to free all sentient beings from their suffering. We imagine ourself surrounded by all mother sentient beings, a vast assembly as extensive as space, and then lead them in the practice of going for refuge. For auspiciousness we imagine all these beings in human form, but with compassion we remember that in reality each one of them is still experiencing the sufferings of their particular realm. Furthermore, we do not go for refuge just for a short time, but continuously, until we and all other living beings have attained the essence of great enlightenment. If we think like this it will strengthen our practice of refuge. Otherwise we may remember to go for refuge when we are experiencing manifest difficulties, but at other times complacency might get the better of us and we will allow our refuge to degenerate.

The last line of this verse reveals the objects of refuge, the Guru and Three Jewels. According to *Offering to the Spiritual Guide*, the principal object of refuge is Je Tsong-khapa, the Unification of Three Holy Beings, or Lama Losang Tubwang Dorjechang. Thus, according to this sadhana, we visualize our Spiritual Guide as Je Tsong-khapa who has Buddha Shakyamuni at his heart, and Conqueror Vajradhara at his heart. Why is this? There are two main reasons. Firstly, we need a common visualization for our Spiritual Guide. It is possible that a practitioner may have more than one Spiritual Guide. If we did not have a common visualization we would need a separate Guru yoga for each Spiritual Guide, which would display a complete misunderstanding of the nature of the Guru. Moreover, if we have a common visualization, when we are practising Guru yoga in a group there is no need to decide whose Guru we should visualize because we all visualize our Spiritual Guide as Lama Losang Tubwang Dorjechang.

The second reason for visualizing our Spiritual Guide as Lama Losang Tubwang Dorjechang is that to attain Tantric realizations it is essential to regard our root Guru as the same nature as all the Buddhas. When we visualize Lama Losang Tubwang Dorjechang we do not think that there are four separate beings in front of us – our Spiritual Guide, Je Tsongkhapa, Buddha Shakyamuni, and Conqueror Vajradhara – but only one being who has four different aspects. In reality they are all the same nature. Conqueror Vajradhara is the subtle Enjoyment Body of Buddha. He appears directly only to highly realized Bodhisattvas to whom he gives Tantric teachings. To benefit those with less fortune, Conqueror Vajradhara manifested a more visible form as Buddha Shakyamuni, who is an Emanation Body aspect. Buddha Shakyamuni gave extensive Sutra teachings to countless beings in this world. There are two types of Emanation Body – a Supreme Emanation Body and an Emanation Body appearing as an ordinary being. Buddha Shakyamuni is a Supreme Emanation Body. Even though it was possible for ordinary beings to see him and receive teachings from him, they had to possess immense good fortune. Compared with beings in these impure times, beings who were born during the golden age when Buddha Shakyamuni was actually teaching had great good fortune. As times became more and more impure and sentient beings' fortunes declined it was necessary for Buddha Shakyamuni to manifest another form as an Emanation Body appearing as an ordinary being. This he did by manifesting in the form of Je Tsongkhapa. Thus, although Je Tsongkhapa appeared in an ordinary form as a Tibetan monk, we can be certain that in reality he is the same nature as Buddha Shakyamuni who, in turn, is the same nature as Conqueror Vajradhara. In fact, Je Tsongkhapa is often referred to as the 'Second Conqueror'. Later, when times had become even more impure, Je Tsongkhapa manifested again as an ordinary being, this time in the aspect of our Spiritual Guide.

If we think in this way we will have no difficulty in regarding Lama Losang Tubwang Dorjechang as one being who has four different aspects. Every time we see our Spiritual Guide we will immediately recognize him as Conqueror Vajradhara, Buddha Shakyamuni, and Je Tsongkhapa; and whenever we think of Conqueror Vajradhara, Buddha Shakyamuni, or Je Tsongkhapa, we will immediately remember our Spiritual Guide. This is a very profound experience. If we achieve this we will easily understand the experiences of great practitioners such as Naropa and Milarepa, and we will have no difficulty in attaining Highest Yoga Tantra realizations.

How do we visualize the objects of refuge? In the space in front we visualize a vast jewelled throne supported by eight snow lions. In the very centre of this there is a much smaller throne of the same type. On this throne, on a seat of a lotus, moon, and sun, we visualize our root Guru in the aspect of Lama Losang Tubwang Dorjechang. He is in the aspect of a fully-ordained monk wearing a golden Pandit's hat. His right hand is in the mudra of expounding Dharma and his left hand, in the mudra of meditative equipoise, holds a jewelled bowl filled with three nectars. Between the thumb and forefinger of his right hand he holds the stem of an upala flower which blossoms at the level of his right ear. Upon this stands a blazing sword of wisdom similar to that held by Manjushri. His left hand holds the stem of an upala flower which blossoms at the level of his left ear. Upon this rests the *Kadam Emanation Scripture.*

There is great meaning in the hand mudras of Lama Losang Tubwang Dorjechang. His left hand symbolizes that his mind, the Truth Body, never moves from meditative equipoise but always remains mixed with emptiness, like water mixed with water. His right hand indicates that without rising from meditation on emptiness he is able to perform activities of subsequent attainment such as giving Dharma teachings. This quality is unique to Buddhas. Even highly realized Bodhisattvas are unable to perform activities of subsequent attainment while remaining in meditative equipoise. When they are in meditation and ultimate truth, emptiness, is appearing directly to their mind they are unable to cognize conventional truths and therefore cannot perform actions such as giving teachings. On the other hand, when they rise from meditation and directly cognize conventional truths, emptiness no longer appears directly to their mind. Buddhas however are able to cognize both truths simultaneously because they have completely abandoned the conception that holds the two truths to be different entities. Their minds realize directly and simultaneously all objects of knowledge. Thus, without their mind moving from a state of single-pointed absorption on emptiness, they are able to talk and give teachings to others.

Lama Losang Tubwang Dorjechang's mudras also have other meanings. His right hand indicates that first we should listen to and contemplate the meaning of Dharma teachings, and his left hand indicates that we should then meditate on the meanings we have understood. In this way we will become free from the four maras. Freedom from the mara of the delusions, the mara of contaminated aggregates, and the mara of uncontrolled death is symbolized by the three nectars within the jewelled bowl held in his left hand. Freedom from the Devaputra maras is symbolized by the mudra of meditative equipoise itself. Thus these mudras indicate both that Lama Losang Tubwang Dorjechang himself is free from the four maras, and that by relying upon him we too can attain the same freedom.

In each of the four cardinal directions around Lama Losang Tubwang Dorjechang is another throne. On the throne to his right sits Maitreya surrounded by all the Gurus of the lineage of the stages of the vast path, such as Asanga and Vasubhandu; on the throne to his left sits Manjushri surrounded by all the Gurus of the lineage of the stages of the profound path, such as Nagarjuna and Chandrakirti; on the throne behind him sits Conqueror Vajradhara surrounded by all the Gurus of the lineage of Secret Mantra, such as Tilopa and Naropa; and on the throne in front of him sits our present root Guru in his normal aspect surrounded by all the other Spiritual Guides from whom we have received teachings in this life, who share the same lineage and view as our root Guru. Above Lama Losang Tubwang Dorjechang are all the Gurus of the lineage of Vajrayana Mahamudra, seated one above the other. At the very top is Conqueror Vajradhara, and beneath him all the other lineage Gurus appear in the aspect of Manjushri. Around these five groups of Gurus are all the other objects of refuge: Deities of the four classes of Tantra, Buddhas, Bodhisattvas, Emanation Hearers, Emanation Solitary Conquerors, Heroes, Heroines, and Dharma Protectors.

Within this visualization, Lama Losang Tubwang Dorjechang, the five groups of lineage Gurus, the Tantric Deities, and the Sutra Buddhas are all Buddha Jewels; and the Bodhisattvas, Emanation Hearers, Emanation Solitary

Gyalwa Ensäpa

Conquerors, Heroes, Heroines, and Dharma Protectors are all Sangha Jewels. Within the mental continuum of each of these beings are special realizations, such as the direct realization of emptiness, as well as permanent cessations of delusions, of suffering, of samsara, and of true appearance. All these realizations and true cessations are Dharma Jewels.

To begin with we should not try to visualize all the objects of refuge clearly but be satisfied with a rough mental image of them. If we try too hard we are likely to end up with no image at all. When visualizing holy beings what matters most of all is to have strong conviction that they are actually appearing in subtle forms in the space before us.

Once we have generated the causes of going for refuge, understood the way to go for refuge, and visualized the objects of refuge, we can actually go for refuge by reciting the refuge prayer three times or more while contemplating its meaning. In the sadhana the refuge prayer is given in Sanskrit:

Namo Gurubhä
Namo Buddhaya
Namo Dharmaya
Namo Sanghaya

The meaning is 'I go for refuge to the Gurus, I go for refuge to the Buddhas, I go for refuge to the Dharmas, I go for refuge to the Sanghas.' Tibetans often recite this prayer in Sanskrit because these were the very first words of Dharma to be spoken in Tibet, and they remind them of the kindness of the original Indian Pandits who brought the Dharma to their country. At one time there was not even the sound of Dharma in Tibet. Then the Tibetan king, Trisong Detsen, invited Padmasambhava and Shantarakshita to come from India to teach Dharma to the Tibetans. They began by trying to teach the Tibetans to say this refuge prayer in Sanskrit. The Tibetans had never heard Sanskrit before and had great difficulty in pronouncing it correctly to start with, rather as western practitioners are currently struggling to pronounce Tibetan. Eventually they mastered the prayer and, to this day, the Tibetans still cherish these precious Dharma words.

It is worth mentioning in this context that for a long time Sanskrit was more important than Tibetan because it was the language in which Buddha taught and the language in which the original scriptures were written. Gradually, however, all the scriptures were translated from Sanskrit into Tibetan. The Tibetans took great care over these translations, consulting Indian scholars at every stage and translating the texts back from the Tibetan into Sanskrit to test their authenticity. Eventually they had translated into Tibetan a collection of over one hundred volumes of Buddha's teachings and more than two hundred volumes of various commentaries to these teachings. These two collections are known as the Kangyur and Tängyur respectively. Subsequently, many of the original Sanskrit scriptures were irretrievably lost and so these days the only complete collection of scriptures is in Tibetan. If the Tibetan scriptures are lost there will no longer be a complete collection of Dharma texts in this world. Moreover, the pure Sanskrit in which the teachings were originally given has gradually become mixed with colloquial strands and these days only impure forms of Sanskrit remain. The written Tibetan language, however, has not undergone the same kind of degeneration. Therefore there is good reason for claiming that, from the point of view of Dharma, Tibetan is now more important than Sanskrit.

As mentioned before, *Offering to the Spiritual Guide* is a preliminary practice for Vajrayana Mahamudra and was compiled principally as a method for practising the fourth great preliminary guide, Guru yoga. However we can, if we wish, collect all four great preliminary guides with this sadhana, in which case we should collect the first great preliminary guide, going for refuge, at this point. The way to do this is explained in *Joyful Path of Good Fortune* and *Guide to Dakini Land*. Both of these books also contain an extensive explanation of the practice of going for refuge.

GENERATING BODHICHITTA

This has two parts:

1 Generating aspiring bodhichitta
2 Generating engaging bodhichitta

GENERATING ASPIRING BODHICHITTA

Having gone for refuge, we now generate a special motivation of bodhichitta. This is done in conjunction with the next verse from the sadhana:

For the sake of all mother sentient beings,
I shall become the Guru-Deity,
And then lead every sentient being
To the Guru-Deity's supreme state.

On the basis of the compassionate wish generated on the occasion of going for refuge, we now generate the wish to become a Buddha to free all mother sentient beings from the sufferings of samsara and lead them to the supreme happiness of Buddhahood.

Because this is a Highest Yoga Tantra practice, we generate a very special bodhichitta wish. This is expressed by the words 'I shall become the Guru-Deity'. To become enlightened for the sake of others we first train on the common paths of Lamrim and Lojong and then enter into the uncommon Vajrayana paths of generation stage and completion stage. The purpose of practising the two stages of Vajrayana is to accomplish the state of our personal Deity. For example, if our personal Deity is Heruka we strive to become Heruka, and if our personal Deity is Vajrayogini we strive to become Vajrayogini. How is this done? The only way to become a Deity is to rely upon a Spiritual Guide whom we regard as being the same nature as that Deity. For example, if we are striving to become Heruka, we regard our root Guru as by nature inseparable from Heruka. With this recognition we perform either an extensive or a brief Guru yoga and dissolve our Guru into our heart. We feel as if our root mind and our Guru's mind have become inseparable, the nature of Guru Heruka. With this special feeling we then generate ourself as Heruka and maintain divine pride of being the Guru-Deity.

To begin with, this is accomplished through correct imagination but eventually, through training in completion stage practices, we will generate a subtle body called the illusory body, which is an actual body of a Deity. Once we have attained the illusory body we have a pure mind and a pure body. Through continuing to improve our experience with the yogas of completion stage, our pure illusory body will become the actual body of a Buddha and our pure mind will become the actual mind of a Buddha. Then we shall have become the actual Guru-Deity, Guru Heruka.

Without first generating a completely new subtle body, the illusory body, there is no way we can become a Buddha. No matter how long we meditate we will never be able to transform our present gross body into a Buddha's body. To generate the illusory body we need to train in the generation stage and completion stage of Highest Yoga Tantra, and to do this we must practise Guru yoga, regarding our Guru as inseparable from the Deity. In other words, the only way to become a Buddha is to practise Guru yoga in conjunction with the two stages of Highest Yoga Tantra. If we understand this we will realize just how precious is the practice of *Offering to the Spiritual Guide*. We will also see that the way of generating bodhichitta according to Highest Yoga Tantra is much more profound and much more realistic than the way of generating it according to Sutra.

We may wonder why it is necessary to rely upon a Guru to practise generation stage and completion stage. Why can we not simply practise these yogas on our own and generate ourself as the Deity? The answer is that at the moment we are completely different from the Deity, and without the Guru we have no way of establishing a connection with the Deity. For example, the Deity Heruka is a transcendental being completely beyond the realms of ordinary experience. The only way we can connect with Heruka is through our Guru. The Guru's extraordinary characteristic is that although in reality he is a transcendental being who is the same nature as Heruka, he is nevertheless able to appear in an ordinary form and communicate with us directly. In this way he is able to introduce us to Deities such as Heruka and guide us through the stages of trans-forming ourself into that Deity. Thus we should regard our Guru as an emanation of the Deity. Without the Guru it would be impossible for us to receive the blessings of Heruka or any other Deity. This is why Guru yoga is called 'the gateway to receiving blessings'. All Tantric realizations depend entirely upon the blessings of the Guru. Without the water of the Guru's blessings our minds are like dry seeds, incapable of spiritual growth.

There is a traditional Tibetan saying that the Guru pos-sesses the four bodies of a Buddha, which are like a large snow mountain, but if the sun of our faith does not rise, the waters of the Guru's blessings cannot melt. Considering this we should develop deep faith in our Spiritual Guide and generate a strong wish to become the Guru-Deity. Then we can lead all other sentient beings to that state, just as our Guru is presently guiding us.

GENERATING ENGAGING BODHICHITTA

With the previous prayer we generated a simple wish to become enlightened for the sake of others. Now, with the next two verses, we transform this wish into engaging bodhichitta by generating a determination to engage in the actual method for becoming enlightened, the profound path of Guru yoga.

For the sake of all mother sentient beings I shall attain as quickly as possible in this very life the state of the Guru-Deity, the primordial Buddha.

I shall free all mother sentient beings from their suffering and lead them to the great bliss of the Buddha grounds. Therefore I shall practise the profound path of the yoga of the Guru-Deity.

When we generate bodhichitta according to Highest Yoga Tantra we generate a special wish to become enlightened as quickly as possible in this very life. This is not because we are impatient, but because our compassion is so strong that we cannot bear sentient beings to suffer for a moment longer.

Another feature of Tantric bodhichitta is expressed by the words the 'primordial Buddha'. This shows the uncommon Tantric method of attaining enlightenment. Since beginningless time all sentient beings have had a very subtle body and a very subtle mind. At present these are obscured by the two types of obstruction: delusion-obstructions and obstructions to omniscience. When through training in the two stages of Highest Yoga Tantra this very subtle body and mind are completely freed from the two obstructions, they become the body and mind of a Buddha. Because the substantial causes of this Buddha's body and mind, our very subtle body and mind, have existed since beginningless time, this Buddha is called the 'primordial Buddha'.

Some people misunderstand the term 'primordial Buddha' and think that all sentient beings have been Buddhas since beginningless time. This is obviously mistaken because if it were true it would follow that ignorance and enlightenment would exist in the same mind at the same time, or that Buddhas experience the sufferings of hell! Je Tsongkhapa explained very clearly that because all sentient beings have a very subtle body and mind they all have Buddha nature – the potential to become a Buddha in the future – but for as long as their very subtle body and mind remain covered by obstructions they are not actual Buddhas.

The second of these two verses also includes the practice of the four immeasurables. The words 'all mother sentient beings' indicate immeasurable equanimity, completely free from discrimination; the words 'I shall free . . . from their suffering' indicate immeasurable compassion; and the words 'and lead them to the great bliss of the Buddha grounds' indicate immeasurable love and immeasurable joy. Finally, the words 'Therefore I shall practise the profound path of the yoga of the Guru-Deity' indicate the special determination of engaging bodhichitta. We should contemplate all this while reciting this verse.

After going for refuge and generating bodhichitta, if we have time we can visualize white lights and nectars flowing from our Guru and all the holy beings in front of us and dissolving into our body. We imagine that our entire body and mind are pervaded by blissful white lights and nectars, which purify all the negative karma we have created since beginningless time, all obstacles to our Dharma practice, all our mental and physical problems and, in particular, all the negative karma we have created with respect to our Spiritual Guide and the other holy beings. We feel completely clean and purified, and pervaded by bliss. Then we visualize yellow lights and nectars flowing from the holy beings and dissolving into us. In this way we receive their blessings to increase our Dharma realizations such as compassion and wisdom realizing emptiness, as well as our lifespan, merit, and wealth.

After this we imagine that lights radiate from Lama Losang Tubwang Dorjechang and pervade all the holy beings around him. They melt into light and gradually dissolve into Lama Losang Tubwang Dorjechang. Then Je Tsongkhapa dissolves into Buddha Shakyamuni, who in turn dissolves into Conqueror Vajradhara. Finally, Guru Vajradhara, who is the very nature of our Spiritual Guide and all objects of refuge, comes to the crown of our head and, entering through our crown, dissolves into our root mind at our heart. We feel that our mind mixes with our Guru's mind of spontaneous great bliss, like water mixing with water, and as a result our mind also transforms into spontaneous great bliss. Because our Guru's mind is a mind of spontaneous great bliss, and because we have mixed our root mind with our Guru's mind, we have a perfect reason for thinking that our mind has actually become a mind of spontaneous great bliss. We should develop strong conviction that this fusion of minds has actually taken place and try to generate a special feeling of bliss. The essence of Highest Yoga Tantra is to generate spontaneous great bliss and then to meditate on emptiness with this mind so as to remove the subtlest obstructions from our mental continuum and thereby attain Buddhahood. At the moment we are not able to generate actual spontaneous great bliss but by mixing our mind with our Guru's mind we attain a similitude of it, and with this we can engage in actual Highest Yoga Tantra practices.

SELF-GENERATION AS THE DEITY

As already mentioned, *Offering to the Spiritual Guide* is primarily a preliminary practice for Vajrayana Mahamudra. The meaning of 'Mahamudra' is as follows: 'maha' means 'great', and refers to spontaneous great bliss; and 'mudra' means 'unchangeable' or 'seal', and refers to emptiness. Thus the actual Mahamudra is the union of spontaneous great bliss and emptiness that is accomplished in dependence upon the completion stage practices of Highest Yoga Tantra. In *Clear Light of Bliss*, three types of Mahamudra are explained, of which the union of spontaneous great bliss and emptiness is the first. In dependence upon this union we attain the union of the two truths, which is the union of illusory body and clear light; and in dependence upon this union we attain the union of body and mind, which is the resultant Mahamudra, or enlightenment. Before we can engage in the completion stage practices of Mahamudra, we must first practise generation stage. With generation stage practices we generate ourself as a Buddha primarily through the force of correct imagination, and then with completion stage practices we transform that imagined body of a Buddha into an actual body of a Buddha.

According to Secret Mantra, the root of samsara is not just self-grasping but also ordinary conception and ordinary appearance. The purpose of generation stage is to overcome ordinary conception and ordinary appearance by generating ourself as the Deity. Therefore, at this stage in the sadhana we practise self-generation as the Deity. Moreover, during the sadhana we have to perform certain rituals such as blessing the inner offering and making the secret offering, and to perform these rituals we must first generate ourself as the Deity.

As already explained, when we practise Highest Yoga Tantra we have to generate a special motivation of bodhichitta, wishing to become the Guru-Deity as quickly as possible in this very life. In particular, we need to generate the wish to become a Tantric Buddha. This is sometimes referred to as 'the resultant Mahamudra, the state possessing the seven pre-eminent qualities of embrace'. These seven qualities are:

1 A Form Body endowed with the major signs and minor indications
2 Continuously in embrace with a wisdom knowledge woman
3 A mind always abiding in a state of great bliss
4 This mind of bliss always mixed with emptiness, lack of inherent existence
5 Endowed with great compassion that has abandoned the extreme of attachment to solitary peace
6 Uninterruptedly manifesting Form Bodies that pervade the whole world
7 Unceasingly performing enlightened deeds

Any being who possesses these seven qualities is a Tantric Buddha. When we generate Tantric bodhichitta, we generate the wish to become a Buddha possessing these seven qualities.

Tantra is characterized by bringing the result into the path, that is, identifying with the result of our training right now as a method for accomplishing that result more swiftly. When we perform self-generation we are generating bodhichitta by bringing the result into the path. We have already generated the wish to become the Guru-Deity as quickly as possible, and now we imagine that this wish is actually

Khädrub Sangye Yeshe

fulfilled, by generating ourself as a Tantric Buddha endowed with the seven pre-eminent qualities of embrace.

According to some Tibetan commentaries to *Offering to the Spiritual Guide* we should generate ourselves as Yamantaka at this point, but according to the first Panchen Lama we should generate ourself as our personal Deity. Thus, if we usually practise *Yamantaka Tantra* we should generate as Yamantaka at this point, but if we usually practise *Heruka Tantra* we should generate as Heruka, and so on.

As already explained, when we practise *Offering to the Spiritual Guide* it is very beneficial to try to receive the blessings of the three principal Deities: Yamantaka, Guhyasamaja, and Heruka. One way to do this is to regard Lama Losang Tubwang Dorjechang as the same nature as Yamantaka, visualize the thirty-two Deities of Guhyasamaja within his body, and generate ourself as Heruka. Even if our normal practice is Vajrayogini, we can still generate ourself as Heruka for the purposes of this sadhana because Heruka and Vajrayogini are the same nature, and if we visualize ourself as Heruka we necessarily visualize ourself as Vajrayogini.

There now follows a brief explanation of how to perform self-generation as Heruka. If we have the time we can practise a more extensive self-generation according to the sadhana entitled *The Quick Path*, which can be found in Appendix II, but if we do not have much time or if we are performing *Offering to the Spiritual Guide* as a group puja, we can practise instantaneous self-generation as follows.

Having dissolved the objects of refuge and mixed our mind with our Guru's mind we strongly imagine that our mind has transformed into spontaneous great bliss mixed with emptiness, and we meditate on this for a while. Then we imagine that our whole body is pervaded by blissful blue light, the nature of our mind. This light slowly spreads outwards from our body, dissolving the entire universe and its inhabitants into light. Gradually, from the outer edges of the universe everything then dissolves inwards, leaving behind only emptiness, until everything has dissolved into our body. Then our body slowly dissolves from below and above until it completely disappears. Now everything has become emptiness. At this point we imagine that our mind of spontaneous great bliss, which is completely unified with our Guru's mind, mixes with emptiness like clear water mixing with clear water. Without losing this experience of bliss and emptiness, one part of our mind identifies this experience as the clear light of a Buddha's Truth Body, and we develop divine pride of being the Truth Body, thinking 'I am the Truth Body of Heruka.' We meditate on this for a while.

During this meditation one part of our mind is experiencing bliss, another part is perceiving emptiness, another part is meditating on emptiness, and another part is generating divine pride of being the Truth Body. This meditation is called 'bringing death into the path of the Truth Body'. It is a very powerful meditation that performs many functions simultaneously. It purifies the mind, it helps to reduce and eventually to eradicate our self-grasping, it is a powerful method for overcoming ordinary appearance and ordinary conception, it functions to prevent ordinary death, it causes the ripening of the completion stage realization of clear light, it sows the seed to attain the actual Truth Body of a Buddha, and it is a collection of wisdom. When we train in this meditation, we are training in ultimate bodhichitta. Previously we generated conventional bodhichitta by developing the wish to become a Buddha for the benefit of all sentient beings; now without losing this motivation we train in mixing our mind with emptiness. This is training in ultimate bodhichitta.

We meditate like this for a while and then one part of our mind thinks:

> *Even though I have attained the Truth Body of a Buddha, if I remain like this I shall not be able to benefit sentient beings because they are unable to see me. Therefore I must arise from this state as a Buddha's Form Body.*

With this motivation we imagine that our mind of inseparable bliss and emptiness transforms into an oval-shaped beam of blue light, about one cubit in height, standing vertically on a lotus and sun cushion. Without paying too much attention to the actual form of our body we should generate the thought 'Now I have attained the subtle form of a Buddha', and in this way meditate for a while on the divine pride of being the Enjoyment Body. This meditation is called 'bringing the intermediate state into the path of the Enjoyment Body'.

After a while, one part of our mind thinks:

Even this form is too subtle to be seen by most sentient beings. If I am to help all sentient beings I must arise in a more visible form.

With this motivation, we imagine that our mind in the form of blue light gradually expands in size and assumes the form of Heruka, with one face and two hands and embracing Vajravarahi. We then develop divine pride thinking 'I am the Emanation Body Heruka', and meditate on this. This meditation is called 'bringing rebirth into the path of the Emanation Body'. Then, while maintaining the divine pride of being Heruka, we recite the line from the sadhana:

From the state of great bliss I arise as the Guru-Deity.

When we practise self-generation in this way we forget our ordinary, gross body and mind and identify with the completely pure body and mind of Heruka. In this way our mind remains calm and peaceful and our delusions gradually diminish. We never generate anger, attachment, or other impure minds, but see everything purely as a Buddha does. If we are able to maintain divine pride of being Heruka at all times, there will be no basis for self-grasping or self-cherishing to arise, and we shall have attained a 'perfectly pure mind of great virtue'.

These three meditations are called 'bringing the three bodies into the path' because they are a special method for bringing the three resultant bodies of a Buddha into the present path and using them right now as a means to attain enlightenment. Through regular training in these meditations our ordinary appearance and ordinary conception diminish and we gradually purify ordinary death, intermediate state, and rebirth, and transform them into the three bodies of a Buddha. Eventually we become the actual Guru-Deity.

PURIFYING THE ENVIRONMENT AND ITS INHABITANTS

A fully-qualified Tantric practice must include the four complete purities:

1 Complete purity of place
2 Complete purity of body
3 Complete purity of enjoyments
4 Complete purity of deeds

The second of these, complete purity of body, is included within the practice of self-generation; the first and fourth, complete purity of place and complete purity of deeds, are included within this preliminary practice; and the third, complete purity of enjoyments, is included within the next preliminary practice, blessing the offerings.

As already explained, from the point of view of Highest Yoga Tantra the root of samsara is ordinary appearance and ordinary conception. The reason why we see faults in our environment, our friends, and even our Teachers is that we have ordinary, impure appearances. Someone who is free from impure appearances sees everything purely. A pure mind experiences a pure world and an impure mind experiences an impure world. A Buddha, for example, has no impure appearance. He or she has a completely pure body and a completely pure mind. He experiences his environment as a Pure Land and all the beings who inhabit it as Heroes and Heroines; and he experiences all enjoyments as pure enjoyments. Whatever a Buddha eats or drinks, for example, is experienced as nectar; he never experiences anything as unpleasant. Why is this? It is because his mind is completely pure, like a radiant sun unobscured by clouds.

According to the Highest Yoga Tantra method of bringing the result into the path, we have to train right now in experiencing complete purity of place, body, enjoyments, and deeds. By training ourself to see the world in a pure way we will develop pure minds, and as we develop pure minds we will naturally see the world in a pure way.

Having generated ourself as Heruka with a completely pure body and mind, we now imagine that five-coloured lights, the nature of our five wisdoms, radiate from our body and pervade all worlds throughout the ten directions, completely purifying these worlds and the beings who inhabit them. We imagine that all the impurities and imperfections of samsaric environments are purified. All rocky and uneven ground is made smooth, all extremes of heat and cold are removed, deserts are transformed into beautiful parks, floods abate, darkness is dispelled – the whole environment is transformed into Heruka's Pure Land. At the same time all the defilements of body, speech, and mind of sentient beings are purified, their obstructions to liberation and omniscience are eliminated, and they all become Heroes and Heroines within Heruka's Pure Land. Wherever we look we see only immaculate purity; not an atom of impure appearance remains. As we imagine this we recite the words from the sadhana:

Light rays radiate from my body,
Blessing all worlds and beings in the ten directions.
Everything becomes an exquisite array
Of immaculately pure good qualities.

When we become a Buddha we will be able to perform completely pure deeds and transform worlds and beings through the power of our blessings. At the moment we are practising bringing the result into the path by imagining that we have become Guru Heruka and have transformed the world into Heruka's Pure Land and all sentient beings into Deities in Heruka's mandala. This visualization is very powerful. It makes our mind clean and pure and it creates the cause for us to be reborn in a Pure Land, or at least in a good country with few problems. This practice is also a collection of merit, and it causes our Buddha seed to ripen. When we visualize ourself as a Buddha blessing all sentient beings and their environments we are training in bodhichitta by bringing the result into the path.

BLESSING THE OFFERINGS

In general, four types of offering are made during *Offering to the Spiritual Guide* – outer, inner, secret, and suchness offerings. Of these, the outer and inner offerings must be blessed before they are offered. If possible we should actually set out on the shrine at least one row of outer offerings. This should include the four waters – water for drinking, water for bathing the feet, water for rinsing the mouth, and water for sprinkling – as well as flowers, incense, light, perfume, and food. It is not usual in our tradition to set out a substance to symbolize music because music is sound, not visual form. If it is not possible to set out offerings in the traditional manner, any clean offering substances such as pure water, flowers, honey, fruit, or chocolate can be placed on the shrine. In addition to these, we should set out on a table in front of us a skullcup, or similar vessel, containing the substance of the inner offering. A detailed explanation of the inner offering is given in *Guide to Dakini Land*.

Before we offer these substances we need to bless them because it is not appropriate to offer ordinary, impure substances to holy beings. In reality, holy beings experience whatever we offer them as nectar, whether we bless it or not, but so that we can establish a strong connection with them it is very helpful if we bless the offering substances first. Thus, instead of offering ordinary substances in ordinary containers, we imagine that we are offering uncontaminated nectar in jewelled vessels.

If we have time, we can bless the outer offerings and inner offering according to the extensive rituals of the Yamantaka, Heruka, or Vajrayogini sadhanas. The method

70

for blessing offerings according to *Heruka* and *Vajrayogini Tantras* is explained in *Guide to Dakini Land*. Alternatively, we can bless the offerings according to the brief ritual in *Offering to the Spiritual Guide* as follows.

We imagine all the offerings in the space in front of us and above each offering we visualize the three letters: OM AH HUM. Immediately above each substance there is a white OM, the nature of Buddha Vairochana, the vajra body of all the Buddhas; above this is a red AH, the nature of Buddha Amitabha, the vajra speech of all the Buddhas; and above this is a blue HUM, the nature of Buddha Akshobya, the vajra mind of all the Buddhas. These letters are called 'the three vajras' – the body, speech, and mind of all the Buddhas. Countless light rays radiate from these letters and draw back the blessings of all the Buddhas of the ten directions in the aspect of Buddha Vairochana, Buddha Amitabha, and Buddha Akshobya. We imagine that thousands and thousands of these Buddhas appear and dissolve into the three letters. Then the letter HUM turns upside-down, descends, and dissolves into the offering substance, purifying it of all faults and ordinary characteristics such as an unpleasant smell or ordinary colour, and transforming it into a completely clean, pure substance. Then the letter AH turns upside-down and dissolves into the offering substance, transforming it into blissful nectar possessing three qualities: wisdom-nectar that destroys delusions, medicine-nectar that cures sickness, and life-nectar that overcomes death. Finally, the letter OM turns upside-down and dissolves into the offering substance whereby it becomes inexhaustible.

As we visualize this we recite the words from the sadhana:

OM AH HUM

By nature exalted wisdom, having the aspect of the inner offering and the individual offering substances, and functioning as objects of enjoyment of the six senses to generate a special exalted wisdom of bliss and emptiness, inconceivable clouds of

**outer, inner, and secret offerings, commitment
substances, and attractive offerings cover all the
ground and fill the whole of space.**

We strongly imagine that (1) all the offerings appear in
their individual aspects, (2) they are by nature wisdom
because all the wisdom beings of the ten directions have
dissolved into them, and (3) they function as objects of
enjoyment of the six senses to generate spontaneous great
bliss and emptiness in whoever experiences them. We
should visualize a vast array of such offerings covering all
the ground and filling the whole of space.

According to the words of the sadhana we visualize
outer offerings (such as the four waters), inner offerings
(ten substances derived from the body transformed into
blissful nectar), secret offerings (beautiful consorts that we
offer to Guru Vajradhara), commitment substances
(various special substances that we offer to fulfil our
commitments), and attractive offerings (such as parks
containing wild animals).

Sometimes, for example if we are travelling or if our
domestic circumstances do not permit us actually to set out
offerings, we can create offerings with our mind. First we
remember the emptiness of all phenomena and meditate on
this for a while. We contemplate that all phenomena are of
one taste in emptiness, which is the source of all
phenomena. Then, from that state of emptiness, we generate completely new offerings. We imagine that all forms
appear as Rupavajra goddesses, all sounds as Shaptavajra
goddesses, all smells as Gändhavajra goddesses, all tastes
as Rasavajra goddesses, all tactile objects as Parshavajra
goddesses, and all other phenomena as Dharmadhatuvajra
goddesses. All flowers become flower goddesses, all water
becomes water goddesses, and so on. We imagine all the
ground and all of space filled with these offering goddesses, and later, when the time comes to make the actual
offerings, we offer these. More detail on these goddesses
can be found in *Guide to Dakini Land*.

By blessing offerings in the ways described here we create the cause to experience wealth and riches in the future. We will experience only pure objects of enjoyment and we will be free from problems.

Panchen Losang Chökyi Gyaltsän

Visualizing the Field of Merit

The actual practice of *Offering to the Spiritual Guide* has five parts:

1 Visualizing the Field of Merit and inviting and absorbing the wisdom beings
2 Offering the seven limbs and the mandala
3 Making praises and requests
4 Receiving blessings
5 Gathering and dissolving the Field of Merit

VISUALIZING THE FIELD OF MERIT AND INVITING AND ABSORBING THE WISDOM BEINGS

This has two parts:

1 Visualizing the Field of Merit
2 Inviting and absorbing the wisdom beings

VISUALIZING THE FIELD OF MERIT

Having completed the preliminary practices we now visualize Lama Losang Tubwang Dorjechang and all the other holy beings in front of us so that we can offer the seven limbs, make praises and requests, and receive blessings. The assembly of holy beings visualized in front is known as the 'Field of Merit'. If we sow ordinary seeds in an external field we eventually harvest crops such as rice and barley. In the same way, if we sow seeds of faith and the spiritual path in the Field of Merit we harvest the excellent inner crops of increased good fortune, blessings, and Dharma realizations. Conversely, if we do not sow seeds in an external field no crops will grow and, in the same way, if we do not sow seeds of faith and the spiritual path in the Field of Merit we will not receive blessings and realizations.

Sowing seeds of faith and the spiritual path in the Field of Merit is the principal cause of pure happiness. Through this practice, temporarily we will experience peaceful and controlled minds and a gradual reduction of our daily problems, and ultimately we will attain the permanent peace of liberation or enlightenment. Ordinary farmers can generally sow seeds only once or twice a year and the results they achieve are short-lived, but we can sow seeds in the Field of Merit as often as we like and the increased good fortune and spiritual realizations that result bring happiness not only in this life but in all our future lives as well. Milarepa once wrote a song to ordinary farmers in which he said:

> You are farmers of this life,
> But I am a farmer of future lives.
> If you examine carefully you will see
> Who receives more benefit.

Ordinary farmers toil for hours in the fields experiencing many hardships and problems, and even then the results of their labours are not guaranteed. The few temporary benefits that they do receive are mixed with a great deal of misery and frustration. Spiritual farmers, on the other hand, do not experience such problems. By sowing seeds in the Field of Merit we will definitely grow crops such as love, compassion, bodhichitta, concentration, mental and physical suppleness, wisdom, and eventually the unsurpassed joy of full enlightenment. These experiences will bring great peace and happiness to ourself and to all other living beings. Therefore we should consider ourself very fortunate to be able to visualize the Field of Merit and make offerings to it. Such practices are the very essence of a meaningful human life.

According to the words of the sadhana, we visualize the Field of Merit as follows:

Within the vast space of indivisible bliss and emptiness, amidst billowing clouds of Samantabhadra's offerings, fully adorned with leaves, flowers, and fruits, is a wishfulfilling tree that grants whatever is wished for. At its crest, on a lion throne ablaze with jewels, on a lotus, moon, and sun seat, sits my root Guru who is kind in three ways, the very essence of all the Buddhas.

In the space in front of us we visualize a vast plain of lapis lazuli covered with powdered gold. In the middle of this there is an ocean of milk-like nectar, its bed strewn with precious jewels. Rising from the centre of the ocean is a huge wishfulfilling tree. The roots and trunk of the tree are made of pure gold, its branches of silver, and its twigs and leaves of fine, white crystal. The tree is adorned with flowers of exquisite red pearls and fruits of dazzling rubies, emeralds, and other jewels. The entire tree is of unearthly beauty and its leaves and branches whisper with the sound of holy Dharma. If we wish for wealth it bestows wealth, if we wish to be cool it bestows coolness, if we wish to be warm it bestows warmth.

The tree is supported by two naga kings whose bodies are half-immersed in the ocean. The trunk divides into seven large branches – three to the left, three to the right, and one in the centre. On top of the central branch is a vast lotus flower which is white with a reddish tint and has thousands of petals. Upon this is a huge throne made of lapis lazuli supported by eight snow lions, two in each corner. Each snow lion supports the throne with one front paw and holds a jewel with the other.

Snow lions are not ordinary animals but very rare creatures found high up in snow mountains. Some people say they do not exist at all, that they are entirely fictional, but this is not so. They do exist, but can be seen only by those with great good fortune. Many paintings depict the great

Indian Mahasiddhas riding on snow lions. We should visualize the snow lions that support the throne like these, not as ordinary lions. One of the characteristics of snow lions is that if their milk falls on the ground or is stored in an ordinary vessel it immediately turns sour. This is used by Conqueror Vajradhara as an analogy to illustrate the dangers of transmitting Tantric teachings to those who are not blessed with an empowerment.

The lion is generally regarded as the king of animals because it is the most powerful of all animals. In the same way these snow lions symbolize that Lama Losang Tubwang Dorjechang, the principal being in the Field of Merit, has the power to subdue all harmful influences. Specifically, Lama Losang Tubwang Dorjechang has eight special powers: the power of body, the power of speech, the power of mind, miracle powers, the power of being wherever desired, the power of his Pure Land, the power to fulfil wishes, and the power of enlightened actions.

Covering the entire surface of the throne is a lotus flower which has eleven tiers, each tier being slightly smaller in diameter than the one beneath it. The top tier has four petals, one in each of the cardinal directions.

The plain, ocean, tree, and other features are all by nature inseparable bliss and emptiness. As mentioned before, pure view is an essential characteristic of Highest Yoga Tantra. From the point of view of generation stage, pure view entails viewing ourself as the Deity, the environment as the Deity's Pure Land, and all the inhabitants as Heroes and Heroines. From the point of view of completion stage, pure view entails regarding everything as a manifestation of bliss and emptiness. The pure view of completion stage is more difficult to understand than the pure view of generation stage, and we shall understand it fully only when we have actual completion stage realizations.

In completion stage practice we bring our inner winds into the central channel through the force of meditation. As the winds enter, abide, and dissolve within the central channel all impure conceptual minds that depend upon the impure winds that flow through the left and right channels cease. We attain a very subtle, blissful mind of clear light, known as 'spontaneous great bliss'. When this subtle mind meditates on emptiness it readily mixes with emptiness, like clear water mixing with clear water, and we attain a realization of inseparable bliss and emptiness. Here 'bliss' refers to the subjective mind of clear light, 'emptiness' to the object, emptiness, and 'inseparable' to the complete fusion of these two into a state of indivisibility. Subsequently, when we rise from meditation, we experience everything as a manifestation of our mind, which is a union of bliss and emptiness. Therefore, everything is seen as having the nature of indivisible bliss and emptiness.

The words of the sadhana say that we visualize the Field of Merit 'amidst billowing clouds of Samantabhadra's offerings'. There are two ways to understand this. According to Sutra, 'Samantabhadra' refers to one of Buddha Shakyamuni's Bodhisattva disciples who was renowned for his ability to mentally create vast clouds of offerings filling every corner of space. According to Tantra, 'Samantabhadra' means 'thoroughly good', and refers to indivisible bliss and emptiness. Thus we visualize the Field of Merit manifesting from the vast space of indivisible bliss and emptiness amidst masses of beautiful offerings, which themselves are manifestations of indivisible bliss and emptiness.

At the very top of the lotus flower, in the middle of the four petals, we visualize our root Guru in the aspect of Lama Losang Tubwang Dorjechang, sitting on a sun and full moon cushion. The lotus itself symbolizes renunciation, the moon cushion conventional bodhichitta, and the sun cushion ultimate bodhichitta. Together, these three seats symbolize that our root Guru has attained these three realizations.

We may wonder, 'Who is my root Guru?' According to the words of the sadhana, we should recognize as our root Guru the Spiritual Guide from whom we receive the three kindnesses. According to Sutra the three kindnesses are:

to give vows, to give textual transmissions, and to give commentarial explanations. According to Tantra they are: to give empowerments, to give transmissions, and to give special advice based on personal experience. In both cases we regard a Spiritual Guide as our root Guru if he or she holds a pure lineage, leads us to correct spiritual paths, and shows us either of the two types of three kindnesses in relation to our principal daily practice.

When we visualize this Field of Merit, we visualize our root Guru in the aspect of Lama Losang Tubwang Dorjechang and regard him as the essence of all our Spiritual Guides. We should not feel that a Spiritual Guide cannot be our root Guru just because he is not ordained, or because he is not famous. What matters is that he or she helps us to tame our mind. Sometimes our Spiritual Guide will put difficulties in our way, as Marpa did with Milarepa, or even scold us, as Tilopa did with Naropa, but we should regard all these as special blessings that help us to purify our mind and eliminate obstructions.

We visualize our Spiritual Guide as Lama Losang Tubwang Dorjechang by following the words of the sadhana:

He is in the aspect of a fully-ordained monk, with one face, two hands, and a radiant smile. His right hand is in the mudra of expounding Dharma, and his left hand, in the mudra of meditative equipoise, holds a bowl filled with nectar. He wears three robes of resplendent saffron, and his head is graced with a golden Pandit's hat. At his heart are Buddha Shakyamuni and Vajradhara, who has a blue-coloured body, one face, and two hands. Holding vajra and bell, he embraces Yingchugma and delights in the play of spontaneous bliss and emptiness. He is adorned with many different types of jewelled ornament and wears garments of heavenly silk. Endowed with the major signs and minor indications, and ablaze with a thousand rays of light, my Guru sits in the centre of an aura of five-coloured rainbows. Sitting in the vajra posture, . . .

We visualize the external aspect of our Spiritual Guide as Je Tsongkhapa. Altogether, there are eighty different aspects of Je Tsongkhapa. In this aspect, which is the one that Je Tsongkhapa revealed to Mahasiddha Dharmavajra, he appears as a fully-ordained monk wearing a yellow Pandit's hat. His right hand is in the mudra of expounding Dharma and his left hand, in the mudra of meditative equipoise, holds a jewelled bowl brimming with the three nectars. Between the thumb and forefinger of his right hand he holds the stem of an upala flower which blossoms at the level of his right ear. Upon this stands a flaming sword of wisdom similar to that held by Manjushri. This sword has the power to dispel ignorance from the mind of whoever beholds it. Between the thumb and forefinger of his left hand he holds the stem of another upala flower which blossoms at the level of his left ear. Upon this rests the *Kadam Emanation Scripture.*

We may wonder why the sadhana specifically mentions the fact that our Spiritual Guide has one face and two hands, since this is perfectly normal! The reason is that we are visualizing our Spiritual Guide according to Tantra, and many Tantric Deities have more than one face and more than two hands. Heruka, for example, has four faces and twelve hands.

Our Spiritual Guide's body is white with a reddish tint, and his skin is as smooth as a lotus petal. He has a serenely peaceful face, with elongated eyes and a long, high-bridged nose. He gazes down upon his disciples with a smile of delight, as a mother would look at her dearest child.

At Guru Tsongkhapa's heart on a lotus and moon seat is Buddha Shakyamuni who has a golden-coloured body. His left hand, in the mudra of meditative equipoise, holds a precious bowl filled with nectar, and his right hand rests on his right knee with the tips of his fingers touching the seat. At Buddha Shakyamuni's heart is Conqueror Vajradhara who has a blue-coloured body, one face, and two hands. In his right hand he holds a golden vajra and in his left a silver bell. His hands are crossed at his heart embracing his consort, Yingchugma, with whom he sits in sublime union, delighting in the great play of spontaneous bliss and emptiness. Both Conqueror Vajradhara and Yingchugma are adorned with various jewelled ornaments and wear garments of heavenly silk.

As mentioned before, according to Highest Yoga Tantra we strive to attain the state of Buddhahood possessing the seven pre-eminent qualities of embrace. These seven qualities are embodied by Conqueror Vajradhara. All Tantras include methods for transforming attachment into the spiritual path by generating pure, uncontaminated bliss and then using that mind of bliss to meditate on emptiness. The four classes of Tantra are distinguished by the way in which bliss is generated in conjunction with a consort. In Action Tantra, bliss is generated by looking at a consort, in Performance Tantra by exchanging smiles with her, in Yoga Tantra by touching her, and in Highest Yoga Tantra by entering into union with her.

Lama Losang Tubwang Dorjechang is endowed with the thirty-two major signs and eighty minor indications of a Buddha. His entire body is made of light and he sits with his legs crossed in the vajra posture amidst an aura of five-coloured rainbow lights, which are the nature of his five exalted wisdoms.

At first it is difficult to visualize this in detail, and we should be satisfied with a rough image of Lama Losang Tubwang Dorjechang. What matters most of all is to understand the significance of this visualization so that we can develop faith. As it says in the sadhana, we should regard our Spiritual Guide as 'the very essence of all the Buddhas'. To do this we need to recall the instructions from the stages of the path on relying upon a Spiritual Guide, where there are many scriptural citations, analogies, and logical reasons proving that our Spiritual Guide is a Buddha.

According to *Offering to the Spiritual Guide* we regard our Spiritual Guide as an emanation of Je Tsongkhapa, who in turn is an emanation of Buddha Shakyamuni, who in turn is an emanation of Conqueror Vajradhara. We can be certain that our Spiritual Guide is an emanation of Conqueror Vajradhara because Conqueror Vajradhara himself said that in degenerate times he would appear in an ordinary form as a Spiritual Guide. Because Buddhas have completely abandoned self-cherishing they are necessarily non-deceptive; therefore we must believe what Conqueror Vajradhara says.

In the golden age, when Buddha Shakyamuni was teaching, there were sentient beings who had a great deal of merit, and so they were able to see Buddha Shakyamuni directly. Some were even able to see him as a Supreme Emanation Body endowed with the major signs and minor indications. These days, however, when times are degenerate and sentient beings have little merit, we are not able to see Buddha's form directly. Even if a Buddha endowed with the hundred and twelve signs and indications were present in front of us we would be unable to see him. Impure minds can see only impure forms. Therefore, to make themselves accessible to sentient beings in these impure times, the Buddhas have to appear in ordinary forms as Emanation Bodies who appear to take rebirth from ordinary parents and are apparently subject to ageing, sickness, and death. However, they still perform the functions of a Buddha.

If we were to meet Buddha Shakyamuni directly, how would he help us? He would guide us by setting an immaculate example, teaching spiritual paths, and encouraging us in our practice. If we examine the actions of our present Spiritual Guide we will see that he or she is doing just this. Anyone who performs the actions of a Buddha must be a Buddha. Thus, although our Spiritual Guide appears in an ordinary form, we can be certain that he or she is a Buddha.

Everyone who has attained enlightenment in the past has done so with the intention of helping sentient beings, and every Buddha has promised to continue working for the benefit of others until all sentient beings have reached enlightenment. Since it is inconceivable that Buddhas would break their promise, we can be certain that all the Buddhas are still working to help us. If we ask who is helping us right now, the answer is our Spiritual Guide. Therefore, it follows that our Spiritual Guide is an emanation of the Buddhas.

We tend to focus on the external appearance of our Spiritual Guide without considering his actual nature. Because our Spiritual Guide appears to us in an ordinary form it is easy to assent to that appearance and relate to him as an ordinary being. To prevent this ordinary view of our Spiritual Guide we need to contemplate the foregoing reasons again and again. As has already been explained, pure view is an essential part of any Tantric practice. If it is necessary to maintain pure view of ourself, our environment, and our enjoyments, how much more important is it to maintain pure view of our Spiritual Guide? We shall never attain Tantric realizations until we can see our Spiritual Guide and Conqueror Vajradhara as inseparable.

If we see faults or imperfections in our Spiritual Guide we should regard these as the projections of our impure mind and ignore them. The experiences of past Yogis show how deceptive appearances can be. Asanga, for example, saw Maitreya as a dog, and Naropa saw Tilopa as an old man who caught fish and fried them alive. Later, when their minds were purified, these great Yogis saw the real nature of their Gurus. If we maintain a pure view of our Spiritual Guide, later, when we attain the realization of the concentration of the Dharma continuum on the Mahayana path of accumulation, we shall see him as a Supreme Emanation Body, then, when we attain the Mahayana path of seeing, we shall see him as an Enjoyment Body, and finally, when we attain Buddhahood, we shall see him as the Truth Body.

Even if our Spiritual Guide is wrathful with us we should still keep pure view of him. The Kadampa Geshes used to advise 'The Guru who rebukes you is reciting wrathful mantras that pacify your obstacles, and the Guru who beats you is granting empowerments that bestow blessings.' If we cannot put this advice into practice straight away, we should at least try to understand it and generate the intention to practise it in the future.

One reason for visualizing our Spiritual Guide as Lama Losang Tubwang Dorjechang is to remind us that, like Buddha himself, our Spiritual Guide has an outer, inner, and secret aspect. His outer aspect, Je Tsongkhapa, is that of a Hinayana monk; his inner aspect, Buddha Shakyamuni, is that of a Supreme Emanation Body endowed with the signs and indications; and his secret aspect is that of Conqueror Vajradhara. His purpose in showing these three aspects is to demonstrate to his disciples how they should behave in public, how they should be motivated internally, and what they should practise in secret.

Our outer aspect is important because ordinary people, who cannot see internal states of mind, judge us by our external appearance and behaviour. Here, we visualize our Spiritual Guide as a fully-ordained monk wearing the three religious robes: the lower garment, the tang gö, and the two upper garments, the chö gö and the nam jar. The appearance of a Hinayana monk wearing saffron robes pleases everyone's mind because it symbolizes the inner beauty of a peaceful and controlled mind. In the *Namasanghita* Buddha praised the clothes worn by monks and nuns as the best clothes because they create a virtuous impression in everyone. We naturally appreciate and respect someone who wears religious robes, who keeps pure moral discipline by observing the two hundred and fifty three vows of a monk, who has few possessions and few desires, and who always remains with a peaceful and controlled mind.

The external appearance of a saffron-robed monk is the best outer aspect because it naturally induces respect in others and thereby makes it easier for us to help them. However, this does not mean that internally we should keep a Hinayana attitude. By showing his inner aspect as a Supreme Emanation Body possessing the thirty-two major signs and eighty minor indications, our Spiritual Guide demonstrates that our internal motivation should be

Drubchen Gendun Gyaltsän

bodhichitta. A Supreme Emanation Body can be accomplished only by training in the Mahayana paths.

Within the Mahayana there are both Sutra and Tantra paths. By showing a secret aspect as Vajradhara, the principal Tantric Buddha, our Spiritual Guide demonstrates that we should not be satisfied with the Sutra Mahayana paths alone, but should take as our heart practice the stages of the path of Secret Mantra. Thus, our Spiritual Guide demonstrates that externally we should show the aspect of maintaining pure moral discipline by observing the Pratimoksha vows purely, internally we should be motivated by bodhichitta and follow the Bodhisattva's way of life, and secretly we should strive to attain enlightenment as a Tantric Buddha by practising the two stages of Highest Yoga Tantra.

This way of practising Dharma, with an outer, inner, and secret aspect, is very beautiful because not only is it the best way to help others, it is also the supreme method for completing our own spiritual development. Je Tsongkhapa practised in this way. Gungtang Rinpoche once composed a praise to Je Tsongkhapa in which he rejoiced in his outer, inner, and secret aspects:

Externally you appear as a disciplined saffron-robed
    monk keeping purely all your Pratimoksha vows,
Internally you are motivated by the precious mind
    of bodhichitta,
And secretly you are a Tantric Yogi practising the
    two stages;
Only you possess these good qualities.

There is an even deeper significance to the visualization of our Spiritual Guide as Lama Losang Tubwang Dorjechang, which was revealed to Mahasiddha Dharmavajra by Je Tsongkhapa when he appeared to him in this form. To understand this we first need to understand how everyone has a gross body and mind, and a subtle body and mind.

Normally, when we think about our body and mind, we are thinking about our gross body and mind, and the self that we apprehend in dependence upon these is our gross self. Our gross body is formed from the sperm of our father and the blood of our mother. At the time of conception our mind enters into the fertilized ovum in our mother's womb and then we begin gradually to identify these new substances as our body. In reality, however, they are not our body because they are derived from the bodies of others. Moreover, this new form is only a temporary abode for our mind because sooner or later we have to die, at which time we have to abandon this body like a bird leaving one nest to fly to another. Because our gross body is a temporary body it does not make sense to cling to it as our actual body.

Just as our gross body is temporary, so too are our gross minds. At death, our gross minds subside and dissolve into our very subtle mind, the clear light of death. It is only this subtle mind that passes from one life to the next. In the next life, new gross minds arise from the clear light mind; we do not take any gross minds with us from our previous life.

Since the gross body and the gross minds of this life are temporary, it follows that the gross self that is imputed upon them is also temporary. The self of this life did not exist prior to conception, and it will cease to exist at death, because when the body and mind of this life separate irreversibly there is no longer any basis for imputing the self of this life.

After death it is our subtle mind that passes into the next life; thus although our gross minds are temporary, our subtle mind is not. Our subtle mind has existed since beginningless time and will remain for eternity. For this reason it is called 'the continually residing mind'. Sometimes, as at the death time and during sleep, it manifests naturally, but at other times, unless it is intentionally manifested in meditation through completion stage practices, it remains in a latent form.

The subtle mind is mounted on a subtle inner wind from which it is never separated. This subtle wind is our subtle body. Just as the subtle mind is beginningless and endless, so too is the subtle body; thus, the subtle body is called 'the continually residing body'. The self that is imputed upon the subtle mind and body is the subtle self. This subtle self never dies. Death occurs when the body and mind separate irreversibly. Thus, when the gross body and mind separate the gross self dies and the person of this life ceases to exist. The subtle body and mind, however, never separate; therefore the subtle self never dies.

The subtle body is the subtle inner wind located inside the central channel at the heart. For ordinary beings the shape of this body is not fixed. After the clear light of sleep has ceased we arise in a subtle body called the dream body, and after the clear light of death has ceased we arise in a subtle body called the intermediate state, or bardo, body. Each time we dream we assume a different dream body, and each time we die we assume a different bardo body.

By training in the completion stage of Highest Yoga Tantra we learn to manifest our subtle mind and subtle body during meditation. Eventually, through the force of completion stage meditation, our subtle mind transforms into meaning clear light and our subtle body transforms into the pure illusory body, which is the actual body of the Deity. There are two types of illusory body: the impure illusory body and the pure illusory body. When we attain the pure illusory body, we attain the actual vajra body and at that time we pass completely beyond sickness and completely beyond death. By continuing to train in completion stage practices, our mind of meaning clear light transforms into the Truth Body, which is the actual mind of a Buddha, and our illusory body transforms into the Enjoyment Body, which is the actual body of a Buddha. Thus the substantial cause of a Buddha's mind is the mind of meaning clear light, and the substantial cause of this is the subtle continually residing mind. Similarly the substantial cause of a Buddha's body is the illusory body and the substantial cause of this is the subtle continually residing body. From a Tantric point of view, therefore, our subtle body and mind are called our 'Buddha seed' or 'Buddha lineage' because they are the original causes from which the body and mind of a Buddha will eventually develop. Our gross body and mind, however, can never transform into the body and mind of a Buddha because they are temporary and finally have to be abandoned.

Since our Spiritual Guide is a Buddha, his actual mind is the subtle mind of the Truth Body and his actual body is the subtle form of the Enjoyment Body. Ordinary beings, however, are unable to see even ordinary subtle bodies such as dream bodies or bardo bodies, so it goes without saying that they cannot see the completely pure body of the Spiritual Guide, the Enjoyment Body. We can only see the forms of other beings whose karma is similar to our own. Thus we can see other humans and some animals, but we cannot see nagas, gods, or spirits. If a naga were to come into our room we would not see it. Even worldly gods such as Indra have to manifest gross forms to make themselves visible to humans. Therefore, to make himself visible and accessible to ordinary sentient beings, our Spiritual Guide assumes a gross external form. Since this gross form is taken from ordinary parents, it appears to be subject to ageing, sickness, and death like any other gross form. However, our Spiritual Guide's actual body is his vajra body, or Enjoyment Body, and this never dies. The gross form of the Spiritual Guide is like a jewellery box and his vajra body is like a precious jewel inside that box. When we do long-life prayers for our Spiritual Guide we are praying for his gross external form to remain so that he will continue to benefit us directly. There is no need to pray for the long life of his vajra body because it is immortal.

When we visualize our Spiritual Guide as Lama Losang Tubwang Dorjechang, his outer aspect, Je Tsongkhapa, symbolizes our Spiritual Guide's gross external form; his inner aspect, Buddha Shakyamuni, symbolizes his subtle body, the vajra body; and his secret aspect, Conqueror Vajradhara, symbolizes his subtle mind, the Truth Body. In this context, Je Tsongkhapa is called the 'commitment being' because it is a Buddha's commitment to emanate gross forms for the benefit of sentient beings; Buddha Shakyamuni is called the 'wisdom being' because the vajra body of a Buddha is the nature of wisdom; and Conqueror Vajradhara is called the 'concentration being' because the Truth Body of a Buddha never moves from a state of single-pointed concentration on ultimate truth, emptiness. This explanation is based on Ngulchu Dharmabhadra's commentary. According to other commentaries, Je Tsongkhapa and Buddha Shakyamuni are both regarded as commitment beings, Vajradhara as the wisdom being, and the letter HUM as the concentration being.

When we visualize our Spiritual Guide as Lama Losang Tubwang Dorjechang we also visualize within his body the thirty-two Deities of Guhyasamaja. This is indicated by the following words in the sadhana:

> . . . his completely pure aggregates are the five Sugatas, his four elements are the four Mothers, and his sources, veins, and joints are in reality Bodhisattvas. His pores are the twenty-one thousand Foe Destroyers, and his limbs are the wrathful Deities. His light rays are directional guardians such as givers of harm and smell-eaters, and beneath his throne are the worldly beings.

This visualization is sometimes called 'the body mandala of Lama Losang Tubwang Dorjechang'. In this context 'body' refers to various parts of Lama Losang Tubwang Dorjechang's body, and 'mandala' refers to the Deities in whose aspect these various parts appear.

Our Spiritual Guide's five aggregates are the five Buddha families. His aggregate of form is Buddha Vairochana, his aggregate of feeling Buddha Ratnasambhava, his aggregate of discrimination Buddha Amitabha, his aggregate of compositional factors Buddha Amoghasiddhi, and his aggregate of consciousness Buddha Akshobya.

Within our Spiritual Guide's body there are four elements: the earth element, the water element, the fire element, and the wind element. These are the nature of the

91

four Mothers. His earth element is Lochana, his water element Mamaki, his fire element Benzarahi, and his wind element Tara.

Also within our Spiritual Guide's body there are twelve sources: six power sources and six object sources. His six power sources are his eye sense-power, ear sense-power, nose sense-power, tongue sense-power, body sense-power, and mental power. These are the nature of six of the eight great Bodhisattvas. His eye sense-power is Ksitigarbha, his ear sense-power Vajrapani, his nose sense-power Akashagarbha, his tongue sense-power Avalokiteshvara, his body sense-power Sarvanivaranaviskambini, and his mental power Manjushri.

Our Spiritual Guide's six object sources are the forms, sounds, smells, tastes, tactile objects, and other phenomena within his continuum. As we shall see, for auspiciousness it is customary to disregard the last of these and to regard the first five as the nature of the five Bodhisattva goddesses: Rupavajra, Shaptavajra, Gändhavajra, Rasavajra, and Parshavajra respectively.

Our Spiritual Guide's veins and joints are the two remaining Bodhisattvas. The generality of his veins is Maitreya and the generality of his joints is Samantabhadra. These two Bodhisattvas, together with the six Bodhisattvas who are the nature of our Spiritual Guide's sense-powers, are the eight great Bodhisattvas.

Our Spiritual Guide's limbs and the other parts of his body are the ten wrathful Deities of Guhyasamaja. His right hand is Yamantaka, his left hand Aparajita, his mouth Hayagriva, his right shoulder Achala, his left shoulder Takkiraja, his right knee Niladanda, his left knee Mahabala, his crown Ushnishachakravarti, the soles of his feet Sumbharaja, and his secret place Amritakundalini.

All these Deities are visualized in our Spiritual Guide's body as follows. To begin with we visualize at our Spiritual Guide's heart a blue letter HUM which transforms into Buddha Akshobya, the principal Deity of the mandala of Guhyasamaja. He is the same nature as Conqueror

Vajradhara, the concentration being, and he sits in union with Yingchugma. This Buddha Akshobya is not to be confused with the Buddha Akshobya who is our Spiritual Guide's consciousness aggregate and who, as we shall see, also appears in our Spiritual Guide's body, between his heart and navel chakras.

Buddha Vairochana sits in our Spiritual Guide's head with his ushnisha just below our Spiritual Guide's ushnisha and his crossed legs just above his throat chakra. Buddha Amitabha sits with his ushnisha just below our Spiritual Guide's throat chakra and his crossed legs just above his heart chakra. Buddha Akshobya sits between his heart chakra and navel chakra, Buddha Ratnasambhava between his navel chakra and the root of his sex organ, and Buddha Amoghasiddhi between the root of his sex organ and its tip.

Lochana sits in embrace with Buddha Ratnasambhava, Mamaki with Buddha Akshobya, Benzarahi with Buddha Amitabha, and Tara with Buddha Vairochana. Normally, Tara is the consort of Buddha Amoghasiddhi but because she is the nature of our Spiritual Guide's wind element, in this instance she sits in embrace with Buddha Vairochana in our Spiritual Guide's head where, according to this system, the wind mandala is situated.

At both of our Spiritual Guide's eyes sits Ksitigarbha embracing Rupavajra; at both of his ears sits yellow Vajrapani embracing Shaptavajra; at each nostril sits Akashagarbha embracing Gändhavajra; at the root of his tongue sits Avalokiteshvara embracing Rasavajra; near the tip of his sex organ sits Sarvanivaranaviskambini embracing Parshavajra; and at his heart sits red Manjushri. As mentioned before, we do not visualize the phenomena-source goddess, Dharmadhatuvajra, within our Guru's body. The reason for this is that she symbolizes dissolution into emptiness, and not including her is auspicious for the Spiritual Guide not to dissolve his present form into the emptiness of the Truth Body. If we wish to visualize Manjushri embracing a consort, we visualize him embracing Yingchugma; but we do not regard her as one of the thirty-two Deities.

At our Spiritual Guide's crown sits white Maitreya, and at each of his joints sits Samantabhadra. At his right wrist sits Yamantaka, at his left wrist Aparajita, in front of his mouth Hayagriva, at his right shoulder Achala, at his left shoulder Takkiraja, at his right knee Niladanda, at his left knee Mahabala, at his crown Ushnishachakravarti, at the soles of each foot Sumbharaja, and at the tip of his sex organ Amritakundalini.

Originally, the explanation of this body mandala was given by Conqueror Vajradhara in *Vajra Rosary Tantra*. Later a detailed explanation was given by Khädrubje in *Ocean of Attainments of Generation Stage*, which is a commentary to the generation stage of Guhyasamaja. If we cannot visualize all these Deities, it is sufficient simply to regard the various parts of Lama Losang Dorjechang's body as being the nature of these Deities.

Once we have grown used to visualizing this body mandala it is very helpful to apply it in practice, because it is a powerful method for overcoming ordinary appearance and generating strong faith. As already mentioned, the essence of Tantric practice is to maintain pure view at all times, so it is especially important to have pure view of our Spiritual Guide. We need to abandon ordinary appearance of our Spiritual Guide and regard every single part of his body as a Deity. For example, we should regard his right hand as in reality Yamantaka, his mouth as Hayagriva, and so on. Then, if our Spiritual Guide touches us with his right hand we should think that we have received the blessings of Yamantaka, and if he speaks to us we should think that we have received the blessings of Hayagriva. Similarly, if our Spiritual Guide uses wrathful actions, such as beating us with his right hand, or verbally rebuking us, we should also feel that we are receiving the blessings of these Deities. If we are able to overcome ordinary appearance completely and see every part of our Spiritual Guide's body as a Buddha, this is a sign that we have attained very high realizations.

Although Lama Losang Tubwang Dorjechang does not have actual hair pores, within his body we imagine that there are twenty-one thousand principal hair pores. Within each of these there is a Buddha Land complete with its principal Buddha and his entire retinue. The words of the sadhana say 'Foe Destroyers' but the meaning is Mahayana Foe Destroyers, or Buddhas. Our Spiritual Guide is able to manifest these Buddha Lands in his hair pores without his pores becoming larger or the Buddha Lands becoming smaller. Extraordinary powers of a Buddha such as these are difficult to accept at first, but later we will be able to appreciate them. It is very helpful in this context to study the explanations given by Chandrakirti in *Guide to the Middle Way*. More detail on these can be found in the commentary, *Ocean of Nectar*.

There are many stories of great Yogis who could display powers such as these. For example Naropa once showed Marpa the entire mandala of Hevajra on his hand; but his hand did not become larger and the mandala did not become smaller. Also, Milarepa once hid from Rechungpa inside the horn of a dead yak without the horn becoming larger or himself becoming smaller. He then manifested a hail storm and invited Rechungpa to join him for shelter. When Rechungpa was unable to do so, his pride of feeling superior to his Spiritual Guide was subdued.

Lama Losang Tubwang Dorjechang radiates countless rays of light which manifest as the eleven classes of directional guardian, such as givers of harm and smell-eaters. In general there are two types of directional guardian: mundane and supramundane. When we practise *Heruka* or *Vajrayogini Tantra*, for example, we invite eleven types of guardian from the eight great charnel grounds as guests to partake of a torma offering. Usually they assume the aspect of mundane guardians, but when we make torma offerings to them in conjunction with the practice of Heruka and Vajrayogini we visualize each of these guardians in the aspect of Heruka or Vajrayogini. This is because in these practices the guardians in the charnel grounds are emanations of Heruka and Vajrayogini.

In the practice of *Offering to the Spiritual Guide* we imagine that all the mundane directional guardians are beneath Lama Losang Tubwang Dorjechang's throne, indicating that our Spiritual Guide has completely subdued them so that they cannot harm us. The supramundane directional guardians, who are all manifestations of Lama Losang Tubwang Dorjechang, remain in the ten directions, outside the Field of Merit, to pacify outer obstacles.

The reason why all the Buddhas enter into our Spiritual Guide's body is explained by Conqueror Vajradhara in *Vajra Rosary Tantra*. Because ordinary beings cannot see Buddhas directly we cannot, for example, make offerings directly to them. When we make offerings in front of a statue or picture of a Buddha we receive the merit of making offerings to Buddha, but we do not receive the merit of their offering having been directly accepted. However, when we make offerings to the Spiritual Guide all the Buddhas enter into his body so that when the Spiritual Guide accepts our offering we receive the merit of our offering having been directly accepted by all the Buddhas. By the same token, when we make prostrations to our Spiritual Guide we make prostrations to all the Buddhas, when we receive the blessings of our Spiritual Guide we receive the blessings of all the Buddhas, and when we listen to teachings from our Spiritual Guide we are listening to teachings from all the Buddhas. Therefore, it is essential that we disregard the external appearance of our Spiritual Guide and regard his body as a temple in which all the Buddhas abide.

Even if our Spiritual Guide's external behaviour does not conform to our expectations we should still regard his body as a temple and develop faith. If we do this it will benefit us, not our Spiritual Guide. Faith is naturally virtuous because it is never mixed with worldly concerns. With faith we do not need a virtuous motivation to make our actions virtuous; whatever we do out of faith is necessarily virtuous. If we have faith, our mind is calm and peaceful, and non-virtuous minds such as anger, attachment, and jealousy are naturally pacified. If we lack faith our Dharma practice will tend to be mixed with impure motivations, but if we have faith our practice will always be pure. Therefore we should consider the development of faith to be of paramount importance. Regarding our Spiritual Guide's body as a holy temple for all the Buddhas is the supreme means for developing faith.

According to Highest Yoga Tantra, the state of Buddhahood is the resultant Mahamudra that is the union of body and mind. This means that when we become a Buddha our body and mind become the same entity. Thus, unlike ordinary beings, whose body and mind are separate entities, Buddhas' bodies can go wherever their minds go. In the Tantric scriptures it explains that the omniscient mind of a Buddha pervades all objects of knowledge, and so it follows that a Buddha's body also pervades all phenomena. Therefore, not only is our Spiritual Guide's body a temple for all the other Buddhas, it is also present in all phenomena. Thus we are always in the presence of our Spiritual Guide. This is not easy to understand at first but, as we gain some experience of Tantra, we will come to see how true this is.

Even though all the Buddhas are present before us, we are unable to see them because of our karmic obscurations. However, we should not be misled into thinking that they are not present just because we cannot see them. Asanga practised intensive retreat for twelve years before he was able to see Buddha Maitreya directly. When Maitreya finally appeared to Asanga, Asanga asked him where he had been until then. Maitreya replied that he had been with Asanga since the very beginning of his retreat, but it had taken Asanga all this time to purify his mind sufficiently to be able to see him. From this we can see that we do not need to travel long distances or go on long pilgrimages to meet the Buddhas; we have only to purify our minds.

After Milarepa attained enlightenment his disciples asked him to show them the Pure Land where he had attained enlightenment. Milarepa showed them into his cave. Because they still had karmic obscurations all they saw was a cold, empty cave, but for Milarepa it was a Pure Land. Similarly, there are Twenty-four Auspicious Places of Heruka and Vajrayogini in this world where the entire mandala of Heruka, complete with the sixty-two Deities, remains. One of these places is Mount Kailash in Tibet. When tourists go there they see an ordinary mountain, and when practitioners of Hinduism go there they may see Indra's palace; but for pure practitioners of Heruka and Vajrayogini, it is Heruka's mandala. This demonstrates that what we see depends upon our mind. Ordinary minds see ordinary worlds and pure minds see pure worlds. For as long as we have ordinary minds we shall not see all the Buddhas around us, but if we have faith in their presence eventually we will purify our mind and see them directly.

So far we have described the principal figure of the Field of Merit. We now visualize all the other holy beings surrounding him according to the words of the sadhana:

Surrounding him in sequence is a vast assembly of lineage Gurus, Yidams, hosts of mandala Deities, Buddhas, Bodhisattvas, Heroes, Dakinis, and Dharma Protectors.

Since our Spiritual Guide is the essence of all objects of refuge, we visualize all these holy beings as emanations of Lama Losang Tubwang Dorjechang. Thus, from the heart of Lama Losang Tubwang Dorjechang light rays radiate to his right and transform into Maitreya surrounded by all the Gurus of the lineage of the stages of the vast path. Maitreya sits in the centre on a lotus and moon seat. He is orange in colour with one face and two hands, which are held at his heart in the mudra of expounding Dharma. Each hand holds the stem of a flower from a naga tree. On the flower that blooms beside his right ear is a wheel, and on the flower that blooms beside his left ear is a long-necked vase.

He sits in the Bodhisattva posture with one leg slightly extended, like Tara. Seated around him are the fifty-one Gurus of the lineage of the stages of the vast path. They are: Guru Buddha Shakyamuni, Maitreya, Asanga, Vasubandhu, Arya Vimuktasena, Venerable Vimuktasena, Arya Gola, Vinaya Gola, Shantarakshita, Haribhadra, Elder Vidyakokila, Younger Vidyakokila, Lama Serlingpa, Atisha, Dromtönpa, Geshe Gönbawa, Geshe Neusurpa, Geshe Tagmapa, Geshe Lodrag Namseng, Geshe Namkha Gyalpo, Geshe Senge Zangpo, Geshe Gyaltsän Zangpo, Lodrag Drubchen, Je Tsongkhapa, Gyaltsab Dharmarinchen, Togdän Jampäl Gyatso, Khädrubje Tamchäkhyenpa, Baso Chökyi Gyaltsän, Drubchen Dharmavajra, Gyalwa Ensäpa, Khädrub Sangye Yeshe, Panchen Losang Chökyi Gyaltsän (first Panchen Lama), Gendun Gyaltsän, Drungpa Tsöndru Gyaltsän, Drungpa Tabupa, Könchog Gyaltsän, Narga Gyaltsän, Lama Rinchen Döndrub, Panchen Losang Yeshe (second Panchen Lama), Zhadrung Lhakpa, Geleg Gyatso, Losang Namgyal, Kachen Yeshe Gyaltsän, Phurchog Ngawang Jampa, Panchen Palden Yeshe (third Panchen Lama), Khädrub Ngawang Dorje, Ngulchu Dharmabhadra, Yangchän Drubpay Dorje, Khädrub Tendzin Tsöndru, Kyabje Phabhongka Rinpoche, and Kyabje Trijang Rinpoche. Each lineage Guru is in his own aspect, and they all sit facing us. Detailed descriptions of these Gurus are found in the Tibetan works of Kachen Yeshe Gyaltsän.

From the heart of Lama Losang Tubwang Dorjechang light rays radiate to his left and transform into Manjushri surrounded by all the Gurus of the lineage of the stages of the profound path. Manjushri sits in the centre on a lotus and moon seat. He is orange in colour with one face and two hands, which are held at his heart in the mudra of expounding Dharma. Each hand holds the stem of an upala flower. On the flower that blooms beside his right ear is a flaming sword, the nature of the omniscient wisdom of all the Buddhas, and on the flower that blooms beside his left ear is the *Perfection of Wisdom Sutra in Eight Thousand Lines*. Like Maitreya, Manjushri sits in the Bodhisattva posture.

Drungpa Tsöndru Gyaltsän

Seated around him are the forty-six Gurus of the lineage of the stages of the profound path. They are: Guru Buddha Shakyamuni, Manjushri, Nagarjuna, Chandrakirti, Elder Vidyakokila, Younger Vidyakokila, Lama Serlingpa, Atisha, Dromtönpa, Geshe Potowa, Geshe Sharawa, Geshe Chekawa, Geshe Chiwawa, Lungyi Wangchuk, Geshe Drowai Gönpo, Zungchenpa, Tsonawa, Möndrawa, Chökyab Zangpo, Je Tsongkhapa, and Togdän Jampäl Gyatso. From Togdän Jampäl Gyatso up to Kyabje Trijang Rinpoche, the lineage is the same as the lineage of the stages of the vast path.

We may wonder why it is necessary to list the entire lineage. A lineage is a line of instruction that has been passed down from Teacher to disciple, with each Guru in the line having gained personal experience of the instruction before passing it on to others. It is essential for a lineage to be intact if we are to receive the full blessing of the instruction. It is not enough that the written instruction remains. If there is no one left who has personal experience of an instruction, the lineage of that instruction is broken and the blessings are lost. For example, suppose that in the future there is no one left who knows how to make aeroplanes. Even if the manuals and diagrams remained intact, it would be impossible actually to construct an aeroplane without the knowledge and experience of someone who had made one before. If a 'lineage' of experience is necessary to preserve mundane knowledge such as this, how much more important is a lineage that preserves spiritual realizations?

If we were to discover an ancient scripture buried beneath the ground and upon opening it found that it contained instructions on how to become enlightened, we would never be able to attain enlightenment simply by reading the book without receiving teachings on the subject. We would have no means of clarifying doubts or clearing up misunderstandings and, without the blessings of a lineage, we would find it impossible to take the instructions to heart. For us those instructions would be like a locked treasure chest. On the other hand, if we met a Teacher who held the lineage of those instructions, it would be like finding a key that unlocked that chest and led us to a realization of their actual meaning. When we see all the names of the lineage Gurus, therefore, we should consider how fortunate we are to be able to receive instructions that have been preserved purely by so many holy beings since the time of Buddha himself.

From the heart of Lama Losang Tubwang Dorjechang light rays radiate in front of him and transform into our present root Guru surrounded by all our other Spiritual Teachers who share the same lineage and view as our root Guru. Some Kadampa Lamas gave very useful practical advice concerning relying upon more than one Teacher. They would say that if we wish to rely upon more than one Spiritual Guide we should ensure that they all share the same lineage and view as our principal Spiritual Guide, otherwise the blessings of the latter will soon disappear.

We visualize our root Guru in his usual form, except that we do not recall any apparent imperfections but imagine him with a perfect, youthful form. If he is still alive, we visualize him sitting on a meditation seat, not on a lotus and moon seat. His right hand is in the mudra of expounding Dharma and his left hand is in the mudra of meditative equipoise holding a vase filled with long-life nectar. His right hand symbolizes that he destroys our ignorance by giving us teachings, and his left hand symbolizes that he protects us from uncontrolled death. Je Tsongkhapa said that ignorance and uncontrolled death are the two greatest obstacles to attaining enlightenment. Ignorance prevents spiritual realizations and generates confusion about spiritual instructions. Uncontrolled death steals our precious life and deprives us of the opportunity to attain enlightenment. If we lose our money we can always earn more, or at least borrow some, but if we lose this precious life we can never replace it. Therefore we should constantly request our Spiritual Guide to protect us from ignorance and uncontrolled death.

From the heart of Lama Losang Tubwang Dorjechang light rays radiate behind him and transform into the Gurus of the lineage of Secret Mantra. These appear in five columns, with the foot of each column slightly behind Lama Losang Tubwang Dorjechang. At the top of the central column is Conqueror Vajradhara. Beneath him is Manjushri, and beneath him are all the Gurus of the Ensa Whispered Lineage, from Je Tsongkhapa to Kyabje Trijang Rinpoche, all appearing in the form of Manjushri. To the right of this column there are two more columns. In the column to the far right are the lineage Gurus of the Guhyasamaja practice and in the right column nearest to the centre are the lineage Gurus of the Yamantaka practice. On the far left are the lineage Gurus of the Heruka practice and between these and the central column are the lineage Gurus of the sixteen Deities of the Kadampa tradition. These last are the principal Deities of the Kadampa Teachers. The principal Deity is Thousand-Armed Avalokiteshvara (Chenrezig Gyalwa Gyatso). In his heart, is four-armed Chenrezig, in his heart is two-armed Chenrezig, in his heart is Tara, in her heart is Buddha Shakyamuni, in his heart is Maitreya, in his heart is Achala, in his heart is Atisha, and so on. To receive detailed instructions on these it is necessary to receive the empowerment of the sixteen Deities. We do not visualize the Deities themselves, just the lineage Gurus of this tradition.

The four principal groups of Gurus appear in space as emanations from the heart of Lama Losang Tubwang Dorjechang. Around him, on the four petals of the top tier of the lotus, there are the principal Deities of Highest Yoga Tantra. On the petal to Lama Losang Tubwang Dorjechang's right is Guhyasamaja surrounded by the thirty-two Deities of Guhyasamaja. Guhyasamaja is blue with three faces and six arms and embraces his consort, Parshavajra, who is also blue with three faces and six arms. All his retinue have three faces and six arms and hold various implements.

On the petal in front is Yamantaka surrounded by the thirteen Deities of Yamantaka. Yamantaka is dark blue with

nine faces and thirty-four arms and embraces Vajra Ben-
dali. On the petal to the left is Heruka surrounded by the
sixty-two Deities of Heruka. He is dark blue with four faces
and twelve arms and embraces Vajravarahi. On the petal
at the back is Hevajra surrounded by the nine Deities of
Hevajra. He is sky-blue with eight faces and sixteen arms
and embraces Nairatma.

On the tier of lotus petals below this, which is slightly
wider in diameter with more petals than the one above it,
are all the other Deities of Highest Yoga Tantra such as
Guhyatara, Hayagriva, Vajrayogini, and Kalachakra,
together with their retinues. On the third tier, which is
larger still, are all the Deities of Yoga Tantra such as Kun-
griya Sarvavirti, who is white in colour with four faces and
two arms. On the fourth tier are all the Deities of Performance Tantra such as Bhagawan Vairochana Abhisam-
bodhi, who has one face and two hands. He is yellow and
has a large retinue of a hundred and seventeen Deities. On
the fifth tier are all the Deities of Action Tantra such as
Tarsig Sanka who is yellow with one face and two hands,
Amitayus, White Tara, Green Tara, Ushnisha Vijaya,
Eleven-Faced Mahakaruna, Bhagawan Vajra Akshobya,
Sitapatri, and Achala.

On the sixth tier are all the Sutra Buddhas such as the
Thousand Buddhas of this Fortunate Aeon, the Seven
Medicine Buddhas, and the Thirty-five Confession
Buddhas. On the seventh tier are all the Bodhisattvas such
as the eight great disciples of Buddha Shakyamuni:
Manjushri, Avalokiteshvara, Vajrapani, and so forth. On the
eighth tier are all the Emanation Solitary Conquerors and
on the ninth tier are all the Emanation Hearers, including
the sixteen Arhats: Mayaparitaka, Chudapartaka, and so
forth. In general, Solitary Conquerors and Hearers are
Hinayanists, the former being superior to the latter in terms
of both merit and wisdom. In this instance, however, we
regard them all as emanations of Lama Losang Tubwang
Dorjechang appearing in the aspect of Hinayana practitioners. On the tenth tier are all the Heroes and Heroines

such as the Heroes and Heroines of the Twenty-four Auspicious Places of Heruka. These are the Tantric Sangha who assist Tantric practitioners. In particular, they help to increase bliss, to fulfil wishes, and to bestow attainments. Whenever we make a tsog offering we regard all those present as an assembly of Heroes and Heroines. Finally, on the eleventh tier, the one that covers the surface of the largest throne, are all the Dharma Protectors such as Mahakala, Kalindewi, and Kalarupa. These are supramundane beings who manifest a wrathful aspect, but who in reality are manifestations of our Guru's wisdom. Their main function is to protect Dharma practitioners from adverse conditions and to create favourable conditions for their practice.

The inner realizations of all these holy beings appear in the form of scriptures which rest on small tables on either side of them. Thus, all Three Jewels are included within this visualization. The first six tiers, the Gurus, Deities, and Sutra Buddhas, are all Buddha Jewels; the remaining five tiers, the Bodhisattvas, Solitary Conquerors, Hearers, Heroes and Heroines, and Dharma Protectors, are all Sangha Jewels; and the emanated scriptures beside each holy being symbolize the Dharma Jewels.

It does not matter if we cannot visualize the entire assembly in detail. We should be satisfied with a rough image, rather as we would visualize a large crowd, and try to focus on the principal figure, Lama Losang Tubwang Dorjechang. The main thing is to have conviction that all these holy beings are present and that they are all emanations of our Spiritual Guide. This last point is very important because we will never gain Tantric realizations if we regard our Spiritual Guide as different from the Three Jewels. In particular, we must be firmly convinced that our Spiritual Guide and our Deity are the same nature.

On one occasion, Marpa was woken from his sleep by his Spiritual Guide, Naropa, who informed him that his Deity, Hevajra, had manifested in his room. Marpa leapt out of bed and prostrated to Hevajra. Naropa scolded him, saying that it was inauspicious to prostrate to the Deity before prostrating to the Spiritual Guide because the Deity was manifested by the Spiritual Guide. Then, to demonstrate this point, he reabsorbed Hevajra into his body!

The main reason we find it difficult to believe that our Deity is manifested by our Spiritual Guide is that we see our Spiritual Guide as an ordinary being and readily assent to this appearance. This is a great obstacle to our Tantric practice. If we regard our Guru and Deity as one, we will be able to practise the essence of Deity yoga and make use of very powerful methods for accumulating merit and wisdom. For example, if we see our Guru and Deity as one, every time we practise self-generation we will be performing Guru yoga. Then every time we eat, for example, we will be making offerings to our Spiritual Guide. With profound practices such as these we can attain enlightenment very quickly.

We need to make the most of the precious opportunity that now faces us. Although we are living at a time when Buddha's teachings are rapidly degenerating in this world, there is a prophesy that at this time the practice of Tantra will flourish briefly, just as a candle flame flickers brightly for a few seconds before it is finally extinguished. It is not certain how long this phase will last, but while it does we have a very rare opportunity to receive Tantric teachings and engage in Tantric practices with relative ease. Since Tantric realizations depend principally upon faith, it is essential that we develop and increase our faith if we are to make the most of this precious opportunity.

These days sentient beings have very strong attachment, which would normally be a huge obstacle to gaining Dharma realizations but, through the kindness of Buddha's Tantric teachings, we are able to transform this attachment into the spiritual path and harness all this otherwise negative energy as a powerful force in our spiritual development. Therefore we should not be discouraged but engage in the practice of Tantra purely and sincerely.

Even people who have been very evil can attain enlightenment swiftly through the practice of Tantra because Tantra includes extremely powerful methods for purification. For example, according to the Hinayana Sutras it is impossible for anyone who has committed any of the five heinous actions such as killing their father or mother to gain the path of seeing for many lives, but according to Tantra such people can become Buddhas in that same life. If we meet a fully-qualified Tantric Master and rely upon him purely with great devotion, we can purify even the heaviest negative karma very quickly. Therefore we should constantly strive to prevent ordinary appearance of our Spiritual Guide and see him as one with the Deity.

INVITING AND ABSORBING THE WISDOM BEINGS

The holy beings whom we initially visualize are called the 'commitment beings' because it is our commitment to visualize the Buddhas every day and to make offerings and perform other acts of devotion to them. However if we are not very skilful we may feel that these beings exist only in our imagination and that there are no actual Buddhas in front of us. To overcome such doubts we now invite the actual Buddhas and other holy beings, who are known as the 'wisdom beings', to come from their abodes, enter into our visualization, and remain one with it while we make offerings and so forth. The sadhana says:

> **Their three doors are marked by the three vajras. Hooking light rays radiate from the letter HUM and invite the wisdom beings from their natural abodes to remain inseparable.**

We begin by visualizing the three letters, OM AH HUM, at the three channel wheels, or chakras, of each holy being. In general the phrase 'three doors' refers to our body, speech, and mind, which are the doors through which we perform all our actions, but here when the sadhana says 'their three doors', it is referring to the three principal places of the holy beings' body, speech, and mind. The principal place of the body is the crown chakra, the principal place of the speech is the throat chakra, and the principal place of the mind is the heart chakra. It is easy to see why the throat chakra is the principal place of the speech, but it is not so easy to understand the other two. As for the heart chakra, this is where the subtle mind is located. At death, all our gross minds absorb into the subtle mind at our heart, and in the next life new gross minds evolve from that subtle mind. Therefore, our root mind is the subtle mind at our heart. This is why the heart chakra is regarded as the principal place of the mind.

It is a little more difficult to understand why the crown chakra is regarded as the principal place of the body; after all, in his *Four Hundred*, Aryadeva says that the body sense-power pervades the entire body. The reason why the crown chakra is regarded as the principal place is that it is the main source of the white drops. All the elements of the body originate from the white and red drops that come from the bodies of our parents. Our drops are the source of all the growth and vitality within our body. If our drops increase we become strong and healthy, but if our drops diminish our body weakens. Generally the red and white drops flow through the channels within our body, but the main concentration of the red drops is at the navel and the main concentration of the white drops is at the crown.

The main reason why our crown chakra is the principal place of our body, our throat chakra the principal place of our speech, and our heart chakra the principal place of our mind is that these are the three doors through which our body, speech, and mind receive the blessings of the Buddhas' body, speech, and mind.

At Lama Losang Tubwang Dorjechang's crown we visualize a white letter OM, at his throat a red letter AH, and at his heart a blue letter HUM. These three letters are known as the 'three vajras' because they are the nature of the vajra body, the vajra speech, and the vajra mind of all the Buddhas. A Buddha's body, speech, and mind are called 'vajras' because they are immortal and indestructible, completely beyond birth, ageing, and death. The synthesis of the vajra body of all Buddhas is Buddha Vairochana, the synthesis of the vajra speech of all Buddhas is Buddha Amitabha, and the synthesis of the vajra mind of all Buddhas is Buddha Akshobya. OM is the seed-letter of Buddha Vairochana, AH the seed-letter of Buddha Amitabha, and HUM the seed-letter of Buddha Akshobya.

From the letter HUM at the heart of each holy being, light rays radiate and invite the wisdom beings to arise from the emptiness of the Truth Body, here referred to as 'their natural abode', and appear in the same form as the visualization in front of us. Since the Truth Body pervades all phenomena it is present wherever we are, so we do not need to invite the wisdom beings to come from a long way away; however, if it serves to strengthen our conviction that every single Buddha in the universe has been invited we can imagine hooking rays of light pervading the ten directions and drawing back the wisdom beings. We imagine that instantaneously all the Buddhas appear in the space above our visualization, each Buddha assuming the form of the entire Field of Merit.

The sadhana continues with two verses of invocation:

You who are the source of all happiness and goodness,
The root and lineage Gurus of the three times, the
**   Yidams, and Three Precious Jewels,**
Together with the assembly of Heroes, Dakinis,
**   Dharmapalas, and Protectors,**
Out of your great compassion please come to this
**   place and remain firm.**

Even though phenomena are by nature completely
**   free from coming and going,**
You appear in accordance with the dispositions of
**   various disciples**
And perform enlightened deeds out of wisdom
**   and compassion;**
O Holy Refuge and Protector, please come to this
**   place together with your retinue.**

The first verse is quite straightforward; it is simply inviting all the holy beings out of their great compassion to come before us and remain firmly conjoined with the commitment beings whom we have visualized. The second verse however requires a little more explanation. All phenomena have two natures: a conventional nature and an ultimate nature. So long as we are satisfied with the mere appearance to mind of a phenomenon, it exists and functions for us. This mere appearance is its conventional nature. If, without being satisfied with this mere appearance to mind, we investigate more deeply in the hope of discovering a phenomenon that exists from its own side, we will find nothing. The ultimate nature of all phenomena is emptiness. Thus, although from the point of view of their conventional natures things come and go, from the point of view of their ultimate nature there is no coming or going. According to the Madhyamika philosophy, ultimately all phenomena are free from eight extremes: coming, going, production, cessation, existence, non-existence, singularity, and plurality.

A similar point is made by Venerable Milarepa in one of his songs where he says that from the point of view of ultimate truth there is no samsara and no nirvana, there are no spiritual paths, no results of those paths, no meditators, no objects of meditation, no enlightenment, and no Buddhas. All these phenomena, he says, are merely imputed by conception. Thus, although ultimately there are no Buddhas, conventionally, from the point of view of mere appearance to mind, Buddhas exist.

In the second invocation verse, we remember that ultimately all phenomena are free from coming and going, and we request the Buddhas to arise as mere appearances to mind in whatever forms are beneficial for the various disciples, performing enlightened deeds for their benefit. Thus, when we invite the wisdom beings we do not think that they exist from their own side; rather we invite them merely as appearances to mind, as mere imputations. Indeed it is only because Buddhas do not exist from their own side, because they are mere imputations, that they can arise in a variety of forms according to the needs of disciples. If we invite the wisdom beings with this recognition our action will be an uncontaminated action because it will be free from grasping at inherent existence.

Having invited all the wisdom beings, we imagine that they assemble in the space above the commitment beings, each one in the form of the entire Field of Merit. We then recite:

OM GURU BUDDHA BODHISATTÖ DHARMAPALA
SAPARIWARA EH HAYE HI: DZA HUM BAM HO
The wisdom beings become inseparable from
the commitment beings.

The words 'OM GURU', refer to Lama Losang Tubwang Dorjechang, 'BUDDHA BODHISATTÖ DHARMAPALA' refers to all the other holy beings, 'SAPARIWARA' refers to their retinues, and 'EH HAYE HI' is a mantra of invocation. When we recite 'DZA' we imagine that the wisdom beings come to the crowns of their commitment beings; when we recite 'HUM', we imagine that the wisdom beings dissolve into the commitment beings; when we recite 'BAM', we imagine that the wisdom beings and commitment beings merge completely into one; and when we recite 'HO' we imagine that their union becomes utterly unchangeable.

As mentioned before, the purpose of inviting and absorbing the wisdom beings is to strengthen our conviction that all the Buddhas exist within the body of our Spiritual Guide. Buddha said that he would appear wherever faithful disciples invited him. Buddhas have clairvoyance and so they hear our requests whenever we pray to them. They come immediately because they have great love for us, just as a mother comes immediately when she hears her child calling. Because Buddhas' bodies are the same nature as their mind they are not obstructed by physical objects or distance. By inviting the wisdom beings and imagining that they enter into our Spiritual Guide's body we are left with a special feeling of our Spiritual Guide being like a temple for all the Buddhas. This is very helpful for preventing ordinary appearance and increasing our faith.

Whenever we invite the wisdom beings of the Field of Merit in *Offering to the Spiritual Guide*, thousands and thousands of Buddhas come. Therefore, any place where this sadhana is performed naturally becomes blessed.

If we are unsure about the ability of Buddhas to enter into our Spiritual Guide's body, we have only to think about oracles. In Tibet there were many oracles who would invite spirits to enter into their body and make predictions. These invocations were witnessed by many people, and there were very clear signs that the spirit had actually entered into the oracle's body and taken over. If mundane beings such as spirits can enter into an oracle's body, there can be no doubt that Buddhas can enter into our Spiritual Guide's body.

In his commentary to *Guhyasamaja Tantra*, Nagarjuna says that we should always regard our Spiritual Guide's body as superior even to Conqueror Vajradhara's. Why is this? Even though Conqueror Vajradhara is very precious, being the embodiment of all five Buddha families, we shall not be able to see his body or receive teachings directly from him until we reach the first Bodhisattva ground, and by that time we shall be highly realized meditators. Who will help us in the meantime, when we have no realizations and very little merit? It is our Spiritual Guide, who appears to us now and guides us on the spiritual path by giving us instructions directly. Therefore he is more precious for us even than Conqueror Vajradhara.

Imagine that there is a beggar who is completely impoverished. In such a state of destitution he has no opportunity to meet with kings and queens or other important figures in society. Suppose a kind benefactor takes that beggar into his care, feeds him, and provides him with employment so that later, as a result of the gradual improvement of his fortunes, he then has an opportunity to meet with important people. Even though he would be grateful to them for receiving him into their company, he would be even more grateful to his original benefactor who had helped him in his hour of need. In the same way, even though it will be marvellous when we finally meet Conqueror Vajradhara face to face, it is far more wonderful to meet with our kind Spiritual Guide right now.

Könchog Gyaltsän

Offering the Practice of the Seven Limbs

Having invited the Field of Merit and absorbed the wisdom beings, we now offer the practice of the seven limbs together with the mandala. The seven limbs are:

1 Prostration
2 Offering
3 Confession
4 Rejoicing
5 Requesting the turning of the Wheel of Dharma
6 Beseeching the Spiritual Guide not to pass away
7 Dedication

These practices are called 'limbs' because they support the main body of our practice, the actual meditations on the stages of the path of Sutra and Tantra. The practice of the seven limbs has two main functions: to accumulate merit and to purify the mind. More specifically, the practices of prostration, offering, requesting, and beseeching accumulate merit; the practices of rejoicing and dedication increase merit; and the practice of confession purifies negative karma.

Merit, or good fortune, is the positive energy that results from virtuous actions. In general we all need merit because we cannot fulfil our wishes without it. Even to fulfil worldly aims we require merit, so how much more necessary is it to fulfil our spiritual hopes? In the Sutras Buddha said that those who have merit can fulfil all their wishes and overcome all their obstacles, and so they can easily attain enlightenment. Buddhas have two principal bodies: the Form Body and the Truth Body. Unlike the contaminated bodies of samsaric beings that are produced from the poisons of the delusions, a Buddha's bodies are produced from pure causes. The main cause of the Form Body is the collection of merit, and the main cause of the Truth Body is the collection of wisdom. Therefore, if we want to meet with success in our spiritual practices and finally attain enlightenment, we need to accumulate a great amount of merit. As already explained, Lama Losang Tubwang Dorjechang and all the other holy beings are a supreme Field of Merit. By offering the practice of the seven limbs to them we will quickly accumulate a vast collection of merit and fulfil all our wishes.

PROSTRATION

To prostrate is to show respect. There are three types of prostration: physical, verbal, and mental. We make physical prostrations when we use our body to show respect to the holy beings. We can make full-length prostrations, half-length prostrations, or simply place our palms together at our heart. We make verbal prostrations when we recite praises and so forth to the holy beings, and we make mental prostrations when we develop a mind of faith and respect towards them. We should try to perform all three types of prostration together. Of these three, the most important is mental prostration because faith is the root of all good qualities and all spiritual attainments. Generating faith and respect by contemplating our Spiritual Guide's good qualities and remembering his kindness is not only mental prostration, it is also a sublime offering because it is untainted by worldly concerns. The great Indian Buddhist Master Phadampa Sangye said:

> O People of Tingri, the Spiritual Guide will lead you wherever you wish to go. To repay his kindness, offer your faith. Faith is the supreme offering.

If we wish for a human rebirth our Spiritual Guide will lead us there, if we wish for liberation he will lead us there, if we wish to be reborn in a Pure Land he will lead us there, and if we wish to attain enlightenment he will lead us there. No one is kinder than our Spiritual Guide. To repay his kindness we have only to develop and increase our faith in him. This is the offering that will please him the most.

The practice of prostration in *Offering to the Spiritual Guide* has five parts:

1 Prostrating to the Spiritual Guide as the Enjoyment Body
2 Prostrating to the Spiritual Guide as the Emanation Body
3 Prostrating to the Spiritual Guide as the Truth Body
4 Prostrating to the Spiritual Guides as the synthesis of all Three Jewels
5 Prostrating to the lineage Gurus and Three Jewels

PROSTRATING TO THE SPIRITUAL GUIDE AS THE ENJOYMENT BODY

Spiritual Guide with a jewel-like form,
Who out of compassion bestow in an instant
Even the supreme state of the three bodies, the
**   sphere of great bliss,**
O Vajra Holder I prostrate at your lotus feet.

The actual, ultimate body of a Buddha is the Truth Body. From this arises the subtle Enjoyment Body, which is a Buddha's actual Form Body. However, this body is too subtle for most living beings to see and so the Enjoyment Body manifests the Emanation Body. The principal Emanation Body is the Supreme Emanation Body possessing the signs and indications of a fully enlightened being. This body manifests countless other Emanation Bodies appearing in ordinary forms for the benefit of migrators.

In this verse, we focus on the Enjoyment Body aspect of our Spiritual Guide, represented by Conqueror Vajradhara at the heart of Lama Losang Tubwang Dorjechang, and make prostrations. Although we usually see our Spiritual

Guide in an ordinary aspect we need to remember that in reality he is Conqueror Vajradhara, the 'Vajra Holder', and develop faith in him accordingly. Our Spiritual Guide is like a jewel because he is so precious. Among all jewels, the most precious is the legendary wishfulfilling jewel, but even this can grant only mundane wishes. Our Spiritual Guide on the other hand can fulfil all our wishes. He can grant us not only mundane happiness but also the supramundane attainment of full enlightenment.

A Buddha's three bodies – the Truth Body, the Enjoyment Body, and the Emanation Body – are completely pure because they arise from the inseparable union of bliss and emptiness. This is indicated by the words 'sphere of great bliss'. In this context, 'sphere' refers to emptiness. Although we can attain a union of bliss and emptiness before we attain enlightenment, the union that is referred to here is the inseparable Union of the resultant Mahamudra, or Buddhahood. By relying upon our Spiritual Guide we can attain this union in one short human life. For example, out of his great compassion Dharmavajra bestowed great enlightenment on his disciple Losang Döndrub in three short years. Compared to the life of a hell being, this is like an instant. Therefore, the sadhana says 'Who out of compassion bestow in an instant'.

This extraordinary wishfulfilling quality of the Spiritual Guide is praised in many scriptures. For example, in *Heruka Tantra* it says that rather than making offerings to all the Buddhas and Bodhisattvas it is better to make offerings to our Spiritual Guide because he alone can bestow spontaneous great bliss, which is the means to attain enlightenment in one short human life. Similarly, in *Five Stages of Completion Stage* Nagarjuna says that if we fell off a cliff we would fall to the ground below whether we wanted to or not and, in the same way, if we rely sincerely upon our Spiritual Guide we will be liberated from samsara even if we wish not to be. This is illustrated by the lives of many great Bodhisattvas. Out of their great compassion, courageous Bodhisattvas often generate the wish to remain in samsara to help sentient beings, even if it means spending aeons in the hell realms, but because they rely sincerely upon their Spiritual Guides they cannot help attaining liberation. Nagarjuna's Spiritual Guide, the great Yogi Saraha, said that if we rely sincerely upon our Spiritual Guide we will definitely attain spontaneous great bliss, but if we abandon our Spiritual Guide, no matter how hard we try or for how long we practise, this attainment will be impossible.

Contemplating the extraordinary qualities of our Spiritual Guide, we should develop deep faith and respect and prostrate to him with body, speech, and mind. The Tibetan word for prostrate is 'chag tsäl' in which 'chag' means to sweep away impurities and defilements and 'tsäl' means to request all good qualities. Therefore, when we say 'I prostrate' we are saying that we want to cleanse ourself of all faults and defilements and attain all the good qualities of our Spiritual Guide.

PROSTRATING TO THE SPIRITUAL GUIDE AS
THE EMANATION BODY

Exalted wisdom of all the infinite Conquerors
Out of supremely skilful means appearing to suit
disciples,
Now assuming the form of a saffron-robed monk,
O Holy Refuge and Protector I prostrate at your
lotus feet.

As already mentioned, because ordinary sentient beings cannot see the Enjoyment Body it manifests the Emanation Body, which is a gross form that is visible to ordinary beings. Even then, the Supreme Emanation Body is not visible to those who have not attained the Mahayana path of accumulation, unless they have very pure karma. When we reach the third stage of the Mahayana path of accumulation, known as the 'great stage', we attain a realization known as the 'Concentration of the Dharma Continuum'. At this point we are able to recall all the Dharma teachings we have heard throughout all our previous lives, and we never forget any new teachings that we receive. With this realization we are also able to see and receive teachings directly from the Supreme Emanation Body. However, for those who have not yet attained this state, the Supreme Emanation Body manifests other Emanation Bodies. So as to be visible to ordinary beings, these emanations appear in ordinary forms, appearing to take rebirth from ordinary parents and to be subject to ageing, sickness, and death. We should not be misled by this ordinary appearance into thinking that these emanations are ordinary beings. We should remember that the apparently ordinary characteristics of our Spiritual Guide are manifested for our benefit, and that without this ordinary aspect we would not be able to see him at all. Therefore, we should think that our Spiritual Guide is by nature the exalted wisdom of all the Buddhas, who out of supremely skilful means manifests in whatever form is most suitable for his disciples, for example as a saffron-robed monk, and then prostrate to him with great faith.

A Supreme Emanation Body manifests countless other bodies for the benefit of sentient beings. Thus, Buddha Shakyamuni for example manifested millions of forms simultaneously in countless different worlds. In some worlds he manifested taking birth, while in others he was manifesting passing away. In some he demonstrated turning the Wheel of Dharma, while in others he appeared as an ordinary monk, or as a king or queen. Sometimes he appeared as a non-Buddhist such as Indra, sometimes as an ordinary man or woman, sometimes as a spirit, sometimes as an animal, sometimes as a handicapped person, sometimes as a crazy person, and sometimes even as a heavily deluded person. A Buddha's manifestations are completely beyond the scope of ordinary imagination. In *Guide to the Bodhisattva's Way of Life*, Shantideva says that, if it benefits sentient beings, Buddhas even manifest as inanimate objects such as bridges, boats, trees, and even whole countries. Because of our karmic obscurations we have no way of telling whether or not something is an emanation of Buddha. Something or someone may seem perfectly ordinary to us, but they could easily be an emanation. In fact, the more we think about it, the more it seems that everything around us could be an emanation.

The Buddhas have spent aeons investigating which is the best way to help sentient beings, and they have concluded that it is to manifest in an ordinary form as a Spiritual Guide, demonstrate a perfect example, and guide sentient beings by giving Dharma teachings. If our Spiritual Guide were to display clairvoyance and miracle powers it would not benefit us. Buddhas cannot remove our delusions with their hands, nor can they grant us realizations like giving us a present; all they can do is to show us the path and encourage us to follow it. Contemplating this, we realize that there is no one kinder than our Spiritual Guide, who appears in an ordinary form, sets an immaculate example for us to follow, and leads us on the path to liberation and enlightenment by giving flawless teachings.

PROSTRATING TO THE SPIRITUAL GUIDE AS THE TRUTH BODY

**Abandonment of all faults together with their imprints,
Precious treasury of countless good qualities,
And sole gateway to all benefit and happiness,
O Venerable Spiritual Guide I prostrate at your lotus feet.**

As mentioned before, the actual, ultimate body of a Buddha is the Truth Body. There are two types of Truth Body: the Wisdom Truth Body and the Nature Truth Body. The former is the actual omniscient mind of a Buddha and the latter is the emptiness, or ultimate nature, of that mind. These two bodies are not separate entities but are the same nature. To attain enlightenment it is necessary to remove two types of obstruction from the mind: the delusion-obstructions and the obstructions to omniscience. Any mind that is free from these two obstructions is a Wisdom Truth Body, and the emptiness of that mind is the Nature Truth Body. The Nature Truth Body is the ultimate true cessation. It is referred to in the first line of this verse as the 'abandonment of all faults together with their imprints'. The Wisdom Truth Body is referred to in the second and third lines.

In the *Diamond Cutter Sutra* Buddha says that those who think that his body is a physical object and that his speech is sound are mistaken because his actual body is the Truth Body. The same applies to our Spiritual Guide. Without some experience of Secret Mantra it is difficult to understand this. When we attain enlightenment, it is not this present body of flesh and bone that becomes a Buddha's body; rather we develop a completely new body, an ultimate illusory body that is one nature with the ultimate clear light of the Truth Body.

It is also difficult for us to understand how the Wisdom Truth Body is the source of all good qualities and the sole gateway to all benefit and happiness. To understand this point we need to improve our experience of Secret Mantra. According to Secret Mantra, the definitive Guru is the indivisible bliss and emptiness of the Truth Body, and the Guru that appears to us in various forms is the interpretative Guru. The definitive Guru is in reality the synthesis of all phenomena, because all phenomena are manifestations of bliss and emptiness. This is explained in the yoga of the complete purity of all phenomena in the *Heruka* and *Vajrayogini Tantras*.

PROSTRATING TO THE SPIRITUAL GUIDES AS THE SYNTHESIS OF ALL THREE JEWELS

Essence of all Guru-Buddhas and Deities,
Source of all eighty-four thousand classes of holy
   Dharma,
Foremost amongst the entire Superior Assembly,
O Kind Spiritual Guides I prostrate at your lotus
   feet.

With this verse we prostrate to the five groups of Spiritual Guides in the Field of Merit, including the Gurus of the Mahamudra lineage, but we pay particular attention to Lama Losang Tubwang Dorjechang as the synthesis of all holy beings. In *Heruka Tantra* it says:

The Guru is Buddha, the Guru is Dharma,
The Guru is also Sangha.
The Guru is the creator of all;
To all Gurus I prostrate.

This means that we should regard our Spiritual Guide as the synthesis of all Three Jewels: Buddha, Dharma, and Sangha. According to *Vajra Rosary Tantra*, we should regard our Spiritual Guide's mind as Buddha, his speech as Dharma, and his body as Sangha, and make offerings and prostrations to him accordingly. When the *Heruka Tantra* says that our Spiritual Guide is 'the creator of all', it does not mean that he has created the whole universe; rather the meaning is that all pure happiness is created by Spiritual Guides. In samsara there is no uncontaminated happiness; this is to be found only by relying upon our Spiritual Guide. Remembering this, we should make prostrations to all the Spiritual Guides in the Field of Merit.

PROSTRATING TO THE LINEAGE GURUS AND THREE JEWELS

To the Gurus who abide in the three times and the
   ten directions,
The Three Supreme Jewels, and all other objects
   of prostration,
I prostrate with faith and respect, a melodious
   chorus of praise,
And emanated bodies as numerous as atoms in the
   world.

This verse is particularly important for our practice, and if possible we should memorize it and recite it whenever we do prostrations. It explains to whom we should prostrate, with what motivation we should prostrate, and how we should prostrate. First it says that we should make prostrations to all the Gurus in the three times and the ten directions. There are countless Gurus throughout the universe, there have been countless Gurus in the past, and there will be countless Gurus in the future. For example, if we consider the lineage of the stages of the profound path, there are only forty-six Gurus named, starting with Guru Buddha Shakyamuni, but Buddha Shakyamuni had a Guru, who in turn had a Guru, and so on without beginning.

Besides the Gurus and Three Jewels, there are countless other objects of prostration such as all those who are not yet Buddhas but who guide others on the path by giving vows, teachings, and so forth; those who observe purely any of the three types of moral discipline; Dharma books and other representations of the Three Jewels; and spiritual friends who set a good example or give helpful advice. We should develop a motivation of faith and respect for all of these countless objects of prostration and prostrate to them all with body, speech, and mind.

As for how we should prostrate, we make mental prostrations by developing a mind of faith and respect, and we make verbal prostrations by imagining a melodious chorus of praise resounding throughout the universe. To make physical prostrations, we imagine that from every pore of our body we manifest another body, and that each of these bodies in turn manifests countless other bodies, and so on, until the whole universe is filled with our bodies, and then we imagine that they all make prostrations. By prostrating in this way we receive incalculable benefits.

We have had countless bodies in the past, but we have wasted them all. Now we should try to derive some meaning from this present body by using it to make prostrations to the holy beings. Prostrations are very precious. If we do prostrations regularly it will be good for our health, our mind will become happy and clear, we will accumulate vast amounts of merit, and we will purify our negative karma. The Tantric scriptures say that we should continue to make offerings and prostrations to our Spiritual Guide even after we have attained enlightenment. Je Tsongkhapa, for example, was already enlightened, but to show a good example to others he performed three and a half million prostrations to the Thirty-five Confession Buddhas – a hundred thousand to each Buddha – while in retreat at Ölga Chölung. As a result, he accomplished a special vision of the Thirty-five Buddhas. If holy beings such as Je Tsongkhapa make prostrations, how much more important is it for us to do this practice? More detail on prostrations can be found in *Joyful Path of Good Fortune* and *The Bodhisattva Vow*.

OFFERING

The practice of offering has seven parts:

1 Offering the outer offerings and the five objects of desire
2 Offering the mandala
3 Offering our spiritual practice
4 Inner offering
5 Secret offering
6 Suchness offering
7 Offering medicines, and ourself as a servant

OFFERING THE OUTER OFFERINGS AND THE FIVE OBJECTS OF DESIRE

This has two parts:

1 Offering the outer offerings
2 Offering the five objects of desire

OFFERING THE OUTER OFFERINGS

**O Guru, Refuge, and Protector, together with your retinue,
I offer you these vast clouds of various offerings:**

According to *Offering to the Spiritual Guide* there are ten outer offerings:

1 Water for drinking
2 Water for bathing
3 Water for the mouth
4 Water for sprinkling
5 Flowers
6 Incense
7 Light
8 Perfume
9 Food
10 Music

These substances have already been set out on the shrine and blessed as part of the preliminary practices. After they have been blessed, we develop three recognitions: (1) their nature is the exalted wisdom of bliss and emptiness, (2) they appear in the aspect of the individual offering substances, and (3) they function as objects of enjoyment of the six senses to generate a special wisdom of bliss and emptiness in whoever experiences them.

Although we visualize these offerings in their usual aspect, we do not think of them as ordinary substances but as having the nature of bliss and emptiness. In the Sutras Buddha taught how to regard all phenomena as manifestations of emptiness. Thus, in the *Heart Sutra* he says:

Form is empty; emptiness is form. Emptiness is not other than form; form also is not other than emptiness.

This means that forms such as water, flowers, and incense are empty of inherent existence and do not exist from their own side. Flowers, for example, are merely a manifestation of the emptiness of flowers. Thus, when we offer substances such as flowers we should do so with the recognition that the three spheres of the offering – the person making the offering, the offering itself, and the recipient of the offering – are all empty of inherent existence.

When we make offerings in Highest Yoga Tantra practices, we go one stage further and regard the offerings as manifestations of bliss and emptiness. The essence of Secret Mantra is the attainment of the union of bliss and emptiness. To accomplish this we first generate a mind of spontaneous great bliss and then mix this mind with emptiness, like mixing water with water. From the point of view of the experience of Tantric practitioners, therefore, there is no difference in entity between the subjective mind, spontaneous great bliss, and the object emptiness upon which it is focused. Accordingly they see all phenomena not just as manifestations of emptiness, but as manifestations of bliss and emptiness, because for them the two are indivisible. Even though we have not yet attained the realization of the union of bliss and emptiness, it is very beneficial to try to understand it intellectually and then to regard all phenomena as manifestations of bliss and emptiness.

According to the sadhana, we should offer 'vast clouds' of offerings to the Field of Merit, which means that we should imagine all our offerings to be vast and extensive. The first four outer offerings are known as the 'four waters'. These are offered with the words:

The purifying nectars of the four waters gently flowing
From expansive and radiant jewelled vessels perfectly arrayed;

As we recite these words, we perform the appropriate hand gestures and visualize countless offering goddesses emanating from our heart carrying jewelled vessels filled with delicious nectar for drinking. They offer this to the Field of Merit who partake and thereby experience uncontaminated bliss. Then the goddesses reabsorb into our heart and we manifest new goddesses carrying vessels of water with which they bathe the feet of the holy beings. After these are reabsorbed, we manifest more goddesses who offer water for refreshing the mouth, and then we manifest goddesses who offer sprinkling water for refreshing the body. In each case we should imagine that the water is the nature of

Panchen Losang Yeshe

exalted wisdom nectar and that it functions to induce uncontaminated bliss in the holy beings.

When we set out the four waters on the shrine, we should try to offer water that is cool, delicious to taste, light, soft, clear, sweet-smelling, good for the digestion, and soothing on the throat. Offering cool water causes us to develop pure moral discipline, offering delicious water ensures that we will always find delicious food and drink in future lives, offering light water will cause us to experience the bliss of physical suppleness, offering soft water makes our mind calm and gentle, offering clear water makes our mind clear and alert, offering sweet-smelling water brings easy and powerful purification of negative karma, offering water that is good for the digestion reduces our illnesses, and offering water that soothes the throat makes our speech beautiful and powerful. If we cannot find water that possesses these eight qualities we should imagine that we are offering such water, and then we shall receive the same benefits.

Beautiful flowers, petals, and garlands finely arranged,
Covering the ground and filling the sky;

After offering the four waters we manifest countless offering goddesses, some carrying single flowers, some carrying flower garlands, and some carrying flower petals for scattering. We visualize these flowers as breathtakingly beautiful, with heavenly scents, and we imagine that they cover the ground and fill the sky. The goddesses offer these flowers to the holy beings, causing them to experience uncontaminated bliss. Then we reabsorb the goddesses into our heart.

By offering flowers in this way, we create the cause to have a pleasant appearance in future lives and to see everything around us in a pleasant aspect. If we could see everything and everyone as beautiful we would not develop anger or jealousy but would feel affectionate love for all living beings. On the basis of this we would find it very easy to generate compassion and bodhichitta. More-over, if we could experience everything as pleasant we would not generate attachment because our mind would always be balanced. From this we can see that immense benefits come from making qualified offerings.

> **The lapis-coloured smoke of fragrant incense**
> **Billowing in the heavens like blue summer clouds;**

When we offer incense we manifest countless offering god-desses holding precious bowls of gold, silver, and lapis, filled with many different types of incense. The swirling smoke from this incense billows in the sky like blue sum-mer clouds, and when the holy beings experience its aroma they generate uncontaminated bliss. By offering incense we create the cause always to experience pleasant smells and never to be reborn in unpleasant places.

> **The playful light of the sun and the moon,**
> **glittering jewels, and a vast array of lamps**
> **Dispelling the darkness of the three thousand**
> **worlds;**

Next we offer light by manifesting countless goddesses holding butter lamps, glittering jewels, and many other sources of light, including the sun and the moon. Each lamp radiates light from which other lamps manifest, and so on, until all the three thousand worlds are illuminated by this offering. Temporarily, offering light makes our mind clear and sharp during meditation and creates the cause to have clear eyesight. Moreover, offering candles with steady, long-lasting flames creates the cause to have a long life. Princi-pally, however, offering light is a powerful method for destroying the darkness of ignorance and increasing our wisdom. Practitioners of Mother Tantras such as *Heruka* or *Vajrayogini Tantra* emphasize the attainment of the wisdom of clear light and so they should make many light offerings.

Traditionally, light is offered in the form of butter lamps, or oil lamps. The significance of this offering is as follows. The wick symbolizes self-grasping, the butter or oil symbolizes the ocean of samsaric suffering, and the flame symbolizes wisdom realizing emptiness. As the flame burns the wick and consumes the butter or oil, we imagine that the wisdom realizing emptiness is destroying our self-grasping and thereby consuming the ocean of samsara. Alternatively, we can think of the butter or oil as the lower realms and the wick as all the different types of rebirth in those realms, and as the flame burns we imagine that the three lower realms are being completely purified.

> **Exquisite perfume scented with camphor,
> sandalwood, and saffron,
> In a vast swirling ocean stretching as far as the eye
> can see;**

Next we offer perfume by manifesting countless goddesses holding precious vessels filled with camphor, sandalwood, saffron, and other sweet-smelling substances. We imagine that the holy beings experience these and generate uncontaminated bliss. As with all the other offerings, the holy beings have no need of such substances, but they accept them for our benefit. When we offer perfume we create the cause to attain pure moral discipline.

> **Nutritious food and drink endowed with a
> hundred flavours
> And delicacies of gods and men heaped as high as
> a mountain;**

The text says that we offer food 'with a hundred flavours', which literally means a hundred and eight flavours. There are six principal flavours: sweet, sour, bitter, astringent, hot, and salty; and each of these can be produced in combinations such as sweet-sweet and sweet-sour, making a total of thirty-six flavours. Each of these flavours can be strong, middling, or weak – making a total of a hundred and eight different flavours. We emanate goddesses bearing foods endowed with all these flavours and offer them to the holy beings. The benefits of offering food are that in the future we shall always find nourishing food and drink, and that we shall be sustained by the food of concentration.

> From an endless variety of musical instruments,
> Melodious tunes filling all three worlds;

When we offer music, we emanate countless goddesses playing musical instruments such as flutes, drums, and lutes, and singing melodious songs. The sound of this music fills all three realms – the human realm, the god realm above, and the Naga realm below – and induces uncontaminated bliss in all the holy beings. By offering music we create the cause to hear only pleasant sounds in the future, especially the sound of Dharma, and never to hear bad news.

OFFERING THE FIVE OBJECTS OF DESIRE

> Delightful bearers of forms, sounds, smells, tastes,
>   and objects of touch –
> Goddesses of outer and inner enjoyments filling
>   all directions.

Secret Mantra is sometimes called the Path of Attachment because it is the method for transforming attachment into the spiritual path. As already mentioned, the essence of Secret Mantra is the generation of spontaneous great bliss. Initially great bliss is generated through the force of attachment but, once it is generated, it destroys the attachment that gave rise to it, rather as a fire that is started by rubbing together two pieces of wood then consumes that wood. For ordinary beings the most powerful objects of attachment are the five objects of desire – attractive forms, sounds, smells, tastes, and tactile objects. In Secret Mantra these objects are visualized in a pure form and then enjoyed so as to generate bliss.

At this stage in the sadhana, we offer the five objects of desire to the Field of Merit. Because all the beings in the Field of Merit are emanations of Lama Losang Tubwang Dorjechang they are all enlightened beings, thus they have no need for objects of desire because they abide eternally in a state of spontaneous great bliss. However, by offering these objects to them we create the cause for us to generate spontaneous great bliss.

There are two types of sense object: inner and outer. Inner sense objects are those that are conjoined with consciousness, for example the forms, sounds, smells, tastes, and tactile objects within the continuum of a person; and outer sense objects are those that are not conjoined with consciousness, for example the taste or smell of an apple. We begin by offering outer sense objects.

From our heart we manifest countless Rupavajra goddesses who are white in colour and extremely attractive. They each hold precious mirrors in which are reflected all the beautiful forms throughout the three thousand worlds. We imagine that when the holy beings behold these forms they generate spontaneous great bliss. We then reabsorb the Rupavajra goddesses into our heart and manifest countless Shaptavajra goddesses. They are blue in colour and play various musical instruments that delight the holy beings. After reabsorbing them we manifest countless Gändhavajra goddesses who are yellow and hold white conch shells brimming with exotic perfumes, whose fragrance delights the holy beings. Then we manifest countless Rasavajra goddesses who are red and hold bowls filled with many types of delicious food which they offer to the holy beings. Finally we manifest countless Parsha-vajra goddesses who are green and hold heavenly silks that induce great bliss when touched. We imagine that the holy beings enjoy all these objects and generate spontaneous great bliss. Offering the five outer sense objects in this way creates the cause to be able to transform them into the path in the future.

Offering the five inner sense objects is especially important for practitioners of completion stage because it is a special method for generating spontaneous great bliss. It is important to know what spontaneous great bliss is. We should not think that because it is such an advanced realization we do not need to know about it yet. By developing an intellectual understanding of spontaneous great bliss now we create the cause actually to generate this mind in the future. Spontaneous great bliss is not simply a pleasurable feeling, nor is it the bliss of suppleness induced by tranquil abiding, or the bliss of tranquility experienced by Foe Destroyers. Spontaneous great bliss is a special bliss that arises when, through the force of completion stage meditation, the winds enter, abide, and dissolve within the central channel causing the drops therein to melt and flow. There are different methods for causing the winds to enter, abide, and dissolve within the central channel, such as tummo (or inner fire) meditation and vajra recitation. These will be explained below. When the winds dissolve into the central channel, the various knots that usually constrict that channel are loosened. Then, through the force of the blazing of the inner fire, the drops melt and flow, thereby inducing great bliss.

There are four stages to the development of this bliss. As the white drop in the crown channel wheel melts and descends to the throat channel wheel, the first level of bliss, known simply as 'joy' is generated. When it descends to the heart channel wheel the second level of bliss, known as 'supreme joy', is generated; when it descends to the navel channel wheel the third level, 'extra-ordinary joy', is generated; and finally when it descends to the tip of the sex organ the fourth level, 'spontaneous great joy', is generated. Each level of bliss is more power-ful than the preceding one, and spontaneous great joy is the most powerful. For experienced practitioners of com-pletion stage the drops never leave the central channel. They remain at the tip of the sex organ for a while and then rise again through the central channel, giving rise to another four levels of spontaneous great bliss, which are even more powerful. In this way, an accomplished practi-tioner is able to keep the drops flowing up and down the central channel all day and thereby experience sponta-neous great bliss for extended periods of time.

It is important to distinguish spontaneous great bliss from the feeling of bliss that is induced by ordinary sexual intercourse. During ordinary intercourse, the tummo heat is increased, causing the drops to flow through the channels and induce a feeling of bliss; but in this case the drops flow through the outer channels, not the central channel, and are eventually ejaculated or collect in the uterus. Thus the bliss of ordinary sex is a gross, contaminated mind that is short-lived. In completion stage practices, however, the winds are gathered and dissolved into the heart channel wheel inside the central channel, and this gives rise to a very special bliss that is pure and uncontaminated. This bliss is non-conceptual and free from distraction, and when it focuses on emptiness it readily mixes with it like water mixing with water. Because at this stage the practitioner's drops never leave the central channel, spontaneous great bliss can remain completely absorbed in emptiness for long periods of time without distraction. Thus it is able to eliminate self-grasping and its imprints very quickly. This is why Secret Mantra is a quick path to enlightenment.

Once we are able to meditate on emptiness with spontaneous great bliss, we shall be able to attain enlightenment through this practice alone. We shall not have to perform external actions such as prostrations or offerings, nor shall we have to do other types of meditation. Meditation on the clear light of bliss is at once a collection of merit and a collection of wisdom, and so it is the cause of both the Form Body and the Truth Body of a Buddha. According to Sutra, a Bodhisattva cannot accumulate both the collection of wisdom and the collection of merit simultaneously within one single meditation, but has to accumulate wisdom principally during the meditation session and then rise from meditation to accumulate merit during the meditation break. However in Secret Mantra both these collections can be accumulated within one single meditation, the meditation on spontaneous great bliss. Hence, whereas it is said that a Bodhisattva on the Sutra path takes three countless great aeons to attain enlightenment, Tantric practitioners can complete the path in a matter of years.

By contemplating these points, we will increase our faith in Secret Mantra and develop a strong desire to generate spontaneous great bliss. In some Sutras it says that apart from the fourth Buddha, Buddha Shakyamuni, only the eleventh and the last of the thousand Buddhas of this Fortunate Aeon will teach Secret Mantra. The reason these teachings are so rare is that they are easily misunderstood or misused, and so there are very few suitable disciples who can practise them purely. Therefore, we should consider ourself extremely fortunate even to be able to read these instructions, and we should generate a strong determination to practise them purely while we have the opportunity.

With an understanding of the nature and function of spontaneous great bliss, we can appreciate the importance of offering the five inner sense objects. This practice was explained by Je Tsongkhapa in his Guhyasamaja and Heruka sadhanas, and the following explanation is based on those texts.

We begin by offering inner forms. From the HUM at our hearts we manifest countless knowledge women who are breathtakingly beautiful and skilled in the sixty-four arts of love. We imagine that the holy beings generate spontaneous great bliss simply by beholding their beautiful forms and sensuous postures. These goddesses are then reabsorbed and we manifest countless other knowledge women who induce bliss with the sound of their voices. Then we manifest countless knowledge women whose bodies have a heavenly fragrance that induces great bliss in whoever experiences it. These are followed by knowledge women who induce bliss with the taste of their kisses, and finally by knowledge women whose vaginas induce bliss in whoever touches them.

The Heruka sadhanas include another method for offering the five objects of desire. According to this method we begin by imagining that all the countless worlds gather into one. We then imagine that all the forms in this world transform into attractive Rupavajra goddesses, all the sounds into Shaptavajra goddesses, all the smells into Gändhavajra goddesses, all the tastes into Rasavajra goddesses, and all the objects of touch into Parshavajra goddesses. These goddesses are then offered to the holy beings who generate spontaneous great bliss. If we do this practice regularly we will gradually come to perceive all sense objects as Rupavajra goddesses and so forth, and in this way we shall overcome ordinary appearances. If we enjoy objects of desire with such pure appearance, there is no danger of our committing non-virtue or breaking our vows. Pure appearance is the essence of Secret Mantra practice and the foundation of Tantric moral discipline.

OFFERING THE MANDALA

O Treasure of Compassion, my Refuge and
Protector, supremely perfect Field of Merit,
With a mind of devotion I offer to you
A thousand million of the Great Mountain, the
four continents,
The seven major and minor royal possessions, and
so forth,
A collection of perfect worlds and beings that give
rise to all joys,
A great treasury of the desired enjoyments of gods
and men.

In this context, the mandala is the entire universe visualized as completely pure and offered to the Field of Merit. When we offer the mandala, we imagine that we are holding the entire universe in our hands, but our hands do not become larger and the universe does not become smaller. If we find this difficult to understand, we can think about how large images can be reflected in a small mirror, or how whole cities can be shown on a television screen.

We do not offer just the world in which we live, but all worlds. According to Buddhist cosmology our world is flat with a large mountain, Mount Meru, in the centre. This is surrounded by four continents, each of which has two major and many minor sub-continents. A thousand such worlds together is called 'the thousand worlds', a thousand of these is called 'the two thousand worlds', and a thousand of these is called 'the three thousand worlds'. When we offer the mandala, we imagine the three thousand worlds in our hands and, regarding them as Pure Lands, offer them to the holy beings.

We do not need to doubt the existence of such worlds. Buddhas and others who have attained clairvoyance confirm the existence of countless worlds besides our own, all of which are inhabited by a great variety of living beings. Moreover, we should be careful not to reject the view of the world as flat with a large mountain and four continents simply because it does not appear that way to us. The way the world appears depends upon the mind that is viewing it, and Buddha described the world in many different ways depending upon the karma of the disciples he was addressing. The essential point about a mandala offering is to visualize the world as a Pure Land, and for this purpose it is most helpful to follow the description given by Buddha. When we offer the mandala it does not matter that we cannot picture all the different worlds in detail. We should be like a blind man who lives in a beautiful house. Though he cannot see the house he knows that it is beautiful and is pleased by it.

Because we are offering the entire universe in a pure form, it is easy to make this offering without miserliness, and without the stains of the eight worldly concerns. Therefore, mandala offerings are very powerful and produce great results. With each offering we accumulate a vast amount of merit and create the cause to be reborn in a Pure Land. Even if we are not reborn in a Pure Land, we will be reborn in a beautiful, peaceful environment.

In the space above the four continents we visualize the seven major and minor possessions of a chakravatin king. A chakravatin king is an extremely fortunate being who has accumulated a vast amount of merit and as a result has

taken rebirth as a king with dominion over all four continents, or at the very least over one of the four continents.
At present there are no chakravatin kings in our world, and
there is no one who has complete dominion over our
continent, Jambudipa.

Because of their unusual merit, chakravatin kings have
a hundred and twelve bodily features that are very similar
to a Buddha's thirty-two major signs and eighty minor
indications, and their retinues also have special features.
They also have seven special possessions: a precious wheel,
a precious jewel, a precious queen, a precious minister, a
precious elephant, a precious horse, and a precious householder or a precious general. The last two are not the same,
but either can act as his servant.

The precious wheel is made of gold and has a thousand
spokes. It is five hundred miles in diameter and serves as a
chariot for the king. It is like a huge sun aloft in the sky and
it can convey the king and his entire entourage three times
round the three thousand worlds in a single day. The wheel
is symbolic of the king's sovereignty, for he reigns wherever
it goes. In the scriptures the precious wheel is used as an
analogy for Dharma. When Buddha revealed the entire path
to enlightenment he was said to have 'turned the Wheel of
Dharma' because wherever the Wheel of Dharma is present
deluded minds are brought under control.

The precious jewel is made of lapis lazuli, is octagonal,
and radiates five-coloured lights that illuminate the three
thousand worlds. Its light transforms night into day, radiates warmth in cold regions, and cools hot regions. It has
the power to prevent sickness and untimely death wherever the king reigns.

The precious queen is very beautiful and completely free
from imperfections. Her body has a naturally pleasant
fragrance and she induces bliss in whoever touches her.
She has great love for all her subjects, caring for them like
a mother, and eliminating sorrow wherever she reigns.

Unlike ordinary ministers, who are biased and preju-
diced, the precious minister has complete equanimity and

causes harm to no one. All his actions are in accordance with Dharma. He is very skilful in administering the king's affairs and he intuitively knows the king's wishes and fulfils them without being asked.

The precious elephant is shaped like an ordinary elephant but it is so large that it looks like a snow mountain! It has seven limbs: four legs, a trunk, a tail, and an erect penis. It is as strong as a thousand ordinary elephants but is so tame it can be led by a fine thread. It can convey the king round the three thousand worlds three times in a day, always maintaining a very smooth gait that induces bliss in the rider. It instinctively recognizes the king's enemies and subdues them effortlessly.

The precious horse is white and adorned with celestial jewels. It does not require reins because it knows the thoughts of its rider. Although it is as fast as the wind, the ride is always extremely smooth. It too instinctively protects its rider from harm.

The precious householder is the keeper of the king's treasury. He ensures that the treasury is always brimming with gold, silver, and many rare jewels; but in all his dealings he never deceives anyone. He brings wealth to all the king's subjects and, because of his love, compassion, and very stable mind, he is respected by everyone and regarded as a father by all.

The mandala offering and its contents are not a Tibetan invention. These things were described by Conqueror Vajradhara in the *Guhyasamaja Tantra* where he says:

Those who wish for attainments
Should mentally and skilfully fill this universe
With the seven precious objects.
By offering them every day,
Their wishes will be fulfilled.

Those who have received Highest Yoga Tantra empowerments have a commitment to offer the mandala six times a day to their Spiritual Guide. The reason we are given this commitment is that we need to accumulate a vast amount of merit to receive Secret Mantra realizations.

In addition to the seven major royal possessions listed above, chakravatin kings also have seven minor possessions: the precious sword, the precious skin, the precious bedding, the precious garden, the precious house, the precious cloak, and the precious boots.

If a chakravatin king is attacked by an enemy he needs only to hold the precious sword aloft and his enemy is immediately subdued without any blood being shed or any harm being inflicted.

The precious skin is a naga skin five miles long that shines like the sun and the moon. It is fire-proof and water-proof and it keeps the wearer cool in summer and warm in winter. Whoever wears this skin experiences great bliss.

The precious bedding is soft and comfortable and whoever falls asleep on it naturally develops concentration. Even if a dull-minded person were to sleep on it, he or she would wake up with a clear and fresh mind. It also has the power to overcome anger and attachment.

The precious garden is extremely beautiful and peaceful and is inhabited by gods and goddesses playing various musical instruments. Whoever enters this garden naturally develops a virtuous mind. If a heavily deluded, malevolent person were to enter it his mind would immediately be pacified. Everyone who enters the garden has their wishes fulfilled; for example, if someone wishes for a son, they are granted a son, if they wish for a daughter, they are granted a daughter, and so on.

The precious house is made of jewels. It has transparent walls and sparkles with light, day and night. It is frequented by gods and goddesses and always has a happy, tranquil atmosphere. Anxiety and discontent are calmed just by entering this house, and those who are sorrowful or depressed are uplifted by its atmosphere.

The precious cloak is light and smooth, and wearing it induces great bliss. Just like a god's robe, when it is unfolded it covers the whole ground, but when it is rolled up it fits beneath a fingernail.

Whoever wears the precious boots can walk on water as easily as on dry land, and they can travel great distances without difficulty. Wearing them induces great bliss and cures all diseases associated with the feet and legs.

We visualize all these precious objects in the space above the four continents, together with the various offering goddesses, the sun and the moon, the precious umbrella, the victory banner, and all the treasures of gods and men. In short, we amass everything precious throughout the three thousand worlds and offer it to our Spiritual Guide.

If we have time we can offer a long mandala together with other shorter verses at this point. There are two short verses that are especially powerful:

> The ground sprinkled with perfume and spread
>   with flowers,
> The Great Mountain, four lands, sun and moon,
> Seen as a Buddha Land and offered thus,
> May all beings enjoy such Pure Lands.

> I offer without any sense of loss
> The objects that give rise to my attachment, hatred,
>   and confusion,
> My friends, enemies, and strangers, our bodies and
>   enjoyments;
> Please accept these and bless me to be released
>   directly from the three poisons.

These verses are very blessed. The first verse was composed by Dharmodgata in response to requests by Sadaprarudita. It describes the seven-point mandala and shows that we should make mandala offerings with the prayer that all living beings be born in Pure Lands and constantly experience pure enjoyments.

Offering the mandala with the second verse is a powerful method for overcoming the three poisons: attachment, hatred, and confusion. Like any mind, these delusions can arise only in dependence upon their objects. Attachment arises in dependence upon objects of attachment; hatred, or anger, in dependence upon objects of anger; and confusion in dependence upon objects of confusion. Without these objects, the delusions cannot arise, just as a bird cannot land if there is no ground. Therefore, to prevent our delusions arising, we imagine that all the objects that give rise to our attachment, hatred, and confusion are transformed into pure objects and offered to our Spiritual Guide. Because they have been offered we can no longer grasp at them or allow the mind to indulge in them, and in this way we are protected from delusions.

There are four types of mandala offering: outer, inner, secret, and suchness. We offer the outer mandala by visualizing the universe transformed into a Pure Land as already described. To offer the inner mandala, we imagine that our body transforms into a Pure Land and then offer this to our Spiritual Guide. Thus we imagine that our skin splits open and becomes an extensive vajra ground, and our blood and other bodily fluids become perfume anointing this ground. Our trunk becomes Mount Meru, our four limbs the four continents, our fingers the sub-continents, our head Indra's palace on top of Mount Meru, our two eyes the sun and the moon, and our inner organs the precious objects. Offering the mandala in this way is a powerful method for overcoming cherishing our body.

The outer and inner mandalas are explained in both the Sutras and Tantras, but the secret and suchness mandalas are explained only in the Tantras. To offer these we must first generate ourself as the Deity with a mind of great bliss mixed with emptiness. We then imagine that this inseparable union of bliss and emptiness transforms into a mandala in the usual aspect, and we offer this to our Spiritual Guide. Because the mandala is the nature of bliss it is a secret offering, and because it is the nature of emptiness it is a suchness offering. Offering the mandala in this way is very profound and produces great results in the future.

If we do not have much time there is no need at this point to recite the long mandala or the two short verses mentioned above; rather it is sufficient to recite only the verse from the sadhana. If we wish to collect mandala offerings

Losang Trinlay

as one of the four great preliminary guides we can do so either here or at the end of the seven limb practice.

OFFERING OUR SPIRITUAL PRACTICE

O Venerable Guru, I offer these pleasure gardens,
Both actually arranged and emanated by mind, on
    the shores of a wish-granting sea,
In which, from the pure white virtues of samsara
    and nirvana,
There arise offering substances of broad, thousand-
    petalled lotuses that delight the minds of all;
Where my own and others' mundane and
    supramundane virtues of the three doors
Are flowers that bring colour to every part
And emit a multitude of scents like
    Samantabhadra's offerings;
And where the three trainings, the five paths, and
    the two stages are the fruit.

In general, an offering is anything that pleases the Spiritual Guides and other holy beings. According to the Kadampa Geshes, a real Spiritual Guide is pleased not so much by offerings of material gifts or money as by his disciples practising his teachings purely. Therefore it is said that offering our spiritual practice is the supreme offering.

We offer the virtuous practices of ourself and others – both the mundane virtues of ordinary beings and the supramundane virtues of Superior beings – as well as the results of all these practices. These are offered as beautiful forms such as flowers, trees, and lakes. Thus, whereas the actual offering is our virtuous practices and their results, the basis of the offering is external forms. The basis of the offering can be either actual external objects, such as flowers that we have arranged on the shrine, or just mentally imagined forms.

According to the sadhana, our roots of virtue from maintaining pure moral discipline transform into a vast wish-granting sea adorned with beautiful lotuses. Within the sea there are exotic islands on which grow exquisite trees. The roots come from our virtues of listening to Dharma, the branches from our virtues of contemplating Dharma, and the flowers from our virtues of meditating on Dharma. Our realizations of the three higher trainings, the five Mahayana paths, and the two Tantric stages appear as delicious fruits adorning the trees. We visualize countless islands adorned with these trees and offer them to our Spiritual Guide.

Another way to offer our practice is to visualize our virtues of keeping pure moral discipline as water, our faith as flowers, our virtues of keeping the three vows as incense, our virtues of listening to Dharma as light, our virtues of training in concentration as food, our wisdom realizing emptiness as music, and our virtues of maintaining virtuous mental factors, such as sense of shame and consideration, as the five objects of desire.

If we simply offer our faith, for example, this is not an outer offering because we are offering an inner virtue; but if we mentally transform our faith into the aspect of flowers and offer it, it becomes an outer offering.

According to *Offering to the Spiritual Guide*, the outer offerings are made in association with the vase empowerment. When we receive a Highest Yoga Tantra empowerment, the Vajra Master grants four separate empowerments: the vase empowerment, the secret empowerment, the wisdom-mudra empowerment, and the word empowerment. The vase empowerment is so called because it is granted by means of certain rituals associated with a vase. During this empowerment, the Vajra Master emanates from his heart goddesses who bestow the empowerment and thereby help the disciple to overcome ordinary appearances. When we make the outer offerings, we also emanate offering goddesses from our heart, and this practice also helps us to overcome ordinary appearances. Therefore the outer offerings and the vase empowerment are said to be similar in terms of both method and result.

INNER OFFERING

**I offer this ocean of nectar with the five hooks, the
five lamps, and so forth,
Purified, transformed, and increased,
Together with a drink of excellent tea
Endowed with a hundred flavours, the radiance of
saffron, and a delicate aroma.**

The inner offering is unique to Highest Yoga Tantra and is
made in association with the secret empowerment. During
the secret empowerment, the Vajra Master gives the disciples nectar that is derived from the inner drops of the
male and female Deities. Because it is very easy for those
who have not received empowerments, and for those with
Hinayana inclinations, to misunderstand the nature and
function of this nectar it is called a 'secret substance', and
the disciples are advised not to reveal it to others. In a
similar fashion, the inner offering involves the transformation of ten substances – the five meats and the five nectars
– into nectar which is then offered to the holy beings. Once
again, the nature and function of these substances can
easily be misunderstood and so practitioners are advised
also to treat these substances as secret.

The inner offering is so called because the basis of the
offering, the five meats and the five nectars, are inner substances, that is substances that are derived from the continuum of living beings. A detailed description of these
substances and the method for transforming them into the
inner offering is given in *Guide to Dakini Land*. In *Offering
to the Spiritual Guide* the five meats are called the 'five
hooks' and the five nectars are called the 'five lamps' because they are the means for swiftly gathering and illuminating all the Highest Yoga Tantra attainments.

To make the inner offering at this point, we hold both
the vajra and the skullcup containing the nectar with our
right hand, and then with the left hand, which is also
holding the bell, we dip the tip of the ring finger into the
nectar and flick a little into space. At the same time we

imagine countless Rasavajra goddesses emanating from our heart. These goddesses hold skullcups with which they scoop up nectar from our skullcup and offer it to the Field of Merit. We imagine that the holy beings taste the nectar and generate uncontaminated bliss. We then dissolve the goddesses back into our heart.

If we regularly bless the inner offering with strong concentration, offer it to the holy beings, and taste it ourself, this practice will increase our lifespan and make our body and speech very powerful. The principal function of the inner offering, however, is to bless our channels, winds, and drops, thereby increasing our experience of the spontaneous great bliss of completion stage. The inner offering substance can also be used to cure disease in others.

If we wish to make a tsog offering, the actual ritual for doing so in conjunction with *Offering to the Spiritual Guide* is appended to the main sadhana and may be included at any one of a number of places depending upon the particular practice that is being emphasized. If we are emphasizing the swift attainment of realizations we make the tsog offering after the requests, just before the prayer of the stages of the path; if we are emphasizing purification we make the tsog offering in the middle of the seven limb practice, just before the confession verse; and if we are emphasizing accumulating great merit by making offerings, such as in a long life puja, we make the tsog offering at this point, just after the inner offering.

The main purpose of making the tsog offering is to restore broken commitments, to delight the Heroes and Heroines, and to receive special blessings from our Spiritual Guide. If possible the offering should be made by a group of practitioners who have a close connection with each other and who view themselves with divine pride as an assembly of Heroes and Heroines.

The substance of the tsog offering is meat and alcohol, usually referred to by their Sanskrit names, bala and madana, as well as any pure, clean food. The substances are blessed in the same way as the inner offering. The tsog offering is then made in sequence to the Spiritual Guides, Yidams, Three Jewels, Heroes, Heroines, and Dharma Protectors, and all mother sentient beings. From the Spiritual Guides we request blessings, from the Yidams we request Tantric attainments, from the Three Jewels we request Dharma realizations, from the Heroes, Heroines, and Dharma Protectors we request help with our Dharma practice, and when we make the tsog offering to all sentient beings we pray that they will swiftly overcome mistaken appearances and pass beyond suffering.

There then follow two special verses with which the whole assembly makes the tsog offering to their root Guru, after which the tsog offering is tasted by everyone present. We recite 'AH HO MAHA SUKHA', which means 'Oh what great bliss!' and try to generate an experience of great bliss which we offer to the Deities dwelling within our body.

A plate of offerings is then collected for the spirits who do not have the karma to enjoy untouched food but rely upon others giving them food that they have already tasted. Since this is offered as part of the practice of giving, it is sent out just before the verse on the perfection of giving in the prayer of the stages of the path.

SECRET OFFERING

And I offer most attractive illusory mudras,
A host of messengers born from places, born from
  mantra, and spontaneously-born,
With slender bodies, skilled in the sixty-four arts
  of love,
And possessing the splendour of youthful beauty.

The secret offering is also unique to Highest Yoga Tantra. It is performed in association with the wisdom-mudra empowerment because it involves offering a knowledge woman to Guru Vajradhara.

By making this offering we create the cause to generate spontaneous great bliss ourself in the future by relying upon a consort, or mudra. As already explained, the essence of Secret Mantra is to generate spontaneous great bliss by bringing the winds into the central channel. This can be done only to a limited extent by meditation alone; to complete the practice we need to accept an action mudra. Through completion stage meditation we can completely loosen the knots in the channel wheels at the crown, throat, navel, and secret place, and by relying upon vajra recitation in particular we can partially loosen the knots at the heart channel wheel. However we cannot completely loosen these knots by meditation alone. These will naturally loosen completely at death, but if the practitioner wants this to happen before death he or she must accept an action mudra at this stage. Through the force of the two central channels uniting during embrace, the downward-voiding wind of the consort will enter the practitioner's central channel and loosen the knots at the heart channel wheel. Then the practitioner can complete the path to enlightenment in that life.

The correct time to rely upon an action mudra is after having gained the experience of dissolving some of the winds into the central channel at the heart channel wheel. When through this practice, we are able to perceive clearly the eight signs of dissolution from the mirage-like appearance to the clear light, and we have attained the experience of isolated body, isolated speech, and isolated mind, it is appropriate to enter into union with an action mudra.

A mudra is called a 'messenger' because she fulfils our wishes by bringing great bliss. There are three types of messenger: outer, inner, and secret. These are explained in detail in *Guide to Dakini Land*. A knowledge woman is an outer messenger. The verse from the sadhana mentions three types of outer messenger: those born from places, born from mantra, and spontaneously-born. The first are Dakinis from the Twenty-four Holy Places of Heruka, the second are messengers with realizations of generation stage or the first stages of completion stage, and the third are messengers with a realization of the union of clear light and illusory body that is either the union that needs learning or the Union of No More Learning.

We visualize countless action mudras of all three types emanating from our heart, merging into one, and dissolving into Yingchugma, who is sitting in union with Guru Vajradhara at the heart of Lama Losang Tubwang Dorjechang. We imagine that through the force of this offering our Guru generates spontaneous great bliss. It is important to make this offering to the Guru in his secret aspect as Vajradhara and not in his outer aspect as a fully-ordained monk. Once again, from the side of the Guru there is no need to make this offering because he abides immovably in a state of great bliss. The purpose of making this offering is only to create the cause for us to generate spontaneous great bliss in the future.

We should visualize all the knowledge women as extremely youthful and attractive. According to the words of the sadhana these consorts are 'skilled in the sixty-four arts of love'. In the Sutras Buddha explained sixty-four arts in connection with sports such as archery, but in the Tantras he explained sixty-four arts of love as methods for inducing spontaneous great bliss. There are eight basic arts: embracing, kissing, biting, scratching, enticing walking, whistling, performing the actions of a man, and lying on top. Each of these can be performed in eight different ways, making sixty-four arts in all.

In the *Guhyasamaja Tantra* Vajradhara stresses the importance of Tantric practitioners making the four types of offering every day, and he places special emphasis on the secret offering as a method for generating great bliss.

SUCHNESS OFFERING

I offer you the supreme, ultimate bodhichitta,
A great, exalted wisdom of spontaneous bliss free
from obstructions,
Inseparable from the nature of all phenomena, the
sphere of freedom from elaboration,
Effortless, and beyond words, thoughts, and
expressions.

The suchness offering is made in association with the fourth empowerment, the word empowerment. In this context, 'suchness' means 'thatness', or 'emptiness', the ultimate nature of all phenomena. Strictly speaking, we offer not emptiness but the realization of ultimate bodhichitta, which is a mind of spontaneous great bliss mixed inseparably with emptiness. Thus we imagine that as a result of entering into union with a mudra during the secret offering, Guru Vajradhara generates this mind. Although our Guru already has ultimate bodhichitta, we imagine that he generates it anew, as an auspicious cause for us to gain this realization in the future.

In Secret Mantra, the red and white drops that flow through the channels are sometimes called 'bodhichittas' because they are the main cause of developing actual ultimate bodhichitta. This is an example of a cause being named after its effect. Without these drops, we would have no means of gaining any completion stage realization, let alone ultimate bodhichitta. Beings who are reborn in Pure Lands such as Sukhavati, for example, do not have red and white drops and so they are not able to practise Highest Yoga Tantra. Bodhisattvas in these Pure Lands make continuous prayers to be reborn in a human form so that they can practise completion stage and attain enlightenment swiftly.

According to the words of the sadhana, Guru Vajradhara's exalted wisdom of spontaneous great bliss is 'free from obstructions', which means that it has completely abandoned both the delusion-obstructions and the obstructions to omniscience. Not all spontaneous great bliss is free from obstructions. When we first generate spontaneous great bliss our mind is still covered by obstructions, but by training in the five stages of completion stage these are gradually removed. When the mind is finally freed from both obstructions we attain enlightenment. Thus the words of the sadhana indicate that Guru Vajradhara is a Buddha because his ultimate bodhichitta is free from obstructions.

The phrase 'Inseparable from the nature of all phenomena, the sphere of freedom from elaboration' is very profound and difficult to understand without some experience of Secret Mantra. The term 'sphere' indicates emptiness and the term 'elaboration' indicates inherent existence, so the meaning is that ultimate bodhichitta is inseparable from emptiness or lack of inherent existence. Once we have a rough understanding of emptiness we should try to generate spontaneous great bliss by training in tummo meditation. When the winds are gathered and dissolved within the central channel, all our gross minds will cease and the very subtle mind of clear light will manifest. This mind is very peaceful and calm, completely free from conceptions, and totally undistracted. It is hundreds of times more powerful than the concentration described in the Sutra teachings. When this mind meditates on emptiness it immediately mixes with it, like water mixing with water, and it feels as if the subjective mind, the clear light, and its object, emptiness, have become completely one.

The reason the clear light mind can mix so easily with emptiness is that it is completely free from conceptual distraction. When the winds are completely gathered and dissolved within the central channel the gross winds are absorbed, and so the gross minds that depend upon these winds cease to function. If there are no gross minds there are no gross objects; thus with respect to the mind of clear light it is as if gross objects do not exist. It is rather like when we fall asleep. At that time, because the gross minds of the waking state absorb, all the objects that appear to them disappear. Thus, for the dream mind it is as if the objects of our normal waking state do not exist.

Being completely free from gross objects, the mind of clear light mixes with emptiness in a space-like meditative equipoise. With respect to this mind, all phenomena are of one taste in space-like emptiness. Thus it is said that this mind is inseparable from the ultimate nature of all phenomena.

The mind that is described as ultimate bodhichitta in Sutra is not an actual ultimate bodhichitta because it still has subtle appearances of conventional phenomena. Therefore, if we want to attain the actual ultimate bodhichitta we need to improve our experience of Secret Mantra practices. Once we understand how the mind of ultimate bodhichitta is inseparable from the nature of all phenomena, we will understand the real nature of the Guru. The actual Guru is definitive Vajradhara, or definitive Heruka. Vajradhara is called 'kyab dag' in Tibetan, which means 'pervading all natures'. This means that the ultimate bodhichitta that is Guru Vajradhara's Truth Body is inseparable from the nature of all phenomena. To fully appreciate this we also need to understand how the two truths are the same nature. This is more difficult to understand than emptiness itself because it is harder to abandon the mind grasping the two truths as separate entities than it is to abandon self-grasping. Hinayana Foe Destroyers, for example, have abandoned the latter but not the former. Only Buddhas are completely free from grasping the two truths as separate entities.

According to the sadhana, ultimate bodhichitta is 'beyond words, thoughts, and expressions.' This is because ultimate bodhichitta is necessarily a direct experience of emptiness, free from conceptuality. It is said that someone who has a direct experience of emptiness cannot adequately describe this experience in words, but can only point to it by means of analogies, such as the analogy of water mixing with water. Even so, great beings such as Je Tsongkhapa are able to give very clear descriptions of emptiness. Thus Changkya Rolpai Dorje praises Je Tsongkhapa, saying:

Emptiness is said to be inexpressible, but you have described it as clearly as something seen with the eyes.

OFFERING MEDICINES, AND OURSELF AS A SERVANT

**I offer many different types of excellent medicine
That destroy the four hundred and four diseases
  of the delusions,
And to please you I offer myself as a servant;
Please keep me in your service for as long as space
  exists.**

The final offering is the offering of medicines, and ourself as a servant. We do not offer medicines for the Guru's benefit because Buddhas are completely beyond pain, disease, and sickness; rather we offer them for our own benefit. Although advanced practitioners can transform the adverse conditions of sickness into the spiritual path, at our stage sickness can often be an impediment to our practice. By offering medicines we create the cause for good health and to overcome the disease of the delusions.

To offer medicines, we emanate countless offering goddesses who hold precious bowls containing a variety of powerful medicines which they offer to the Field of Merit; and we imagine that in accepting this offering the holy beings generate uncontaminated bliss.

According to Dharma, the root cause of disease is the delusions. There are a hundred and one categories of disease that arise from attachment, a hundred and one categories that arise from anger, a hundred and one categories that arise from confusion, and a hundred and one categories that arise from all three together – making a total of four hundred and four categories of disease. We imagine that the medicine we offer can cure all these diseases.

The potency of medicine depends not so much upon the ingredients from which it is made as upon the power of the blessings from the person making it. In the medical scriptures, Buddha taught how to bless medicines in conjunction with the Medicine Buddha sadhanas. Authentic medicine made in this way by highly realized beings can cure all physical diseases as well as the mental afflictions of the delusions, and so we should imagine that the goddesses are offering medicine such as this.

Offering our body is a supreme method for overcoming the strong cherishing we have for our body, and it also accumulates a vast amount of merit. Basically there are three ways in which we can offer our body to our Spiritual Guide: transforming our body into nectar and offering this, transforming our body into a wishfulfilling jewel and making offerings, and offering our body into the service of our Spiritual Guide.

An example of the first way is the kusali tsog offering that is included in the Vajrayogini sadhana. This is explained in detail in *Guide to Dakini Land*. According to the second way, we imagine that our body transforms into a wishfulfilling jewel that radiates infinite rays of light. At the end of each light ray we imagine offering goddesses who make a multitude of offerings to our Spiritual Guide. According to the third way, we offer our body into the service of our Spiritual Guide and strongly feel that from then on it actually belongs to him. This method is very effective. Normally we cherish our body greatly, constantly worrying about whether it is hot or cold, hungry or thirsty, comfortable or uncomfortable, and so on; and out of this self-concern we commit many negative actions. By surrendering our body to our Spiritual Guide our cherishing of our body is naturally reduced and minds such as love, compassion, and bodhichitta grow more easily. Moreover, if we regard our body as belonging to the Guru and Three Jewels we will be protected from harm by spirits and other non-humans, rather as a servant of a king receives uncommon protection. When we offer our body to our Spiritual Guide we should offer not just our present body but also all our future bodies. This creates the cause to be cared for by our Spiritual Guide in all our future lives.

The second of the seven limbs, making offerings, is now completed. At this point, it is customary to restore our Bodhisattva and Secret Mantra vows. The reason this practice is included here, between the second and third limbs, is that maintaining our vows and commitments purely is part of offering our practice and so is included within the second limb, offerings; and restoring our broken or degenerated vows and commitments is part of the third limb, confession.

It is very important for practitioners of Secret Mantra to keep their vows and commitments purely because these are the basis of all attainments. It is impossible to gain realizations of Vajrayana Mahamudra if we do not keep our vows purely. Since at our present stage it is difficult to avoid transgressions of our Bodhisattva and Secret Mantra vows, we need to retake them as often as possible to ensure that we always have pure vows on our continuum. Once we have received Bodhisattva vows from a qualified Spiritual Guide, we can retake them as often as we wish by visualizing our Spiritual Guide and renewing our promise in front of him. As for our Secret Mantra vows, we first need to complete a close retreat of actions on the Deity before we are qualified to retake them on our own.

To retake our Bodhisattva vows, we imagine that Lama Losang Tubwang Dorjechang says the following words three times and that we repeat them while mentally making a firm promise to keep our Bodhisattva vows purely:

I go for refuge to the Three Jewels
And confess individually all negative actions.
I rejoice in the virtues of migrating beings
And hold with my mind a Buddha's enlightenment.

The first three lines – going for refuge, confessing non-virtue, and rejoicing in virtue – are preliminary practices, and the last line is the actual taking of the vows. This is a concise ritual for retaking Bodhisattva vows. Those who are new to the practice are advised to use a more extensive ritual such as the one given in *The Bodhisattva Vow*. An explanation of the root and secondary downfalls of the Bodhisattva vows can also be found in that book.

To retake our Secret Mantra vows we can recite the following ritual three times, imagining that we are repeating the words as they are spoken by Lama Losang Tubwang Dorjechang:

All Buddhas and your Sons
And all Heroes and Dakinis
Please listen to what I now say.
From this time forth
Until I reach the essence of enlightenment,
I, whose name is . . .

Drubwang Losang Namgyal

Shall generate the sacred, unsurpassed mind of
  enlightenment,
Just as all the Conquerors of the three times
Have assured themselves of enlightenment in this way.

From now on I shall maintain the vows
That come from Buddha [Vairochana],
The unsurpassed Three Jewels
Of Buddha, Dharma, and Sangha.
I shall also firmly maintain
The three types of moral discipline:
Training in pure discipline, gathering virtuous Dharmas,
And benefiting other living beings.

I shall perfectly maintain
The vajra, bell, and mudra
Of the great, supreme Vajra Family,
And shall rely upon my Spiritual Guide.
I shall observe the pleasing commitments
Of the great Ratna Family,
Always performing the four types of giving
Six times every day.

Concerning the great, pure Pāma Family,
Arisen from the great enlightenment,
I shall maintain individually the sacred Dharmas
Of the outer, the secret, and the three vehicles.

Concerning the great, supreme Karma Family,
I shall perfectly maintain individually
All the vows that I have taken
And make as many offerings as possible.

I shall generate the sacred, unsurpassed mind of
  enlightenment,
And for the sake of all living beings
I shall keep every one of my vows.

I shall deliver those not delivered,
Liberate those not liberated,
Give breath to those unable to breathe,
And lead all beings to a state beyond sorrow.

There are two types of Secret Mantra commitment: the individual commitments and the general commitments. The individual commitments are the nineteen commitments of the five Buddha families. There are six commitments of the Family of Buddha Vairochana, four commitments of the Family of Buddha Akshobya (the Vajra Family), four commitments of the Family of Buddha Ratnasambhava (the Ratna Family), three commitments of the Family of Buddha Amitabha (the Pāma Family), and two commitments of the Family of Buddha Amoghasiddhi (the Karma Family).

The six commitments of the Family of Buddha Vairochana are:

1 To go for refuge to Buddha
2 To go for refuge to Dharma
3 To go for refuge to Sangha
4 To refrain from non-virtue
5 To practise virtue
6 To benefit others

The four commitments of the Family of Buddha Akshobya are:

7 To keep a vajra to remind us of great bliss
8 To keep a bell to remind us of emptiness
9 To generate ourself as the Deity
10 To rely sincerely upon our Spiritual Guide

The four commitments of the Family of Buddha Ratnasambhava are:

11 To give material help
12 To give Dharma
13 To give fearlessness
14 To give love

The three commitments of the Family of Buddha Amitabha are:

15 To rely upon the teachings of Sutra
16 To rely upon the teachings of the two lower classes of Tantra
17 To rely upon the teachings of the two higher classes of Tantra

The two commitments of the Family of Buddha Amoghasiddhi are:

18 To make offerings to our Spiritual Guide
19 To strive to maintain purely all the vows we have taken

When we recite the ritual for restoring these commitments, we begin by asking all the Buddhas and Bodhisattvas to bear witness to our promise and then take the vows using the secret name we received during the empowerment. For example, if we were given the lineage of Buddha Vairochana we say 'I whose name is Vairochana'. If we have taken many empowerments and received a number of secret names we should use Buddha Akshobya's name.

After promising to keep each of the individual commitments, we make a promise to generate bodhichitta again and again and to keep all our vows purely for the sake of all living beings. When we say 'I shall deliver those not delivered' we promise to help all beings abandon the obstructions to liberation; when we say 'Liberate those not liberated' we promise to help all beings abandon the obstructions to omniscience; when we say 'Give breath to those unable to breathe' we promise to free all beings from suffering; and when we say 'And lead all beings to a state beyond sorrow' we promise to lead all beings to full enlightenment.

In addition to the individual commitments of the five Buddha families we also have to maintain the general commitments. These are included within the root vows and secondary commitments of Secret Mantra. It is particularly important to avoid the fourteen root downfalls because if we incur any of these we break our Secret Mantra vows. All the vows and commitments of Secret Mantra are enumerated in *Guide to Dakini Land*.

If we are to avoid breaking our vows it is very necessary to memorize them and understand clearly what they mean. Even if we cannot keep them all purely at the moment, we should generate a sincere wish to keep them purely in the future. So long as we hold on to this wish we are keeping our vows purely, but if we give up this wish and lose interest in our vows we break them completely.

CONFESSION

**In the presence of the great Compassionate Ones
I confess with a mind of great regret
All the non-virtues and negative actions that, since beginningless time,
I have done, ordered to be done, or rejoiced in;
And I promise that from now on I shall not commit them again.**

If we want to overcome problems and experience happiness, and if we want to meet with success in our spiritual practices, we must purify the negativity in our mental continuum. If we do not purify our negative karma it will be very difficult for pure minds such as bodhichitta and wisdom realizing emptiness to arise. A mind filled with non-virtuous imprints cannot give rise to pure states of mind because the cause is impure. If the mind itself is impure the objects that appear to it will also be impure; therefore without purifying the mind the pure appearances of generation stage and completion stage will be unattainable. If our room, our clothes, or our body are dirty we clean them straight away. In the same way, if our mind is unclean we should clean it immediately. Having a dirty room or dirty clothes will cause us only minor problems, but having an impure mind will cause great suffering in this and future lives. If a clear, blue sky becomes obscured by clouds, rain will fall. Similarly, if our minds are obscured by negative imprints, suffering and problems will rain down upon us.

We have been accumulating negative actions since beginningless time, and the burden of this negativity weighs heavily upon us. We can know that we have created a great deal of negativity in the past simply by examining our experiences in this life. For example, we can train in spiritual practices for a long time and accomplish almost no results, and yet we can commit negative actions spontaneously, without any effort. Why is this? It is because we have inherited from our previous lives a strong familiarity with non-virtue. By examining an effect, we can discover its cause. If in this life we have an affinity for non-virtue, this can have arisen only from regular acquaintance with non-virtue in the past.

If we do not purify all the negativity in our mental continuum we will have to experience its effects again and again in future lives. Humans are extremely fortunate because they alone have the opportunity to purify negative karma. If having taken a precious rebirth such as this we do not use it to purify our minds, what will we do when we fall into lower realms in the future and are completely overwhelmed by the painful effects of our negative karma? If we lose this life it will be difficult to find another opportunity such as this.

To purify our negative karma we need to apply the four opponent powers: the power of reliance, the power of regret, the power of promise, and the power of the antidote. We apply the first power by going for refuge in Lama Losang Tubwang Dorjechang and generating a motivation of bodhichitta. Then, in the presence of all the holy beings, we generate regret by contemplating the consequences of all the negative actions we have committed since beginningless time, all those we have encouraged others to commit, and all those in which we have rejoiced. The effectiveness of our purification depends very much upon the power of our regret. To generate genuine regret we need strong conviction in the laws of karma, and in particular we need to be convinced that our present and future suffering are the results of our own negative actions.

Often when we experience suffering or misfortune we look outside ourself for the cause. For example, we may suffer from bad headaches and conclude that they are caused by eating sugar, but while it may be true that we develop headaches whenever we eat sugar, the question we need to ask is 'Why does this happen to *me* and not to others?' If we think about this we will see that the principal cause of our headaches is the ripening of our own negative karma, and that eating sugar is merely a contributory condition. If eating sugar were the main cause of headaches, everyone who ate sugar would suffer from headaches. Similarly, if someone attacks us or steals something from us we think that it is the other person who is causing the harm and that we are innocent victims of their evil nature; but once again we need to think 'Why did he attack *me* and not someone else?' Again we are forced to the conclusion that the reason we were attacked and others were not was that we had created the cause and others had not. In reality it was our negative karma ripening that caused the other person to attack us; from their side they had no choice. If we think deeply about this we will come to a definite conclusion that all our suffering arises from our negative karma, and that if we do not purify this karma we will have to experience even greater suffering in the future. If we die without purifying, we will almost definitely take rebirth in the lower realms. When we see a pig wallowing in muck we cannot bear to look, but what will we do if we are born as a pig in our next life? By thinking like this we will develop a strong desire to purify all the negative karma we have accumulated in the past. This mind is the power of regret.

Purification also depends upon making a strong promise to refrain from negative actions in the future. We need to be skilful in the way we make such promises. To begin with it is better to promise to refrain for a short time and then gradually to extend the duration of our promise, rather than to make promises that we cannot keep. Breaking promises made to our Spiritual Guide is a huge obstacle to our spiritual development.

There are many different antidotes that we can use to purify the effects of our negative actions, but the two most effective are meditation and recitation of Vajrasattva, and making prostrations to the Thirty-five Confession Buddhas in conjunction with the *Mahayana Sutra of the Three Superior Heaps*. The former is explained in *Guide to Dakini Land* and the latter in *The Bodhisattva Vow*. It is especially important for practitioners of Secret Mantra to engage in these practices extensively as a preliminary for actual Mahamudra meditation. If we have time, at this point in the sadhana we can recite the *Mahayana Sutra of the Three Superior Heaps*, or the *General Confession* by Ashvagosha, but there is no fault if they are omitted. If we wish, we can also pause at this point to collect prostrations as a preliminary practice.

REJOICING

Though phenomena have no sign of inherent
   existence,
From the depths of our hearts we rejoice
In all the dream-like happiness and pure white
   virtue
That arise for ordinary and Superior beings.

To rejoice is to appreciate something. There are three types of rejoicing: virtuous, neutral, and non-virtuous. Examples of virtuous rejoicing are feeling happy when we see others engaging in virtue, feeling happy when we see others enjoying themselves, or feeling happy about our own virtuous actions. Examples of neutral rejoicing are feeling happy about taking a bath, or enjoying watching a child at play. Examples of non-virtuous rejoicing are feeling happy when we see non-virtuous actions being committed by others, or feeling happy when we see someone we dislike experiencing problems. Non-virtuous rejoicing is negative karma and is one of the objects to be purified by the previous limb, confession.

The fourth limb concerns only virtuous rejoicing. Like faith, this is a naturally virtuous mind; in other words, regardless of our motivation, our mind is always virtuous when we rejoice in virtue. Rejoicing is a very powerful method for accumulating merit, and it is also a very easy practice because all it involves is generating a happy state of mind with regard to virtuous actions. Gungtang Jampälyang praised rejoicing as the easiest and most powerful method for accumulating merit. As he pointed out, this practice can be done even while lying in bed!

We can rejoice in the virtues and good fortune of others and of ourself. If we rejoice in the virtues of someone with higher realizations we will receive half the merit they create, if we rejoice in the virtues of someone with equal realizations we will receive the same amount of merit, and if we rejoice in the virtues of someone with fewer realizations we will receive twice the merit.

According to Haribhadra there are five groups of beings in whom we can rejoice: Buddhas, Bodhisattvas, Solitary Conquerors, Hearers, and ordinary beings. In the words of the sadhana these are all included within two categories: Superior beings and ordinary beings. We can rejoice in the Buddhas by thinking about all their virtuous actions. Buddha Shakyamuni, for example, first generated the supreme motivation of bodhichitta, then trained on the Bodhisattva paths helping countless sentient beings, and finally attained enlightenment and turned the Wheel of Dharma as a Supreme Emanation Body. As a result of Buddha's actions there has been an uninterrupted presence of holy Dharma in this world ever since, and countless beings have attained liberation and enlightenment. Even after he had manifested passing away, Buddha Shakyamuni continued to help the beings of this world through countless emanations, which include the Second Buddha Je Tsongkhapa and our present Spiritual Guide.

We can rejoice in Bodhisattvas by thinking about their extraordinary motivation, their dedication to their spiritual training, their extensive deeds to benefit sentient beings, and their great courage in taking responsibility for the happiness of every single living being. Similarly, we can rejoice in Solitary Conquerors and Hearers by thinking about the special quality of their renunciation; their pure practices of higher moral discipline, higher concentration, and higher wisdom; their eventual abandonment of all delusions; and their attainment of the peace of nirvana.

Rejoicing in ordinary beings, especially in our spiritual companions, is also very important. When we see others engaging in virtuous actions such as making prostrations, making offerings, studying, or meditating, we should try to feel happy, without any trace of jealousy, competitiveness, or pride. Our rejoicing naturally encourages others and also enhances our own development. For example, if two friends are practising Dharma together and one emphasizes study while the other emphasizes meditation, it will be immensely beneficial for them both if they learn to appreciate and rejoice in each other's activities. In this way, the one who is disposed to meditate will also develop an interest in study and the one who is disposed to study will come to appreciate meditation.

Atisha said that we should focus exclusively on others' good qualities and pay no attention to any apparent faults. In this way we will develop calm and peaceful minds and we will get on well with everyone. This is especially important in spiritual communities such as Dharma Centres. If all the members of a community practise rejoicing there will be a happy and harmonious atmosphere, but if jealousy, pride, or competitiveness prevail, the community will be poisoned by disharmony and dissent. Therefore, we should make a strong decision to ignore any faults we see in others and concentrate only on their good qualities.

Rejoicing is especially important for Mahayanists. Every day we pray for all sentient beings to be happy, so it is very necessary that we learn to rejoice in the good fortune and happiness of others. Shantideva says that there are two things we can rejoice in: virtue, which is the cause of happiness, and happiness itself. It is not enough just to rejoice when we see others engaging in virtue, we also have to feel happy when we see them experiencing the results of their virtue. A Bodhisattva is like a mother who delights in the happiness and good fortune of her children. If we want to become Bodhisattvas we must also learn to delight in the happiness, success, relationships, possessions, and even the laughter of others.

In the *Perfection of Wisdom Sutra* Buddha taught that Bodhisattvas on the path of meditation should practise rejoicing while remembering the emptiness of all phenomena. Rejoicing is completely pure only when it is free from grasping at inherent existence, otherwise it remains a contaminated virtue. According to the words of the sadhana, we should rejoice in the 'dream-like happiness and pure white virtue' of others. Learning to see all phenomena as like a dream is the best way to overcome grasping at their inherent existence. In a dream, phenomena appear to be real, existing from their own side, but in reality they are merely projected by the mind. Even though dream objects are merely imputed by mind, they exist and function. As Chandrakirti points out in *Guide to the Middle Way*, a man can dream of an attractive woman during the night and when he wakes up the next day continue to feel attachment towards her. Thus, even though the dream woman is merely an imputation of mind, she can function to generate attachment. In the same way, all the phenomena of our waking life – our environment, bodies, minds, and enjoyments – are merely imputed by mind; but they exist nevertheless and function in many different ways. If we view the happiness and virtues of others in this way when we practise rejoicing, our action will be completely virtuous and will produce very powerful results.

Besides rejoicing in the happiness and virtue of others, we should also rejoice in our own good fortune and its causes. For example, by meditating on the preciousness of this human life we will come to appreciate the virtues performed by our previous incarnation that have resulted in such a beneficial effect; and we will then decide to show a similar kindness to our next incarnation. Rejoicing in our own virtues uplifts the mind and encourages us to practise purely.

REQUESTING THE TURNING OF THE WHEEL OF DHARMA

From the myriads of billowing clouds of your
sublime wisdom and compassion,
Please send down a rain of vast and profound
Dharma,
So that in the jasmine garden of benefit and
happiness
There may be growth, sustenance, and increase for
all these living beings.

By requesting the holy beings to turn the Wheel of
Dharma, we create the cause to meet with emanations of
Vajradhara in all our future lives and to receive teachings
directly from them. When we make this request we should
focus on all the beings in the Field of Merit and request
them to give teachings. In this way we create a karmic link
with all the Buddhas and Bodhisattvas; and if we make
continuous requests we will continuously meet their
emanations. After Buddha Shakyamuni had demonstrated
the manner of attaining enlightenment, Brahma and Indra
requested him to turn the Wheel of Dharma, and as a
result of that request countless sentient beings have
benefited. Even today sentient beings are experiencing the
beneficial effects of that request. From this we can understand that requesting teachings is a very powerful action
that accumulates vast amounts of merit and produces
far-reaching results.

REQUESTING THE SPIRITUAL GUIDE NOT TO PASS AWAY

Though your vajra body has no birth or death,
We request the vessel of the great King of Union
To remain unchanging according to our wishes,
Without passing away until samsara ends.

When we request our Spiritual Guide not to pass away, we
are requesting his Emanation Body to remain with us. As
already explained, our Spiritual Guide's actual body is his

vajra body which is immortal and indestructible, so there is no point in requesting this not to pass away. However, for us the vajra body is invisible and so the Spiritual Guide manifests the outer form of the Emanation Body that presently appears to us. We can think of this body as like a jewellery box and our Spiritual Guide's actual vajra body as like a precious jewel inside. Without the outer form acting as a vessel for our Spiritual Guide's vajra body, we would not be able to communicate with him; and so we would not be able to receive teachings and blessings directly. Therefore it is very important that we request the Emanation Body to remain with us for a very long time.

To attain a vajra body we first need to generate spontaneous great bliss by dissolving the winds into the central channel. When that mind of spontaneous great bliss realizes emptiness we attain the realization of non-ultimate example clear light. This mind realizes emptiness by means of a generic image. Later, when the knots at the heart chakra are completely loosened and the winds have dissolved into the indestructible drop at the heart, we attain ultimate example clear light. This mind is the contributory cause of the illusory body, and the subtle wind associated with it is the substantial cause of the illusory body. When we rise from this meditation we attain the impure illusory body. This body is the actual body of the Deity. Whereas before we had attained a Deity body through the power of correct imagination, now our subtle winds have actually transformed into the Deity's body. At this stage it is known as an 'impure' illusory body because we still have not abandoned the obstructions to liberation.

Our principal practice now is to meditate on the clear light, until we attain the clear light that is a direct realization of emptiness, free from any generic image. This realization is known as 'meaning clear light' and is the direct antidote to the obstructions to liberation. When we rise from this meditation, we have abandoned the obstructions to liberation and attained the pure illusory body, which is the actual vajra body. Once this body is attained we will definitely attain enlightenment in that same life. Eventually, through further meditation on the clear light, we abandon the obstructions to omniscience and attain enlightenment. At that time our mind of meaning clear light becomes the Truth Body and our pure illusory body becomes the Enjoyment Body. These two bodies are completely unified as one nature. It is this vajra body, that is the same nature as the Truth Body, that is referred to in the sadhana as 'the great King of Union' and it is this body that we imagine to be the jewel inside our Spiritual Guide's present Emanation Body.

DEDICATION

I dedicate all the pure white virtues I have
   gathered here, so that in all my lives
I shall never be separated from the venerable
   Guru who is kind in three ways;
May I always come under his loving care,
And attain the Union of Vajradhara.

The purpose of dedication is to prevent all the virtues that we have accumulated from being wasted or destroyed by anger. Dedication also transforms our virtues so that they will produce supreme results. We can think of all the virtues we have collected in this and previous lives as like a horse and dedication as like the reins that direct it. By dedicating our virtues we determine what course our virtues will take and what results they will produce. Thus, if we dedicate our virtues to mundane ends such as another human rebirth, they will become a cause of such a result. Alternatively, if we dedicate our virtues to the attainment of enlightenment for the sake of all living beings, they will become a means to that end.

In general, we should always dedicate our merit for the sake of the poor and needy, the sick, the dying, and all other sentient beings who are experiencing suffering. Similarly we should dedicate for an end to all wars and conflicts, and for peace and happiness throughout the world. Extensive prayers for dedication can be found in the tenth chapter of Shantideva's *Guide to the Bodhisattva's Way of Life*.

Specifically, according to *Offering to the Spiritual Guide* we make two special dedications. First we dedicate so that in all our future lives we will never be separated from our precious Spiritual Guide but always come under his loving care. Secondly we dedicate that we may attain 'the Union of Vajradhara'. There are two types of union: the union that needs learning and the Union of No More Learning. The former is the last stage of our Tantric training and the latter is actual Buddhahood. The meaning of 'Vajradhara' is 'Holder of the Vajra'. In this context 'Vajra' means the union of great bliss and emptiness, and the actual Vajradhara is the indestructible union of bliss and emptiness attained at full enlightenment. This is called the 'definitive Vajradhara'. The Vajradhara who appears with a blue-coloured body embracing Yingchugma is known as the 'interpretative Vajradhara'.

This completes the practice of the seven limbs. If we have time at this point we can make a mandala offering together with the three great requests. We make these requests by reciting the following three times:

Please pour down your inspiring blessings upon myself and all my mothers so that we may quickly stop all perverse minds, from disrespect for our kind Teacher to the most subtle dual appearance.

Please pour down your inspiring blessings so that we may quickly generate pure minds, from respect for our kind Teacher to the supreme mind of Union.

Please pour down your inspiring blessings to pacify all outer and inner obstructions.

The meaning of these requests is explained in detail in *Joyful Path of Good Fortune*. After reciting them three times, we imagine that all the holy beings in the Field of Merit respond by bestowing their inspiring blessings upon us. We visualize streams of blissful lights and nectars flowing from their hearts into our body, pacifying all our negative karma, delusions, and other obstacles; increasing our merit, lifespan, and Dharma realizations; and bestowing the blessings of our Guru's body, speech, and mind upon our body, speech, and mind. We need to receive a constant rain of blessings from our Spiritual Guide if we are to attain Secret Mantra realizations.

If we wish, and if we have the time, at this point we can also recite *The Condensed Meaning of the Swift Vajrayana Path* as well as the *Prayers of Request to the Mahamudra Lineage Gurus*, so as to receive blessings to gain the realizations of the Mahamudra. Both these texts can be found in Appendix II.

Kachen Yeshe Gyaltsän

Making Praises and Requests

After offering the practice of the seven limbs together with the mandala, we make requests to our Spiritual Guide. All requests are included within the three great requests mentioned above. We should make constant requests to our Spiritual Guide for his blessings because without them spiritual progress is impossible. Our mind is like a field, and engaging in spiritual practices such as meditating on the stages of the path of Sutra and Tantra is like sowing seeds in that field; but without the rain of the Guru's blessings nothing will grow. The Tibetan word for blessings, 'jin gyi lob', literally means 'to transform'. When we receive the blessings of our Spiritual Guide our mind is transformed into a powerful, virtuous field in which the crops of Dharma realizations flourish; but a mind without blessings is like a dry, arid field in which nothing virtuous can grow.

By studying the biographies of past practitioners such as Milarepa, Naropa, and the Kadampa Geshes we will come to understand the power of the Guru's blessings. Sometimes the blessings of the Spiritual Guide can be astonishing. For example, Geshe Jayulwa, one of Gampopa's Teachers, was very intelligent, but he much preferred serving his Guru to any other kind of activity. For years he performed menial tasks, caring for his Spiritual Guide. One day, when he was returning from emptying a rubbish bin, he suddenly developed single-pointed concentration and remained in that state for two hours. Afterwards he received many visions of Buddhas and attained a clairvoyance that enabled him to see people five hundred miles away. Even though he had done very little meditation, he had attained tranquil abiding through the power of his Guru's blessings.

His acts of devotion had purified the obstacles in his mind and accumulated a vast amount of merit. This shows that when the conditions are right and obstacles are removed, Dharma realizations are achieved very easily. Therefore we should not become discouraged, thinking 'How can I ever attain authentic realizations?', but should develop deep faith in our Spiritual Guide and constantly request his blessings to create perfect conditions and remove all our obstacles.

According to the sadhana there are four ways of making requests to our Spiritual Guide:

1 Requesting by reciting the name mantra
2 Requesting by remembering his good qualities and his kindness
3 Requesting by expressing his good qualities
4 Single-pointed request

REQUESTING BY RECITING THE NAME MANTRA

At this stage we make requests to our Spiritual Guide by reciting the nine-line *Migtsema* prayer. The term 'name mantra' in this context refers to this prayer and not, as might be supposed, to the Guru's Sanskrit name mantra. The nine-line *Migtsema* prayer is as follows:

Tsongkhapa, crown ornament of the scholars of the
   Land of the Snows,
You are Buddha Shakyamuni and Vajradhara, the
   source of all attainments,
Avalokiteshvara, the treasury of unobservable
   compassion,
Manjushri, the supreme stainless wisdom,
And Vajrapani, the destroyer of the hosts of maras.
O Venerable Guru-Buddha, synthesis of all Three Jewels
With my body, speech, and mind, respectfully
   I make requests:
Please grant your blessings to ripen and liberate
   myself and others,
And bestow the common and supreme attainments.

ngö drub kün jung tub wang dor je chang
mig me tse wai ter chen chän rä zig
dri me khyen pai wang po jam päl yang
dü pung ma lü jom dzä sang wai dag
gang chän khä pai tsug gyän lo zang drag
kyab sum kün dü la ma sang gyä la
go sum gü pai go nä söl wa deb
rang zhän min ching dröl war jin gyi lob
chog dang tün mong ngö drub tsäl du söl

When we recite this we should first recall the benefits of relying upon the Spiritual Guide as explained in Lamrim, and remember his immeasurable kindness. Then with deep faith and devotion we should recite the prayer while contemplating its meaning. We contemplate that our Spiritual Guide, who is inseparable from Je Tsongkhapa, the crown ornament of the scholars of the Land of the Snows, is a manifestation of Buddha Shakyamuni, Conqueror Vajradhara, Avalokiteshvara, Manjushri, and Vajrapani, and that he possesses all the excellent qualities of these holy beings. Regarding our Spiritual Guide as the synthesis of all objects of refuge, with our body, speech, and mind we request him to grant us his blessings. We pray that through these blessings the virtuous potentials within our mental continuum will ripen and create the conditions for us to gain the realization of inseparable bliss and emptiness, thereby liberating us from the two obstructions. In short, we ask him to bestow all the common and supreme attainments. In this context, the supreme attainments are the Union of Vajradhara and the common attainments all the realizations of the stages of the path that lead to this state.

If possible, we should recite the *Migtsema* prayer one hundred times at this point, but if we do not have the time we can recite it just seven or twenty-one times. If we wish to collect requests to the Guru as the fourth of the great preliminary guides we can do so at this point by collecting the *Migtsema* prayer. After reciting the prayer as many times as we wish, we imagine that lights and nectars descend from our Spiritual Guide and dissolve into our body and mind. These blessings purify all the negativities we have created since beginningless time – especially all the negative actions we have created towards our Spiritual Guide, such as showing disrespect, going against his advice, or disturbing his mind. We imagine that all these negativities leave through our lower doors in the aspect of black smoke, and that our body becomes as clear as crystal and our mind like clear light. We concentrate for a while on this feeling of complete purity. This creates the cause for us to receive Mahamudra realizations swiftly.

REQUESTING BY REMEMBERING HIS GOOD QUALITIES AND HIS KINDNESS

This has six parts:

1 Requesting by remembering his good qualities as explained in the Vinaya scriptures
2 Requesting by remembering his good qualities as a Mahayana Spiritual Guide
3 Requesting by remembering his good qualities as a Vajrayana Spiritual Guide
4 Requesting by remembering that he is kinder than all the Buddhas
5 Requesting by remembering that he is kinder even than Buddha Shakyamuni
6 Requesting by remembering that he is a supreme Field of Merit

REQUESTING BY REMEMBERING HIS GOOD QUALITIES AS EXPLAINED IN THE VINAYA SCRIPTURES

Great ocean of moral discipline, source of all good qualities,
Replete with a collection of jewels of extensive learning,
Second Buddha, venerable saffron-robed monk,
O Elder and Holder of the Vinaya, to you I make requests.

We begin by making requests to our Spiritual Guide while praising his good qualities as a Vinaya Teacher. According to the Vinaya, a qualified Teacher must be an elder, which means that he must have been ordained for at least ten years without breaking any of his vows, and he must possess fifteen good qualities. These include: great moral discipline, extensive understanding of the three sets of doctrine, expertise in the rules of the Vinaya, loving compassion for his disciples and for sick people, freedom from any worldly relationships, and skill in teaching Dharma at the appropriate time. Because our Spiritual Guide possesses all these qualities he is like a second Buddha for us, showing us the path and leading us to liberation and enlightenment. Contemplating these excellent qualities, we develop deep faith in our Spiritual Guide and request his blessings.

REQUESTING BY REMEMBERING HIS GOOD QUALITIES AS A MAHAYANA SPIRITUAL GUIDE

You who possess the ten qualities
Of an authentic Teacher of the path of the Sugatas,
Lord of the Dharma, representative of all the
Conquerors,
O Mahayana Spiritual Guide, to you I make
requests.

As a fully-qualified Mahayana Spiritual Guide, our Guru possesses the ten qualities explained by Maitreya in *Ornament for Mahayana Sutras*:

1 A mind that is controlled by the practice of moral discipline.
2 A mind that has become peaceful and undistracted through the practice of concentration.
3 Reduced self-grasping through the practice of wisdom.
4 Greater knowledge than the disciple.
5 Delight in teaching Dharma.
6 A wealth of scriptural knowledge.

7 A deep and stable realization of emptiness.
8 Great skill in explaining Dharma.
9 Compassion and love for his disciples.
10 Enthusiasm for teaching Dharma, being free from discouragement or laziness.

It is particularly important for a Spiritual Guide to have greater knowledge and higher realizations than his disciples. Ashvagosha said that if we follow a Spiritual Guide who has lesser qualities it may cause our own good qualities to degenerate. Disciples naturally follow their Teacher's example, so a Teacher must be authentic, not pretending to have qualities and realizations he does not possess. For example if a Teacher pretends to have realizations but in reality indulges in drinking alcohol, sexual misconduct, or other negative actions, this will cause his disciples' behaviour to degenerate.

It is also essential for a Teacher to have great skill in teaching Dharma and to know what to teach at what time. For example, prematurely introducing disciples to Secret Mantra can cause them great problems, and may even cause them to lose their faith. According to Je Tsongkhapa's tradition, a skilled Teacher will gradually lead his disciples through the stages of Lamrim, Lojong, and Secret Mantra, and show them how to combine all these into a regular practice.

REQUESTING BY REMEMBERING HIS GOOD QUALITIES AS A VAJRAYANA SPIRITUAL GUIDE

Your three doors are perfectly controlled, you have great wisdom and patience,
You are without pretension or deceit, you are well-versed in mantras and Tantra,
You possess the two sets of ten qualities, and you are skilled in drawing and explaining,
O Principal Holder of the Vajra, to you I make requests.

Our Spiritual Guide is also a fully-qualified Tantric Master. A Tantric Master must have many special qualities in addition to those required by a Mahayana Spiritual Guide. Needless to say he must have received all the relevant empowerments and transmissions, and have completed the close retreats of these practices. In addition, he must have thirteen good qualities, which are indicated by the present verse. He must possess:

1 Actions of body, speech, and mind that are fully controlled through the practice of moral discipline.
2 Great wisdom.
3 The three types of patience.
4 Straightforwardness; not pretending to have qualities he does not possess.
5 Honesty; not deceiving others.
6 Knowledge of all the rituals and practices explained in the Tantric texts.
7 Great compassion.
8 Extensive understanding of the three sets of doctrine.
9 The ten outer and ten inner qualities.
10 Expertise in constructing and visualizing mandalas.
11 Skill in explaining Secret Mantra.
12 Great experience of Secret Mantra.
13 A mind controlled by the three higher trainings.

The ten outer qualities referred to here are:

1 Expertise in drawing and constructing mandalas.
2 Skill in visualizing mandalas.
3 The concentration of the preparatory practice of the Deity. This is a very precise practice of self-generation, the first of the 'three concentrations' explained in the *Heruka* and *Guhyasamaja Tantras*. Any practice that involves these three concentrations is an extensive self-generation sadhana.
4 The concentration of emanating mudras from the heart. This is the second concentration and involves more elaborate visualizations than the first.

5 The concentration of the ritual of the mandala. This is the third concentration and is the most complex.
6 Skill in granting empowerments.
7 Skill in performing the 'Earth Dance', which is a ritual for purifying a site before constructing a mandala.
8 Skill in performing offering dances.
9 Skill in reciting mantras.
10 Skill in reabsorbing mandalas at the conclusion of a session.

The ten inner qualities are:

1 Expertise in visualizing protection circles to eliminate obstacles.
2 Competence in drawing and blessing wheels to be worn as amulets.
3 Experience in conferring the vase empowerment and the secret empowerment.
4 Experience in conferring the wisdom-mudra empowerment and the word empowerment.
5 The ability to perform wrathful actions when they are required.
6 Expertise in making authentic tormas.
7 The ability to use the ritual dagger, or curved knife.
8 Skill in reciting mantras.
9 Skill in bestowing blessings.
10 Skill in constructing and offering mandalas.

Contemplating how our Spiritual Guide has all these good qualities, we should develop deep faith in him and request his blessings.

REQUESTING BY REMEMBERING THAT HE IS KINDER THAN ALL THE BUDDHAS

To the coarse beings of these impure times who, being so hard to tame,
Were not subdued by the countless Buddhas of old,

You correctly reveal the excellent path of the Sugatas;
O Compassionate Refuge and Protector, to you
I make requests.

Although countless Buddhas have already appeared in this
world, we did not have the good fortune to be their disciples, and so we are still in samsara. Even after Buddha
Shakyamuni passed away, countless realized beings such
as Nagarjuna and Asanga appeared, but again we were not
among their disciples. Even though all these holy beings
had great compassion and wished to help all living beings,
we did not have the faith or the merit to receive their help.
Now we have met our precious Spiritual Guide who
reveals to us exactly the same path that all the previous
Buddhas have revealed. Therefore, for us, our Spiritual
Guide is kinder than all the other Buddhas because it is he
who is helping us directly. Moreover, unlike during the
golden age when Buddha Shakyamuni was teaching,
during these degenerate times it is very difficult to help
disciples because they have so little merit and such strong
delusions; and yet our Spiritual Guide is working continuously to help us by patiently teaching us Dharma, setting
a good example for us to follow, and constantly encouraging us. Who could be kinder than this?

REQUESTING BY REMEMBERING THAT HE IS KINDER EVEN
THAN BUDDHA SHAKYAMUNI

Now, when the sun of Buddha has set,
For the countless migrators without protection or
   refuge
You perform exactly the same deeds as the
   Conqueror;
O Compassionate Refuge and Protector, to you
I make requests.

Buddha Shakyamuni manifested as a Supreme Emanation
Body and performed the twelve principal deeds. Now he
has passed away it is as if spiritually the sun has set, but

because our kind Spiritual Guide has manifested to help sentient beings, the world has not been plunged into spiritual darkness. For all the beings with little merit who did not have the good fortune to meet Buddha Shakyamuni directly, and who would otherwise be without protection and refuge, our Spiritual Guide performs exactly the same deeds as Buddha Shakyamuni himself. During these degenerate times he brings us the precious Dharma Jewel, which is the real refuge and protection. Therefore, for us, he is kinder even than Buddha Shakyamuni.

REQUESTING BY REMEMBERING THAT HE IS A SUPREME FIELD OF MERIT

Even just one of your hair pores is praised for us
As a Field of Merit that is superior to all the
**   Conquerors**
Of the three times and the ten directions;
O Compassionate Refuge and Protector, to you I
**   make requests.**

In general, all Buddhas are a Field of Merit to whom we can make offerings and prostrations but in the *Guhyasamaja Tantra* it says that our Spiritual Guide is the supreme Field of Merit and that making offerings to just one hair pore of his body yields far greater results than making offerings to all the other Buddhas.

As explained above, our Spiritual Guide's body is like a temple in which all the Buddhas of the three times and the ten directions dwell, and when we make offerings or prostrations to him we also make offerings and prostrations to all the other Buddhas. Therefore, for us, he is the kindest of all Buddhas. When we place offerings on the shrine we receive the merit of making offerings, but we do not receive the merit of our offerings being directly accepted. When we make offerings to our Spiritual Guide, however, we do receive this merit. Moreover, even though the Buddhas have given many teachings, these can be of direct benefit to us only if they are brought into focus and presented in a way in which we can understand them and apply them, and it is our Spiritual Guide who does this for us. For example, the sun emits many rays, all of which have the power to burn paper, but without a magnifying glass to bring them into focus on a particular piece of paper, the paper will not ignite. If we think about this deeply we will realize that our Spiritual Guide is kinder than all the other Buddhas.

REQUESTING BY EXPRESSING HIS GOOD QUALITIES

This has four parts:

1 Requesting by expressing his outer qualities
2 Requesting by expressing his inner qualities
3 Requesting by expressing his secret qualities
4 Requesting by expressing his suchness qualities

REQUESTING BY EXPRESSING HIS OUTER QUALITIES

**From the play of your miracle powers and skilful
 means
The ornament wheels of your three Sugata bodies
Appear in an ordinary form to guide migrators;
O Compassionate Refuge and Protector, to you
 I make requests.**

As mentioned before, our Spiritual Guide has an outer, inner, and secret aspect. His outer aspect is that of a fully-ordained monk, Je Tsongkhapa; his inner aspect is that of Buddha Shakyamuni; and his secret aspect is that of Conqueror Vajradhara. The three channel wheels of our Spiritual Guide's outer form are marked by the seed-letters OM AH HUM which symbolize respectively his three enlightened bodies – the Emanation Body, the Enjoyment Body, and the Truth Body. Thus, although the outer aspect of our Spiritual Guide appears as an ordinary form, this form nevertheless displays his enlightened qualities and performs all the actions of an enlightened being.

It is very important to keep a pure view of our Spiritual Guide's outer aspect and not to be misled into thinking that just because he appears as an ordinary being he is an ordinary being. We must always remember that his apparent ordinariness is itself a manifestation of his enlightened qualities. If he were to display extraordinary qualities and miracle powers these would not benefit us in the least, but by appearing in a form to which we can relate and giving us unmistaken advice he gives us immeasurable help. Indeed, it is this very ability to appear in an ordinary form while performing the actions of a Buddha that reveals his real miracle powers and skilful means.

The preciousness of the Spiritual Guide does not exist from its own side, but is dependent upon the mind that perceives it. If a disciple has faith and sees his Spiritual Guide as a Buddha, he will receive the blessings of a Buddha, but if he regards his Spiritual Guide as an ordinary being he will receive no blessings.

Since our Spiritual Guide has assumed an ordinary aspect for our benefit, we must expect this aspect to appear to us to be subject to ageing, sickness, and death; and we should not be surprised or discouraged if he appears to manifest any of these apparently ordinary conditions. All of our Spiritual Guide's actions have meaning, and even when he manifests sickness he is helping us. For example, Sakya Pandita's Spiritual Guide was Dragpa Gyaltsän. Because he was related to him, Sakya Pandita found it very difficult to prevent ordinary appearance of his Spiritual Guide and to show him due reverence. To help him to purify this obstruction, Dragpa Gyaltsän manifested a long illness. In caring for Dragpa Gyaltsän, Sakya Pandita underwent many hardships and as a result of these his mind was purified and he came to see Dragpa Gyaltsän as Manjushri. Thus even the sickness of a Spiritual Guide is a sign of his skill.

REQUESTING BY EXPRESSING HIS INNER QUALITIES

**Your aggregates, elements, sources, and limbs
Are by nature the Fathers and Mothers of the five
Buddha families,
The Bodhisattvas, and the Wrathful Deities;
O Supreme Spiritual Guide, the nature of the
Three Jewels, to you I make requests.**

Although our Spiritual Guide manifests an ordinary outer aspect, internally his body is a temple. As explained above, the different parts of Lama Losang Tubwang Dorjechang's body are the thirty-two Deities of Guhyasamaja. Remembering this, we should develop deep faith and request his blessings.

REQUESTING BY EXPRESSING HIS SECRET QUALITIES

**You are the essence of the ten million circles of
mandalas
That arise from the state of the all-knowing
exalted wisdom;
Principal Holder of the Vajra, pervasive source of
the hundred families,
O Protector of the Primordial Union, to you
I make requests.**

With this verse we express our Spiritual Guide's secret qualities. In reality he is the exalted wisdom of all the Buddhas, from which the ten million circles of mandalas revealed in the Tantric scriptures arise. He is Vajradhara, the 'Principal Holder of the Vajra', in whom all the hundred Buddha families are condensed. Normally we talk about five Buddha families, but each of these has twenty divisions, making a hundred families in all. These can be condensed into three – the families of Vairochana, Amitabha, and Akshobya – and these, in turn, can be condensed into one – Vajradhara. Because our Guru is one with Vajradhara, he pervades all the Buddha families, and so all the Deities and all their mandalas are manifestations of his wisdom.

The words of the sadhana refer to the Spiritual Guide as the 'Protector of the Primordial Union'. This is the Enjoyment Body that is accomplished immediately upon attaining enlightenment. As mentioned before, the substantial cause of this body is the very subtle wind associated with the very subtle mind at the heart. Inside the tiny vacuole at the heart channel wheel that is formed by the knots in the central channel there is a tiny drop known as the 'indestructible drop'. Its upper half, formed from the substance of our father's sperm, is white and its lower half, formed from the substance of our mother's blood, is red. The very subtle mind and the very subtle wind are enclosed within this drop. Normally this drop does not open until death, which is why it is called 'indestructible'.

For ordinary beings, the very subtle mind and very subtle wind within the indestructible drop do not function while they are alive, except when they fall asleep. During sleep, the very subtle wind assumes the shape of the dream body, but this shape is not definite and it dissolves back into the heart channel wheel when we wake. Similarly, at death, the very subtle wind is the substance from which the bardo body arises, but once again this is indefinite and short-lived. For Tantric practitioners, however, the very subtle wind is the substance from which the illusory body arises. As explained above, this is the actual body of the Deity and is immortal. Such a body is completely free from ageing, sickness, death, or any other form of suffering. When we finally remove all the obstructions from the mind and attain enlightenment, the illusory body transforms into the Enjoyment Body; and simultaneously all the other bodies of a Buddha are attained. The Enjoyment Body that is attained when we first become enlightened is known as the 'Protector of the Primordial Union'.

The methods for attaining the illusory body are explained principally in the Father Tantras such as *Guhyasamaja Tantra*, and the methods for attaining the clear light are explained principally in the Mother Tantras such as *Heruka Tantra*. If we wish to attain the body and mind of a Buddha we have to combine these instructions by following the Tantric teachings of Je Tsongkhapa. Both these sets of instructions are combined in the commentary, *Clear Light of Bliss*.

The *Root Tantra of Guhyasamaja* is vajra speech and is very difficult to understand. Within it, twelve analogies are given for the illusory body. Before the time of Je Tsongkhapa, these teachings were frequently misunderstood and many Tibetans thought that the way to attain the illusory body was to visualize one's gross body as light until it actually became light. Je Tsongkhapa gave very clear and precise teachings on the illusory body, showing how its substantial cause is the subtle body, not the gross body, and clearing away many misunderstandings. Je Tsongkhapa's explanations of the illusory body are highly praised by Yogis and scholars of all four schools of Tibetan Buddhism.

REQUESTING BY EXPRESSING HIS SUCHNESS QUALITIES

Pervasive nature of all things stable and moving,
Inseparable from the experience of spontaneous
  joy without obstructions;
Thoroughly good, from the beginning free from
  extremes,
O Actual, ultimate bodhichitta, to you I make
  requests.

With this verse, we contemplate how our Spiritual Guide is the Truth Body. This verse is very difficult to understand. Kachen Yeshe Gyaltsän said that it expresses the very essence of Secret Mantra and that only those with considerable experience of Secret Mantra can fully comprehend it.

The Spiritual Guide's Truth Body is inseparable from bliss and emptiness, and completely free from obstructions. When spontaneous great bliss is initially generated it is covered by both obstructions. Later, when we attain the mind of meaning clear light, this mind is free from obstructions to liberation but it is still covered by the obstructions to omniscience. It is only the spontaneous great bliss of a Buddha's Truth Body that is completely unobstructed.

This inseparable union of bliss and emptiness that is the Spiritual Guide's Truth Body is the nature of all phenomena, both animate and inanimate. This means that all phenomena are manifestations of indivisible bliss and emptiness. For an experienced Tantric Yogi this is easy to understand because this is his or her actual experience, but for ordinary beings it is not so easy. Still, there is great benefit in trying to develop a rough understanding even now.

From the Sutra teachings we understand that all phenomena are manifestations of emptiness, and from the Secret Mantra teachings we understand that the mind of spontaneous great bliss is inseparable from emptiness. Therefore, all phenomena must be manifestations of inseparable bliss and emptiness.

A Tantric practitioner first develops an understanding of profound emptiness and then generates a mind of spontaneous great bliss, which mixes with this emptiness like water mixing with water. At this point, it feels as if the subjective mind of great bliss and the object emptiness are completely one. From the point of view of this experience, conventional objects do not exist; all conventional appearances have subsided into emptiness. When the practitioner rises from meditation and conventional phenomena once again appear to his mind, they appear to arise from the indivisible bliss and emptiness of the previous moment. Thus conventional phenomena appear to such a practitioner to be simply manifestations of bliss and emptiness, and every experience of conventional phenomena induces bliss in him. When he returns to meditation, conventional phenomena once again disappear, as if they were dissolving back into the bliss and emptiness from which they had arisen. Therefore it feels to him as if this inseparable bliss and emptiness is the synthesis of all phenomena. This is the real meaning of 'Chakrasamvara'. 'Chakra' means 'wheel', and here refers to the wheel of all objects of knowledge, and 'samvara' means 'synthesis'. Thus the definitive Chakrasamvara is the union of indivisible bliss and emptiness, which is the synthesis of all objects of knowledge.

When we make requests to our Spiritual Guide with this verse, we are thinking about his ultimate nature as the indivisible bliss and emptiness of the Truth Body. This is the definitive Spiritual Guide. The interpretative Spiritual Guide is the Spiritual Guide who appears as a Deity, or in an ordinary form. This distinction between the definitive and interpretative Spiritual Guide is not unique to Secret Mantra. For example, in the *Diamond Cutter Sutra* Buddha says:

> Whoever sees me as form or sound does not really see me. My actual body is the Truth Body.

However, the precise relationship between these two aspects of the Spiritual Guide is not explained in the Sutras, but is to be found only in the Secret Mantra teachings, especially in *Guhyasamaja Tantra*.

The teaching that all phenomena arise from bliss and emptiness has often been mistaken for the Samkhya view that all phenomena arise from a general principle, but it is infinitely more subtle than this. The great Yogi Saraha once said:

> We do not understand, but if we did we would know that everything is a manifestation of great bliss.

There are two ways to understand this: from the point of view of ultimate truth and from the point of view of conventional truth. According to the first interpretation, all phenomena are the nature of indivisible bliss and emptiness as just explained. According to the second interpretation, all phenomena are manifestations of our root mind, the continually abiding mind. This is a little easier for us to understand.

We can see from our own experience that our world depends upon conceptual thought, because if we withdraw our conceptual minds the world disappears. If we were asked from where do our conceptual minds arise we might be tempted to reply that they arise from the objects that they apprehend, but this cannot be the case because these objects themselves arise in dependence upon conceptual minds. In reality, according to Secret Mantra, conceptual minds arise from gross inner winds, and these in turn arise from the very subtle wind at the heart. For example, when we fall asleep or when we die all our gross winds absorb into the very subtle wind at our heart. At the same time all our conceptual minds cease and the objects that they apprehend disappear. When we wake, or when we are reborn, gross winds once again manifest from the very subtle wind and, at the same time, gross minds and their objects develop. Thus the very subtle wind is the source of all the gross winds, and therefore of all the gross minds and all the phenomena that appear to those minds. Since the very subtle wind is inseparable from the very subtle mind, the continually abiding mind, we can say that all phenomena arise from this mind. As Saraha says:

All phenomena are manifestations of the continually abiding mind. They arise from that mind just as waves arise from an ocean.

SINGLE-POINTED REQUEST

You are the Guru, you are the Yidam, you are the
  Daka and Dharma Protector;
From now until I attain enlightenment I shall seek
  no refuge other than you.
In this life, in the bardo, and until the end of my
  lives, please hold me with the hook of your
  compassion,
Liberate me from the fears of samsara and peace,
  bestow all the attainments, be my constant
  companion, and protect me from all obstacles.

Now, with deep faith and single-pointed concentration, we make a special request to our Spiritual Guide. We regard him as the nature of all Yidams who bestow the mundane and supramundane attainments, as the nature of all Dakas and Dakinis who bestow spontaneous great bliss, and as the nature of all Dharma Protectors who remove obstacles and create favourable conditions; and we request him to care for us and guide us in this and all our future lives.

Tibetans liken this request to driving a stake into the ground. When we drive a stake, if we hit it in the same place every time it will go into the ground easily. Similarly, when we are performing this puja, if we make this request single-pointedly, we will accomplish all the essential meanings of the practice of *Offering to the Spiritual Guide*.

Phurchog Ngawang Jampa

Receiving Blessings

Having made requests to our Spiritual Guide we now receive his blessings. According to *Offering to the Spiritual Guide* this has two parts:

1 Receiving the blessings of the four empowerments and reciting the mantras
2 Receiving the blessings of all the stages of the path

Receiving the blessings of the four empowerments and reciting the mantras has two parts:

1 Receiving the blessings of the four empowerments
2 Reciting the mantras

RECEIVING THE BLESSINGS OF THE FOUR EMPOWERMENTS

Through the force of requesting three times in this way, white, red, and blue light rays and nectars, serially and together, arise from the places of my Guru's body, speech, and mind, and dissolve into my three places, serially and together. My four obstructions are purified and I receive the four empowerments. I attain the four bodies and, out of delight, an emanation of my Guru dissolves into me and bestows his blessings.

When we receive an empowerment directly from our Spiritual Guide we receive four very special potentials into our mental continuum, but unless we subsequently receive regular blessings from our Spiritual Guide it is very easy for these potentials to lose their power. The best method to prevent this from happening is to receive the blessings of the four empowerments. All the practices of generation stage and completion stage are included within this practice, and it sows the seeds to attain realizations very quickly. Therefore, once we have received an empowerment we should try to receive these blessings every day. According to *Offering to the Spiritual Guide* this is done as follows.

We focus on Lama Losang Tubwang Dorjechang, the principal figure in the Field of Merit, and visualize at his crown a white OM, the seed-letter of the vajra body of all Buddhas; at his throat a red AH, the seed-letter of the vajra speech of all Buddhas; and at his heart a blue HUM, the seed-letter of the vajra mind of all Buddhas. To receive the blessings of the first empowerment, the vase empowerment, we imagine that from the letter OM at the crown of Lama Losang Tubwang Dorjechang infinite white light rays and nectars emanate and dissolve into our crown. We imagine that these light rays completely purify all our non-virtuous bodily actions such as killing, stealing, and sexual misconduct, and destroy all sickness and other physical impurities. All ordinary appearances and conceptions of body are purified and we feel completely pure and blissful. This experience empowers us to meditate on generation stage and sows the seed to attain the Emanation Body of a Buddha.

To receive the blessings of the secret empowerment we focus on the letter AH at the throat of Lama Losang Tubwang Dorjechang and imagine that from this letter infinite red light rays and nectars emanate and dissolve into our throat. These purify all our non-virtuous actions of speech, eliminate ordinary appearance and conception of speech, empower us to meditate on the illusory body, and sow the seed to attain the Enjoyment Body of a Buddha.

To receive the blessings of the wisdom-mudra empowerment we imagine that from the letter HUM at the heart of Lama Losang Tubwang Dorjechang infinite blue light rays and nectars emanate and dissolve into our heart. These purify all our non-virtuous mental actions and mental impurities, empower us to meditate on clear light, and sow the seed to attain the Truth Body of a Buddha.

Finally, to receive the blessings of the fourth empowerment, the word empowerment, we focus on all three letters at the three places of Lama Losang Tubwang Dorjechang and imagine that simultaneously white, red, and blue light rays and nectars emanate from these letters and dissolve into our three places. These purify all negativities of body, speech, and mind together, empower us to meditate on the union that needs learning, and sow the seed to attain the resultant Union.

The word empowerment is so called because it is received in dependence upon hearing the words of the Spiritual Guide as he explains Union from his own experience. According to Vajrayana Mahamudra there are three types of union: the union of bliss and emptiness, the union of the two truths (conventional and ultimate), and the union of body and mind. The first is attained when the mind of spontaneous great bliss mixes with emptiness. The second union, which is also called the 'union that needs learning', is attained when the union of meaning clear light and pure illusory body is attained. Although this mind is free from the delusion-obstructions it is still covered by the obstructions to omniscience, rather like a blue sky covered by a thin veil of cloud, and so there is still a need to train in meditation. The third union, which is also called the 'Union of No More Learning', is attained when the obstructions to omniscience are finally abandoned. It is like a clear blue sky completely unobstructed by clouds, and there is now no more training required. This is the resultant Union, the union of a Buddha's body and mind.

We imagine that as a result of receiving the blessings of the four empowerments we have attained the four bodies of a Buddha, and we develop strong divine pride of being the Deity. Lama Losang Tubwang Dorjechang is delighted with us and manifests an emanation who comes to the crown of our head and, entering into our central channel, descends to our heart. We imagine that our subtle body, speech, and mind become of one taste with our Spiritual Guide's body, speech, and mind, and we meditate on this special feeling of bliss for a while.

RECITING THE MANTRAS

With divine pride of being the Guru-Deity, we focus on Lama Losang Tubwang Dorjechang who is sitting at our heart on a lotus, moon, and sun cushion. At his heart, in the centre of a moon cushion, there is a white letter HUM. Around this stands the mantra of all Buddhas, OM AH HUM, with the OM white, the AH red, and the HUM blue. Around this stands the mantra of Conqueror Vajradhara, OM AH VAJRADHARA HUM, which is blue in colour. Around this stands the mantra of Buddha Shakyamuni, OM MUNI MUNI MAHA MUNIYE SÖHA, which is golden in colour. Around this stands the mantra of Je Tsongkhapa, OM AH GURU VAJRADHARA SUMATI KIRTI SIDDHI HUM, which is orange in colour. Finally, around this stands the Sanskrit name mantra of our Spiritual Guide, which is also orange in colour.

We begin by focusing on our Spiritual Guide's name mantra and recite this as many times as we wish while mentally making the three great requests, and in particular requesting his blessings to attain all the realizations of the Mahamudra. It is said that if we recite our Spiritual Guide's mantra with faith this is far more powerful than reciting any other mantra. From this point of view, if we have deep faith it does not matter whether or not our Spiritual Guide has high realizations, but if we have little or no faith, mantra recitation will not help, even if our Spiritual Guide is a fully enlightened being.

There was once an old woman who had great faith in Foe Destroyers. One day, as a joke, a neighbour gave her a dog's tooth saying that it was a relic from a great Foe Destroyer. The woman was delighted and placed the tooth on her shrine, where she made prayers to it four times a day. As a result of her faith, one day the tooth began to radiate light, and later she accomplished many attainments. Even though the basis of her devotion was a dog's tooth, for her it functioned as a holy relic and she received all the benefits of showing devotion to a relic. Therefore, we cannot say that her faith was mistaken.

Atisha regarded Lama Serlingpa as his most precious Guru because he received teachings on bodhichitta from him. However, Lama Serlingpa was a Chittamatrin and, according to the Madhyamika-Prasangika school, it is impossible for those who adhere to this view to progress beyond the Mahayana path of accumulation. For Atisha however, Lama Serlingpa was a Buddha, and through the power of his faith he received a Buddha's blessings from Lama Serlingpa. We cannot say that Atisha's faith was mistaken.

By contemplating these stories, we will realize the importance of deep faith in our Spiritual Guide. Once we have chosen someone as our Spiritual Guide we do not need to check his or her qualifications any further. From that point onwards we should have firm, unwavering faith, and in this way receive the blessings of all the Buddhas.

After reciting our Guru's name mantra, we imagine that it dissolves into Je Tsongkhapa's name mantra. Focusing on this mantra, we recite it as many times as we wish while mentally making requests. This mantra then dissolves into Buddha Shakyamuni's mantra, which we recite. Buddha Shakyamuni's mantra then dissolves into Conqueror Vajradhara's mantra. We recite this mantra and then it dissolves into the mantra of all Buddhas, OM AH HUM, which we then recite. This last mantra may be very short but it has great power. It is called 'the mantra of all Buddhas' because, as already explained, it is the essence of the vajra body, vajra speech, and vajra mind of all Buddhas. These three letters contain all other mantras, and so they are very blessed.

There are three ways to recite the mantra of all Buddhas: by verbal recitation, by mental recitation, or by vajra recitation. Whereas verbal recitation and mental recitation are also practised within generation stage, vajra recitation is exclusively a completion stage practice. This type of recitation is especially emphasized in *Guhyasamaja Tantra*. To do this practice we have to understand how mantra is the nature of the inner winds. We may think that the winds and mantras are different, but this is an ordinary conception of speech and a great obstacle to attaining advanced Tantric realizations. One of the reasons for taking the secret empowerment is to purify this mistaken conception.

When we do vajra recitation on OM AH HUM we do not recite the mantra either verbally or mentally, we simply concentrate on the inner sound of the winds, for they are the mantra. When we inhale, the inner winds just are the sound of OM; as we hold the winds at the heart chakra, they just are the sound of AH; and as we exhale, they just are the sound of HUM. At all three stages, the winds are OM AH HUM, but at any one stage only one of the letters is heard. Thus the in-breath, for example, is OM AH HUM, but only the sound of OM is heard.

Vajra recitation is called the 'precious recitation' because it is a supreme method for loosening the knots at the heart chakra. In *Heruka* and *Vajrayogini Tantras* the practice of tummo is emphasized, but we can also practise vajra recitation once the other channel wheels have been loosened by completion stage meditation. First we should gain some experience of verbal recitation, then we should train in mental recitation as explained in the Vajrayogini practice, and finally we can practise vajra recitation. However, it is very beneficial even now to begin to practise this method.

After reciting the mantra of all Buddhas, we imagine that it dissolves into the white HUM at the heart of Lama Losang Tubwang Dorjechang. We then finish the recitation with a dedication prayer.

RECEIVING THE BLESSINGS OF ALL THE STAGES OF THE PATH

We now recite a long prayer requesting our Spiritual Guide's blessings to accomplish the realizations of all the stages of the path. If possible we should try to combine these requests with actual meditation on the stages of the path. At the very least we should contemplate the meaning of these verses as we recite them. Altogether there are twenty-seven parts to this section, beginning with how to rely upon our Spiritual Guide.

HOW TO RELY UPON OUR SPIRITUAL GUIDE, THE ROOT OF SPIRITUAL PATHS

Through the force of my making offerings and respectful requests
To the venerable Spiritual Guide, the holy, supreme Field of Merit,
I seek your blessings, O Protector, the root of all goodness and joy,
So that you will gladly take me into your loving care.

If we have time, at this point we should practise extensive meditation on how to rely upon the Spiritual Guide according to the Lamrim outlines – remembering the benefits of relying completely upon a qualified Spiritual Guide, the dangers of breaking our commitment to our Spiritual Guide, developing faith by contemplating his qualities, and developing respect by contemplating his kindness. If we do not have time for extensive meditation we can simply make requests by following the words of the sadhana.

It has already been explained how our Spiritual Guide is a supreme Field of Merit in which we can sow the seeds of faith and reap a harvest of Dharma realizations. If the time comes for an ordinary farmer to sow seeds and he neglects to do so it will be a great waste. In the same way, if having met a fully-qualified Spiritual Guide we neglect to sow the seeds of faith and respect, we shall have lost a unique opportunity.

Recognizing that our Spiritual Guide is the source of all goodness and joy, we should try to rely upon him sincerely and, with this verse, make requests for his blessings to be able to do so. We imagine that our Spiritual Guide responds to our requests by bestowing his blessings. Lights and nectars radiate from his heart and dissolve into our body and mind. All the negative karma we have created towards our Spiritual Guide, such as going against his advice or criticizing him, is completely purified, and our body feels as clear as crystal. We receive special blessings to gain the realization of relying upon our Spiritual Guide.

DEVELOPING THE ASPIRATION TO TAKE THE ESSENCE OF OUR HUMAN LIFE

Realizing that this freedom and endowment, found only once,
Are difficult to attain, and yet decay so quickly,
I seek your blessings to seize their essential meaning,
Undistracted by the meaningless activities of this life.

With this verse we request our Spiritual Guide's blessings so that we may gain the realizations of the next two meditations of the stages of the path: meditation on our precious human life and meditation on death and impermanence. Through these meditations we learn to make our present life very meaningful and develop a concern for our welfare in future lives.

If we meditate according to the outlines of the stages of the path, we will recognize that our present human life is very precious because it possesses eight special freedoms and ten special endowments. Such a human life is extremely rare. It is attained only with great difficulty and so we should regard it as being found only once.

Even though this body is so precious, it is not immortal, and one day we shall have to part with it without any choice. Moreover, a human body is as fragile as a water bubble; it can be destroyed by a tiny organism, a small needle, or even by a single drop of water in the wrong place. We must contemplate and meditate on impermanence and death, and on the preciousness of our human life. This will cause us to value every moment of this life. We will not want to waste our precious life on meaningless activities that even animals are capable of performing, but will develop a strong wish to make our lives as meaningful as possible.

What is the essential meaning of our human life? This depends upon our motivation and capacity. The least objective is to avoid falling into the lower realms in our next life by creating the causes to take rebirth as a human or a god. A higher objective is to strive to avoid future samsaric rebirth altogether by attaining liberation. The highest objective, and most meaningful use of a human life, is to strive to attain full enlightenment to be able to free all living beings from the sufferings of samsara. If we do not strive to attain even the least of these objectives we shall be wasting a very rare and precious opportunity. If we are deceived by the meaningless activities of this life into wasting our human potential, we shall lose everything when we die.

Contemplating in this way we make heartfelt requests to Lama Losang Tubwang Dorjechang to bless us so that we can realize the preciousness and impermanence of this human life. Once we have these realizations we will feel that our human life is like a wish-granting jewel, and we will feel a great sense of loss if we waste even a single moment, just as a miser feels a great sense of loss if he has to part with a few coins.

We should not underestimate the power and importance of these preliminary meditations of the stages of the path. Buddha said that just as among all animals an elephant leaves the deepest footprint so too, of all meditations, meditation on death leaves the deepest impression on the mind. We should not feel that just because we are a Mahayanist, or just because we are practising Secret Mantra, we do not need to do meditations such as these. Even highly-realized Yogis rely upon these meditations to give impetus to their practice.

Panchen Palden Yeshe

THE ACTUAL METHOD FOR GAINING THE HAPPINESS OF HIGHER STATES IN FUTURE LIVES

> **Fearing the blazing fires of the sufferings of bad migrations,**
> **From the depths of my heart I go for refuge to the Three Jewels,**
> **And seek your blessings to strive sincerely**
> **To abandon non-virtue and practise the entire collection of virtue.**

Having contemplated the preciousness and impermanence of this human life and developed a wish to experience happiness in future lives, we now consider how this is to be done. The actual method for avoiding lower rebirth and ensuring rebirth in a happy migration is to go for refuge to the Three Jewels and then to observe the laws of karma. These practices are explained in the present verse, which explicitly teaches the refuge of a person of initial scope but implicitly also indicates the refuge of a person of intermediate scope and the refuge of a person of great scope.

The first line of this verse explains the causes of going for refuge: fear of rebirth in the lower realms and faith in the Three Jewels; the second line explains the objects of refuge and the manner of going for refuge; and the last two lines explain the way to observe the laws of karma by abandoning non-virtue and practising virtue, which is the main commitment of going for refuge. Thus all the practices of an initial scope practitioner are included in this verse.

To generate the first cause of going for refuge we have to think about the sufferings we will experience if we take our next rebirth in one of the three lower realms: the hell realm, the hungry ghost realm, or the animal realm. Sometimes we have difficulty in generating fear of rebirth in the hells because we are not convinced that they exist. There seem to be many reasons establishing the existence of emptiness, for example, but few proving the existence of hell.

It is helpful in this context to know about the three different types of phenomenon: manifest, hidden, and deeply hidden. Manifest phenomena, such as tables and chairs, can be known directly by our sense awarenesses, and hidden phenomena can be established by correct reasoning; but deeply hidden phenomena can be known only by relying upon Buddha's scriptures. For us the hells are deeply hidden phenomena, and so we must rely upon the teachings of Buddha to know of their existence.

Dying and taking rebirth in the hells is like falling asleep and experiencing an unending nightmare. Suppose we were to fall asleep and dream of falling into a terrifying abyss in which all kinds of hideous monsters and cruel torturers began attacking us and inflicting unbearable pain, but instead of waking up we stayed in that dream for an inconceivably long time. We would to all intents and purposes be in hell. Similarly, when we die, all the appearances of this life vanish and are replaced by the dream-like appearances of the intermediate state. If heavy negative karma has ripened we will feel as if we are plunging into a dark and terrifying abyss, being dragged down by hideous creatures who are delighting in our discomfort and inflicting all sorts of excruciating pain upon us. These nightmarish appearances will get worse and worse, and will go on and on, appearing to last for an eternity. This is hell.

The hells are not places with distinct geographical locations, nor do they exist from their own side; they are merely appearances to an impure mind, just like a nightmare. As Shantideva says in *Guide to the Bodhisattva's Way of Life*:

Who could have created the weapons
For the beings in the hells?
Who created the blazing iron ground?
Where did the sirens of hell come from?

The Able One has said that all such things
Come from an evil mind.
Thus there is nothing to fear within the three worlds
That has not come from the mind.

In so far as they are both mere appearances to mind, Pure Lands and hell realms are the same. Pure Lands are appearances to pure minds that can be seen only by those who have attained pure view, and hell realms are appearances to impure minds that are seen by those who have heavy negative karma ripening.

Once we have some conviction of the existence of the three lower realms we should contemplate what kind of suffering we would experience if we were born there. At the moment we cannot bear even a slight burn on the hand, but if we are reborn in the hot hells we shall have to experience unbearable torments for inconceivably long periods. It will be like being trapped inside a volcano for an eternity. Similarly, at the moment we cannot bear to miss even a single meal, but if we are reborn as a hungry ghost we shall have to go for years without food or drink, and when we do find a scrap to eat it will turn into a repulsive substance such as pus or blood. In this human life we cannot bear even to be called a dog, but if we are reborn in the animal realm as a dog we shall have to spend our whole life on all fours, with a dull, lethargic mind, scavenging for food, and constantly fending off predators.

If we cannot develop any conviction about the hell realm or the ghost realm, at least we can think about the sufferings of the animal realm and develop a fear of being reborn there. We can imagine being a sheep left out in the open in all weathers with only dirty grass to eat, just waiting to be dragged off to the slaughterhouse and butchered so that others can eat our body; or we can imagine being a lobster being boiled alive, or a toad, or a poisonous snake, or an insect that is swatted or sprayed just because it exists. We have no guarantee that we will not take rebirth in such forms. The time of death is uncertain; we may die tonight and be in an animal body by tomorrow.

By thinking in this way we develop a strong sense of discomfort and start to think about how we can protect ourself from such a hideous fate. By contemplating the special qualities of the Three Precious Jewels we will see that only they have the power to protect us from rebirth in the lower realms, and then our mind will be moved to take refuge in them. Our actual refuge is to practise Dharma, and the Dharma that prevents us from falling into the lower realms is the moral discipline of avoiding non-virtue and practising virtue. Therefore, from the depths of our heart we should request Lama Losang Tubwang Dorjechang to bless us to be able to engage in these practices purely.

We should not think that just because we are practising Secret Mantra we are above such practices and have no need to generate fear of the lower realms. If we cannot go for refuge of the initial scope, there is no way we shall be able to go for refuge of the great scope. It is very important to meditate regularly on the entire cycle of meditations on the stages of the path, such as those presented in *A Meditation Handbook*. It is not enough simply to have an intellectual understanding of the teachings; we have to take them to heart in meditation again and again until our mind genuinely changes. If we meditate regularly on the stages of the path we will develop a special feeling for these practices and we will be delighted whenever we hear Lamrim teachings; but if we do not meditate regularly, listening to such teachings will feel like eating the same food again and again. Moreover, if we take these instructions to heart through regular meditation and our mind is genuinely moved by them, we will have great power to influence others by giving teachings and advice; but someone with little or no meditative experience who tries to teach Lamrim will have no power to help others.

DEVELOPING THE WISH TO GAIN LIBERATION

**Being violently tossed by the waves of delusion
and karma
And tormented by the sea-monsters of the three
sufferings,
I seek your blessings to develop a strong wish for
liberation**

From the boundless and fearful great ocean of samsara.

Whereas the Dharma of a practitioner of initial scope begins with reducing attachment to the happiness of this life and developing a wish for higher rebirth in future lives, the Dharma of an intermediate scope practitioner begins with reducing attachment to the happiness of future lives and developing a wish to gain liberation from all samsaric rebirths. This wish, which is called 'renunciation', does not arise naturally but has to be cultivated intentionally. Without developing this wish we will not make any effort to attain liberation and so we will remain bound within samsara. The root of all Dharma is aspiration. Aspiration induces effort, and effort leads to Dharma realizations. When, through meditation, the wish to escape from samsara arises naturally throughout the day and the night, we have attained a spontaneous realization of renunciation. From then on, all our virtuous actions will be causes of liberation.

The way to develop a wish to gain liberation is to contemplate the teachings of the intermediate scope. According to Je Tsongkhapa in *Great Exposition of the Stages of the Path*, there are two ways to do this: by contemplating the four noble truths and by contemplating the twelve dependent-related links. When we contemplate the present verse from *Offering to the Spiritual Guide* we are practising the first method.

Samsara is like a boundless and fearful great ocean because it is filled with many different types of suffering, just as an ocean is filled with many strange creatures. Moreover, just as an ocean will never dry up no matter how long we wait, so the ocean of samsara will never come to an end of its own accord. The reason we are trapped in this ocean of suffering is indicated by the first line of the verse, which reveals true origins. Our delusions are so strong that they are constantly compelling us to commit negative karma which causes us to take rebirth in samsara again and again. For as long as our minds are under the influence of delusion and karma we have no inner freedom; they are like violent waves tossing us uncontrollably from one state of suffering to another.

The second line shows how to develop a wish to gain liberation from samsara by contemplating true sufferings. According to the stages of the path we have to contemplate the three sufferings, the six sufferings, and the eight sufferings, although only the first of these is mentioned explicitly here. The three sufferings are manifest suffering, changing suffering, and pervasive suffering. Renunciation is not merely a wish to abandon manifest sufferings such as mental and physical pain. Even animals wish to be free from these sufferings, but we would not say that they have renunciation. Similarly, a wish to be free from changing suffering is not genuine renunciation. There are many non-Buddhists for example who recognize that ordinary happiness and enjoyments do not last, but invariably change into suffering and disappointment, and as a result seek a more refined form of happiness through spiritual practice; but even this is not actual renunciation. True renunciation is a mind that recognizes the nature of pervasive suffering and wishes to abandon it.

What is pervasive suffering? It is simply the contaminated aggregates of samsaric beings. For example, when we take rebirth as a human we take on human aggregates, when we take rebirth as an animal we take on animal aggregates, and when we take rebirth as a god we take on god aggregates. If we take on human aggregates we have no choice but to experience the sufferings of the human realm, if we take on animal aggregates we have no choice but to experience the sufferings of the animal realm, and if we take on god aggregates we have no choice but to experience the sufferings of the god realms. All the different types of suffering in samsara arise from samsaric aggregates just as waves arise from an ocean, therefore samsaric aggregates themselves are pervasive suffering. For as long as we remain with contaminated aggregates, whether we abide in the highest god realms or the deepest hell, we will attract suffering just as a magnet attracts iron. If we cling to samsaric aggregates we will take rebirth in samsara, and if we take rebirth in samsara we will experience suffering. Therefore the real object to be avoided is samsaric aggregates, and it is these that the mind of renunciation seeks to abandon. As Geshe Potawa says:

> It is not sickness and death I fear so much as samsaric rebirth.

By contemplating in this way we should develop a deep sense of disgust for samsara and a strong wish for liberation; and we should make heartfelt requests to Lama Losang Tubwang Dorjechang for his blessings to succeed in this practice.

To escape from samsara we have to eradicate all the delusions from our mind. Sometimes it feels as if this is impossible, as if the mind and the delusions are inseparably mixed. Indeed, there is one non-Buddhist school, the Mimasakas, who believe that samsara has no end because the mind and the delusions are the same entity. In reality, however, the delusions can be removed from the mind by abandoning self-grasping, which is the root from which they all arise. Je Tsongkhapa says that self-grasping is like an iron cage in which we are trapped, and that to escape from it we have to realize emptiness; that is, we have to realize that the object of our self-grasping does not exist. Without this realization samsara has no end.

When we are training in these practices, it is very important not to generate false renunciation. For example, renunciation does not entail abandoning our family and friends, nor does it entail living a life of poverty. If poverty were renunciation, poor people would be renunciates and rich people would not. Poverty is simply the result of miserliness, and wealth the result of giving. If possessing wealth were an obstacle to developing renunciation, whoever practised giving would be obstructing their path to liberation! Even though we have to contemplate suffering to generate renunciation, renunciation itself is not a gloomy mind.

It is happy in the knowledge that there is a way to become free from samsaric suffering, and it joyfully engages in the practices that lead to liberation. Whereas an ordinary samsaric mind oscillates between elation and despondency, renunciation is a balanced mind that is constantly positive.

While we are practising the Dharma of the intermediate scope we should not become too tight or too serious. We should continue to associate with our friends and family, look after our health, feed and clothe ourself, and practise Dharma in a comfortable and intelligent manner. A sick person does not enjoy taking medicine but does so out of necessity. In the same way, if we have renunciation, we are not attached to food, clothing, and so forth; but we partake of them in moderation so as to create good conditions for our Dharma practice.

Some people develop renunciation very quickly. Sometimes this is due to the ripening of powerful imprints from previous lives, and sometimes it is due to very skilful practice. When we are training in renunciation we should have a very broad mind and try to use every opportunity to increase our distaste for samsara. A good businessman is always on the lookout for new ways to make a profit, and in the same way we should always be looking around us for more reasons to leave samsara. If we have wisdom, everything we see will teach us something. As Milarepa said:

> I have no need of books because all the objects around me are my books. From these I learn about death and impermanence, the disadvantages of samsara, and the emptiness of all phenomena.

If we practise in this way, always remaining mindful, our everyday experiences will enhance our meditations and our meditations will guide our daily lives. If we mix our entire life with Dharma in this way, we will quickly gain realizations.

If we are followers of the Mahayana and are seeking to enter into Mahayana paths, it is essential to train in renunciation first. Renunciation is a cause of great compassion, which in turn is a cause of bodhichitta. If we are not acutely aware of the suffering nature of our own aggregates, how can we understand the suffering of others and wish to rescue them from samsara? The only difference between training in renunciation and training in compassion is that with the former we focus on our own suffering and with the latter we focus on the suffering of others.

HOW TO PRACTISE THE PATH THAT LEADS TO LIBERATION

**Forsaking the mind that views as a pleasure garden
This unbearable prison of samsara,
I seek your blessings to take up the victory banner
of liberation
By maintaining the three higher trainings and the
wealths of Superiors.**

When we develop a wish for liberation we give up attachment to samsara. We no longer regard samsaric pleasures as desirable objects, but as deceptive objects to be avoided. Although, to the deluded mind, samsara appears to be like a pleasure garden, in reality it is like a prison full of hideous torture chambers. To escape from this prison we need to practise the three higher trainings: training in higher moral discipline, training in higher concentration, and training in higher wisdom. They are called 'higher trainings' because they are motivated by renunciation, which is an exalted mind.

As already mentioned, the root of samsara is self-grasping, and to abandon this we must realize that its object is non-existent by realizing the emptiness of all phenomena. However, an intellectual understanding of emptiness alone is not sufficient actually to abandon self-grasping. For this, a direct realization is needed. Therefore, training in higher wisdom entails striving for a direct realization of emptiness with which to abandon self-grasping. We can attain a direct realization of emptiness

Khädrub Ngawang Dorje

only if our mind is very still and concentrated, so training in higher wisdom depends upon training in higher concentration. To attain actual tranquil abiding we need a pure, undistracted mind and strong mindfulness, alertness, and conscientiousness. These can be attained only by practising pure moral discipline. Moral discipline is like a fence. Just as a fence around a garden keeps out scavenging animals, thereby enabling the plants to grow and produce fruit, so moral discipline keeps out reckless actions that disturb the mind, thereby enabling the tree of concentration to grow and produce the fruit of wisdom.

In summary, training in higher wisdom depends upon training in higher concentration, which in turn depends upon training in higher moral discipline. To cut down a tree we need a sharp axe held by a steady hand and wielded by a strong body. In the same way, to cut self-grasping, the root of samsara, we need the sharp axe of wisdom held by the steady hand of concentration and wielded by the strong body of moral discipline. Therefore we should pray to Lama Losang Tubwang Dorjechang for his blessings to be able to succeed in these practices.

When we attain a direct realization of emptiness we become a Superior being. At that time we become very rich, not because we possess ordinary wealth, but because we possess the seven wealths of Superiors: faith, moral discipline, listening to many teachings, giving, sense of shame, consideration, and wisdom.

HOW TO GENERATE GREAT COMPASSION, THE FOUNDATION OF THE MAHAYANA

Contemplating how all these pitiful migrators are
   my mothers,
Who out of kindness have cherished me again and
   again,
I seek your blessings to generate a spontaneous
   compassion
Like that of a loving mother for her dearest child.

The practices of the intermediate scope should not be seen as ends in themselves, but as preparations for the Mahayana trainings. If we were to practise the three higher trainings simply to gain liberation for ourself alone we would be like a son imprisoned with his mother who finds a way to free himself but leaves his mother behind. When we know how to escape from samsara we should strive to generate a strong wish to free all living beings from this prison of suffering. To be able to do this we need to enter into the Mahayana and attain Buddhahood.

The gateway to the Mahayana is bodhichitta, and the root of bodhichitta is great compassion. Therefore we must begin by training in great compassion. As Nagarjuna says:

> Since the root of bodhichitta is great compassion, whoever seeks enlightenment should cultivate great compassion.

There are two methods for developing great compassion and bodhichitta: the sevenfold cause and effect, and equalizing and exchanging self with others. The first method was passed down from Buddha Maitreya through Chandragomin, and the second was passed down from Buddha Manjushri through Shantideva. *Offering to the Spiritual Guide* explains both methods – the first briefly with the present verse, and the second more extensively in the verses that follow.

According to the first method, we begin by learning to recognize all sentient beings as our mothers by contemplating logical reasons, Buddha's scriptures, and helpful analogies. We need to realize not just that every sentient being *has* been our mother at some time in the past but that every sentient being still *is* our mother. If our mother of this life were to die and take rebirth as a dog, she would not stop being our mother. The fact that she gave birth to us, fed us, and cared for us is not altered by her death. In the same way, all our mothers from our past lives have died and taken rebirth in different forms and, although we no longer recognize them, they are still our mothers. Thus whenever we see any living being, even a tiny ant on the ground, we should think 'This is my kind mother.'

The kindness of our previous mothers is not diminished by the fact that it was in the past that they were kind to us. For example, if someone gave us a hundred pounds last week and someone else gives us a hundred pounds this week, we cannot say that the first person was less kind than the second simply because he helped us in the past. In the same way, even though it was in the past that our previous mothers helped us, they are still kind. If we understand this, we will realize that the kindness of a tiny ant on the ground is equal to the kindness of our present mother.

By contemplating the kindness we have received again and again from all mother sentient beings, we develop a special feeling of warmth and affection for them. This feeling is called affectionate love and is the main cause of the mind of compassion. If we feel affection for someone and we think about their suffering we naturally find their suffering unbearable and want to find ways to stop it. A mind that cannot bear the suffering of others is com-passion. On the other hand, if we do not feel close to someone and we think about their suffering we do not necessarily find their suffering unbearable or develop a wish to protect them. Indeed, sometimes when we think of our enemies experiencing suffering we may even feel pleasure rather than compassion. Generating affectionate love, therefore, is an essential prerequisite for generating compassion. Realizing this, we request Lama Losang Tubwang Dorjechang to grant his blessings so that by generating affectionate love we can develop a spontaneous compassion for all living beings that is as strong as the compassion a mother has for her dearest child.

EQUALIZING SELF AND OTHERS

**In that no one wishes for even the slightest
  suffering,
Or is ever content with the happiness they have,**

**There is no difference between myself and others;
Realizing this, I seek your blessings joyfully to
make others happy.**

The next six verses explain the method for generating great
compassion and bodhichitta by equalizing and exchanging
self with others. These practices are more profound and
more powerful than those of the sevenfold cause and effect,
and they produce a stronger compassion and a superior
bodhichitta, but they are not so easy to practise and in some
cases are open to misinterpretation. Since greater skill and
wisdom are needed to practise this method, for a long time
it was treated as a 'secret Dharma' and passed to suitable
disciples only through the direct oral instructions of the
Spiritual Guide.

The actual method for generating great compassion
according to this system is exchanging self with others,
which means exchanging the object of our cherishing so that
we cherish only others and disregard our own interests, just
as we presently cherish only ourself and disregard the
interests of others. To accomplish this change in attitude we
first need to equalize self and others, which means to learn
to cherish others at least as much as we cherish ourself.

Extensive contemplations for equalizing self and others can
be found in *Meaningful to Behold* and *Universal Compassion*.
In *Offering to the Spiritual Guide*, the first Panchen Lama
gives only brief reasons for consideration. We should think:

> *Just as I wish to be happy, so do all other living beings, and
> just as I do not wish for even the slightest suffering, nor
> does anyone else. From this point of view we are all exactly
> the same. Therefore there is no reason why I should consider
> my own happiness or my own suffering to be more import-
> ant than anyone else's.*

We can add further reasons used by Shantideva in *Guide to
the Bodhisattva's Way of Life*:

> *When I think of my suffering I am thinking about only one
> person, but when I think about the suffering of others I am*

thinking about countless beings. How can I be preoccupied just with my own suffering and ignore everyone else's?

If a mother and her son are in prison together how could the son contemplate his own freedom without also thinking about his mother's? And yet I am in the prison of samsara with countless mothers, so how can I think only about my own welfare and ignore theirs?

By contemplating in this way we will generate the following determination:

From now on I shall care for others just as much as I care for myself.

We then take this resolution as our object of placement meditation, and concentrate on it single-pointedly. In this way we will gradually develop a special affectionate love for all living beings and be able to maintain this love at all times, even during the meditation break.

If we are accustomed to generating kind, loving thoughts, we will feel pleased whenever we meet others, just as a mother is delighted when she sees her dear children. Gradually, others will come to like us, and many of our problems that arise from hatred and jealousy will disappear. Thus even in the short term, affectionate love brings many benefits.

Developing minds such as affectionate love towards all living beings is simply a matter of familiarity. With practice, we can grow used to anything, and if we train in affectionate love sincerely over a long period eventually we will feel love for everyone, including those whom we presently dislike. Shantideva gives many reasons why this can be attained. Therefore we should persevere with trying to generate affectionate love through equalizing self and others, and we should request Lama Losang Tubwang Dorjechang to bless us to be able to succeed in this practice. Once we have generated affectionate love, we will find it very easy to generate great compassion, and with that realization bodhichitta will come very easily. As Mahayanists, we should regard the development of bodhichitta as our heart practice.

THE DANGERS OF SELF-CHERISHING

**Seeing that this chronic disease of cherishing myself
Is the cause that gives rise to unwanted suffering,
I seek your blessings to destroy this great demon
  of selfishness
By resenting it as the object of blame.**

Once we have grown used to cherishing others as much as
we cherish ourself, we then need to go one step further and
learn to cherish others more than we cherish ourself. To do
this we must first realize the many disadvantages of self-
cherishing.

All the sufferings of samsara arise from self-cherishing.
If we check we shall see that all the suffering we experienced in the past, all the suffering we are now experiencing,
and all the suffering we shall experience in the future are
due to self-cherishing. This is because suffering is the result
of negative actions, and all negative actions originate in
self-cherishing.

If our wishes are not fulfilled or we experience problems
we become unhappy. Why? It is only because we are thinking of our own happiness. People who have overcome self-
cherishing never feel unhappy, even when they are sick or
dying. Why are Superior Bodhisattvas able to cut up their
bodies and give them away to others without experiencing
any pain or regret? It is only because they have overcome
their self-cherishing. If we could give up self-cherishing we
would experience many benefits. In the short term we
would solve many of our daily problems and in the long
term we would be able to generate the precious minds of
compassion and bodhichitta.

By contemplating these points we will see that self-
cherishing is the real demon; it is to blame for all our
unhappiness and misfortune. Therefore we should decide
very strongly to stop cherishing ourself, and hold this
decision with single-pointed concentration in placement
meditation. We need to do this meditation again and again
for a long time until the disadvantages of self-cherishing

are obvious to us, and we have a constant wish to abandon it. We pray to Lama Losang Tubwang Dorjechang for his blessings to be able to abandon self-cherishing.

THE BENEFITS OF CHERISHING OTHERS

**Seeing that the mind that cherishes mother beings
and would secure their happiness
Is the gateway that leads to infinite good qualities,
I seek your blessings to cherish these beings more
than my life,
Even if they rise up against me as my enemies.**

Whereas cherishing ourself is the cause of all suffering, cherishing others is the source of all good qualities. Just as we cannot think of a single negative action that does not arise from self-cherishing, so we cannot think of a single virtuous action that does not arise from cherishing others.

If we cherish others, naturally we will perform virtuous actions such as giving, moral discipline, and patience; and as a result we will experience great happiness in the future. We all want happiness, and happiness comes from virtuous actions. If we cherish others we will naturally practise virtue, so cherishing others fulfils all our wishes. It was for this reason that Geshe Langri Tangpa referred to cherishing others as a 'wishfulfilling jewel'.

At the moment when we show love or concern for others we do so with partiality, favouring some and neglecting others. By training in these methods we will come to cherish all living beings equally, without any trace of attachment or bias. With such a pure motivation all our virtuous actions will become very powerful and the cause of great happiness for both ourself and others.

Seeing the great benefits of cherishing others, we should request Lama Losang Tubwang Dorjechang to bless us so that we can cherish all living beings more than our life, even if they rise up against us as our enemies.

EXCHANGING SELF WITH OTHERS

In short, since the childish are concerned for
themselves alone,
Whereas Buddhas work solely for the sake of others,
I seek your blessings to distinguish the faults and
benefits,
And thus be able to exchange myself with others.

Since cherishing myself is the door to all faults
And cherishing mother beings is the foundation of
all good qualities,
I seek your blessings to take as my essential practice
The yoga of exchanging self with others.

These two verses summarize the actual practice of exchanging self with others. Buddhas have attained enlightenment by abandoning self-cherishing and cherishing only others, and so they are able to work continuously for others. Samsaric beings on the other hand are like children because they are concerned only with their own welfare, and as a result they remain trapped within samsara. Since beginningless time we have taken countless rebirths in samsara because of our self-cherishing, but the Buddhas have given up self-cherishing and attained enlightenment. The only difference between us and them is that we cling to self-cherishing whereas they have abandoned it.

Buddhas have not always been Buddhas. At one time they were just like us, but they took on the responsibility of working for others and freed themselves from samsara whereas we remain trapped by our self-concern. As Shantideva says:

But what need is there to say more?
The childish work for their own benefit,
The Buddhas work for the benefit of others.
Just look at the difference between them!

At one time a Yogi called Drugpa Kunleg went to Lhasa to pay homage to a statue of Buddha Shakyamuni. Upon arriving in front of the statue he prostrated to it, exclaiming:

O Buddha, to begin with you and I were exactly the
    same,
But later you attained Buddhahood through the
    force of your effort,
Whereas due to my laziness I remain in samsara;
So now I must prostrate to you.

Again and again we need to contemplate how self-
cherishing is the door to all faults, and generate a determination to abandon it; and again and again we need to
contemplate how cherishing others is the source of all good
qualities, and generate a determination to practise it. By
meditating on these two determinations for a long time and
carrying them in our heart throughout the meditation
break, we will naturally come to cherish others more than
ourself. Therefore we should pray to Lama Losang Tubwang Dorjechang to bless our mind so that we can make
the yoga of exchanging self with others our heart practice.

TAKING AND GIVING

**Therefore, O Compassionate, Venerable Guru,
    I seek your blessings
So that all the suffering, negativities, and
    obstructions of mother sentient beings
Will ripen upon me right now;
And through my giving my happiness and virtue
    to others,
May all migrating beings be happy.**

The practice of taking and giving is an especially powerful
method for developing the realizations of love, compassion, and exchanging self with others. To emphasize its
importance this verse has five lines, whereas all the others
have four. The first line was added by one of the first
Panchen Lama's disciples, Drungpa Taphugpa, with the
Panchen Lama's permission.

When we practise taking and giving, we begin by taking
because sentient beings need to be freed from their sufferings

Ngulchu Dharmabhadra

before they can enjoy the happiness we give them. To meditate on taking, we begin by imagining all the beings of the six realms around us and contemplate their sufferings. In this way we try to develop the compassionate thought:

How wonderful it would be if all these poor beings could be released from suffering and its causes.

Then we generate a special determination:

So that all these poor beings can be free from suffering, I shall take their suffering upon myself.

With this determination we imagine that we draw towards us all the suffering, negativities, and obstructions of all the beings around us in the form of black smoke. This dissolves into our heart where it completely destroys our self-cherishing mind. We think very strongly that this has actually happened, and we develop a great sense of joy. We meditate on this feeling of joy with single-pointed concentration. This is how to meditate on taking by means of compassion.

Having freed all sentient beings from their suffering, we then think about their happiness. Although all sentient beings long to be happy, they never find pure happiness. What little happiness they do find is impure and short-lived. Contemplating this we develop the thought:

How wonderful it would be if all these beings could experience pure, lasting happiness.

and then we develop a special determination:

So that they may experience pure happiness, I shall transform my roots of virtue, my happiness, and my good fortune into whatever each sentient being requires and give it to them.

With this determination, we imagine that our body radiates countless rays of light, which reach all living beings. These rays of light immediately fulfil all their wishes, bringing them whatever they want and bestowing upon them uncontaminated happiness. We strongly think that this has actually happened and feel great joy. We meditate on this feeling of joy with single-pointed concentration. This is how to meditate on giving by means of love.

In *Guide to the Bodhisattva's Way of Life*, Shantideva describes a method whereby we transform our body into a wishfulfilling jewel that radiates light and fulfils the wishes of all living beings. This method is explained on page 242. If we wish, we can incorporate this method into our meditation on giving.

If we find it difficult to take on the sufferings of others, we can start by taking on our own suffering. We begin by taking on the sufferings of ageing, sickness, and death that we will have to experience in the near future, and then we take on the sufferings that we may have to experience in future lives, such as rebirth in the lower realms. We draw all these into our heart in the form of black smoke and imagine that this smoke completely destroys our self-cherishing mind and frees us from having to experience these sufferings in the future. Gradually we can extend the scope of our meditation to take on the sufferings of our friends, relatives, neighbours, and so on, until we are able to take on the sufferings of all sentient beings.

To begin with this practice is done just in the imagination, but as our concentration improves we are able actually to take on others' suffering, as well as our own future suffering. For example, we may have committed a negative action that will result in rebirth in hell, but by practising taking we can experience its effect now in a much diminished form, perhaps as a headache. Cultivating a wish to take on others' suffering combined with a determination to destroy our own self-cherishing is a very powerful form of purification. However, as with most purification, this practice often entails experiencing a little suffering now to purify much greater potential suffering.

If we gain some experience of taking and giving, we can transform all difficult circumstances into the path to enlightenment. We will be free from obstacles, and even evil spirits will be unable to harm us. Because we shall have the ability to transform difficulties into our spiritual practice, we shall be happy when things are going well and happy when they are not; in other words we shall be happy all the time.

When we are familiar with taking and giving, we can mount this practice upon the breath. With the motivation of compassion, each time we inhale we imagine that we are breathing in the suffering of all sentient beings in the form of black smoke. This descends to our heart and destroys our self-cherishing mind. With the motivation of love, each time we exhale we imagine that we are breathing out our happiness and virtue in the form of light which reaches all living beings and brings them happiness and joy. Because our mind is closely related to our inner winds, such a practice is very powerful in harnessing our inner winds to the development of great compassion.

We should make heartfelt requests to Lama Losang Tubwang Dorjechang for his blessings to be able to succeed in the practice of taking and giving. We imagine that our Spiritual Guide bestows his blessings in the form of powerful lights and nectars which radiate from his heart and fill our whole body. All our obstacles to the practice of taking and giving are dispelled and our mind is blessed with the realizations of love and compassion.

The presentation of the stages of the path in *Offering to the Spiritual Guide* is very special. As mentioned before, this entire practice is a preliminary for Mahamudra meditation. Usually we regard only practices such as collecting refuge prayers and collecting prostrations as the preliminaries for Mahamudra meditation, but in reality the practice of Lamrim is the real preliminary. If we can accomplish an authentic change of attitude through practices such as taking and giving, this is the best foundation on which to build a Vajrayana Mahamudra practice.

Some people might think that the Gelugpa tradition has no preliminary practices, but in fact every stage of Lamrim prepares the mind for Vajrayana Mahamudra meditation by helping us to develop a pure motivation and a correct view. If we have these, we will find Mahamudra meditation easy; but if we lack them Mahamudra meditation will bring no results. Therefore, it is very important to emphasize authentic changes of mind through Lamrim practice. For example, the prayers for the six preparatory practices for meditation on the stages of the path include practices for purifying negativities, accumulating merit, and receiving blessings. If we practise these sincerely and then go on to gain some experience of renunciation, bodhichitta, and wisdom realizing emptiness, we shall be very well prepared for Mahamudra meditation. In addition to these practices, we should also prepare our mind by collecting with a good motivation a hundred thousand refuge prayers, a hundred thousand prostrations, and so forth. These preliminary practices will support both our Lamrim and our Mahamudra meditations, and will help both to be successful.

It is utterly impossible to attain Tantric realizations without bodhichitta motivation. There is a story of one practitioner of Hevajra who had renunciation but no bodhichitta. Although he meditated extensively on the generation and completion stages of Hevajra, he was able to attain only the level of a Hinayana Stream Enterer. Later scholars explained that this was because he lacked the motivation of bodhichitta.

Gampopa had a high opinion of his meditative achievements and boasted to Milarepa that he could meditate undistracted for seven whole days. Unimpressed, Milarepa replied:

Even if you could remain concentrated in meditation for aeons, undistracted even by a drum banging in your ear, it would not begin to compare with my meditation on the short-AH.

Meditation on the short-AH is a profound Mahamudra technique for causing the tummo, or inner fire, to blaze. Comparing Gampopa's meditation to this is like comparing a lame donkey to a thoroughbred stallion because it would never give rise to spontaneous great bliss. However, by meditating on the short-AH inside the central channel at the navel the central channel will open, the inner fire will blaze, and this will give rise to the mind of spontaneous great bliss. Nonetheless, if we do this meditation without bodhichitta motivation we will not attain actual realizations. All Secret Mantra realizations depend upon bodhichitta motivation. Therefore, it is most important to prepare for Mahamudra meditation by meditating on the stages of the path. Realizing this, we should make constant requests to Lama Losang Tubwang Dorjechang for his blessings to gain all the realizations of the stages of the path.

THE THIRD TO THE SEVENTH POINTS OF TRAINING THE MIND

Though the world and its beings, filled with the
    effects of evil,
Pour down unwanted suffering like rain,
This is a chance to exhaust the effects of negative
    actions;
Seeing this, I seek your blessings to transform
    adverse conditions into the path.

In short, whether favourable or unfavourable
    conditions arise,
I seek your blessings to transform them into the
    path of improving the two bodhichittas
Through practising the five forces, the essence of
    all Dharmas,
And thereby maintain a happy mind alone.

I seek your blessings to make this freedom and
    endowment extremely meaningful
By immediately applying meditation to whatever
    I meet
Through the skilful means of the four preparations,
And by practising the commitments and precepts
    of training the mind.

The seven points of training the mind enumerated by Bodhisattva Chekawa are:

1 The preliminary practices of training the mind
2 The main practice: training in the two bodhichittas
3 Transforming adverse conditions into the path to enlightenment
4 How to integrate all our daily practices
5 The measurement of success in training the mind
6 The commitments of training the mind
7 The precepts of training the mind

The first point involves meditation on our precious human life, on impermanence and death, on actions and their effects, and on the faults of samsara. These have already been covered in the previous instructions. The second point concerns training in the two bodhichittas: conventional bodhichitta and ultimate bodhichitta. The method for generating conventional bodhichitta is explained in the next section, and the method for generating ultimate bodhichitta will be explained below. The present verses, therefore, are concerned primarily with the third to the seventh points.

Beings in these degenerate times encounter many obstacles to their Dharma practice but, rather than being discouraged by them, Mahayanists striving to attain enlightenment for the sake of all living beings should transform them into the path and use them to strengthen their practice. There are two ways to do this: transforming adverse conditions into the path by adopting a special line of thought, and transforming adverse conditions into the path through the practice of the four preparations.

There are two ways of transforming adverse conditions into the path by adopting a special line of thought: transforming adverse conditions into the path by means of method, and transforming adverse conditions into the path by means of wisdom. According to the first, we should respond to adverse conditions by using them to strengthen our renunciation and compassion. Thus, when we are experiencing suffering we should remember that this is because we have taken rebirth in samsara, and that if we do not want even worse suffering in the future we need to gain liberation in this life. In this way our suffering urges us to practise Dharma more purely. We can also follow Atisha's advice in *Lamp for the Path* and use our experience of pain to make us aware of the much greater pain experienced by countless other sentient beings. In this way we will increase our compassion. Motivated by compassion, we can then practise taking on the suffering of others.

In *Guide to the Middle Way*, Chandrakirti explains how a Bodhisattva on the Mahayana path of accumulation is able to cut up his body and give it away even though it causes him great pain, because he uses his own suffering as an example of the much greater suffering experienced by all other beings. In this way, he develops great courage and resolves to attain enlightenment as quickly as possible to free all living beings from pain.

To transform adverse conditions by means of wisdom, we need to contemplate how the difficulties we experience are mere imputations of mind. Although they appear to exist from their own side, in reality they are empty. Thus whenever we experience pain, for example, we should contemplate that we, the pain, and the cause of the pain all lack inherent existence; and then remain with our mind peacefully absorbed in emptiness.

Transforming adverse conditions through the practice of the four preparations entails accumulating merit, purifying negativities, giving food to obstructive spirits, and making offerings to Dharma Protectors. The main reason we experience difficulties and fail to fulfil our wishes is that we lack merit. Therefore, rather than being discouraged when difficulties arise, we should remember that good fortune arises only from good causes and try to accumulate more merit. Similarly, we should remember that all suffering and misfortune is the ripening effect of negative karma, and that if we do not want to experience more suffering in the future we need to practise purification now. Since all the problems we experience are the results of our own negative karma, only we can experience them; no one else can experience the results of our karma for us. If we patiently forbear difficulties, the karma that gave rise to them will be completely purified. If we respond to adverse conditions in this way they become like Dharma teachings for us and always produce positive results.

Quite often the problems we encounter are caused by obstructive spirits who have become jealous or annoyed by our actions. To pacify them and reassure them that we mean no harm we should give them food, either in the form of a traditional torma or in some other form. If we have no actual food to give them we can simply visualize it. Finally, we can make offerings to the Dharma Protectors who have vowed to protect Dharma practitioners from obstacles and create favourable conditions for their practice.

Children get very excited when they make sandcastles, but when the sea washes them away they become upset. Buddha said that we are like children in this respect because we are happy when things are going well, but become miserable and depressed as soon as we encounter difficulties. Samsaric pleasure is necessarily impermanent, and sooner or later turns into suffering; we would be foolish to expect anything else. Therefore we need to develop equanimity with respect to good and bad situations. We need to think 'If things go well, fine; if they do not, that's fine too.' Whatever comes up, we can turn it to our advantage. As Shantideva says, suffering has many good qualities because it purifies our negative karma, increases our renunciation and compassion, reduces our pride, and helps us to overcome bad mental habits. If we think in this way we will feel that difficult circumstances are our best friends. When our mind is balanced in this way it becomes as stable as Mount Meru, and nothing can cause it to shake.

The fourth point of training the mind concerns integrating all our daily practices. There are many different practices taught in the Mahayana and we may wonder how it is possible to practise them all. The answer is to integrate them all into the practice of training in the two bodhichittas by means of the five forces. As mentioned before, the two bodhichittas are conventional bodhichitta and ultimate bodhichitta. Conventional bodhichitta is the spontaneous wish to attain enlightenment for the sake of all living beings, and ultimate bodhichitta is a direct realization of emptiness maintained by conventional bodhichitta. If we wish to attain enlightenment for the sake of others we need to train continuously in these two bodhichittas.

To maintain a constant, uninterrupted training in the two bodhichittas we must be able to sustain our practice in all situations, whether good or bad. It is especially important to be able to maintain our practice as death approaches, and to use our death to train in the two bodhichittas. To integrate our practices to this extent we need to rely upon the five forces: the force of motivation, the force of familiarity, the force of white seed, the force of destruction, and the force of aspirational prayer.

Motivation, or aspiration, is the root of all Dharma. If we have the wish to do something we will engage in it happily and see it through to completion, but if we have no wish, or only a weak wish, we will be reluctant to engage in the task, or we will not be able to finish it. Therefore, if we want to train in the two bodhichittas continuously we need to generate a strong motivation at the beginning. It is very important to begin our training while our body and mind are still strong. If possible we should motivate ourself to continue our training for the rest of our life, and then practise steadily and conscientiously without letting our original resolve weaken. If we find this difficult, we can commit ourself to train continuously for a shorter period, say three years, one year, or three months, and then examine our actions regularly to make sure that our practice does not degenerate. Every day, as soon as we wake up, and again when we go to bed, we should remind ourself of our commitment and renew our determination. We should make requests to our Spiritual Guide for blessings to be able to maintain a strong and pure motivation.

Yangchän Drubpay Dorje

Having generated a motivation to train in the two bodhi-chittas, we then need to become familiar with these two minds. We should listen to many teachings, contemplate their meaning again and again, and meditate on what we have understood as often as we can. To practise the force of familiarity with conventional bodhichitta, we begin by training in affectionate love and great compassion. During the meditation break we should use our everyday experiences to improve our compassion. When we see poor or sick people we should generate compassion for them, and when we see rich and famous people we should feel compassion for them too. Whoever is trapped within samsara is an object of compassion – some are experiencing great suffering now, others will experience great suffering in the future – but no one in samsara is free from suffering.

To become familiar with ultimate bodhichitta we need to begin by improving our understanding of emptiness and then train in seeing the empty nature of phenomena. In the *Perfection of Wisdom Sutras* Buddha said that we should contemplate emptiness at all times, whether we are sitting, standing, coming, or going. Whatever appears to any of our six senses is empty, just like objects in a dream. Milarepa said:

Last night's dream is my Teacher. Is it the same for you?

Buddha gave many analogies to help us understand the emptiness of phenomena, and we should try to become familiar with these. In this respect emptiness is easier to understand than the subtle laws of karma because it is much more difficult to find analogies to illustrate these.

To sustain and protect our training in the two bodhi-chittas we need to engage in two activities: accumulating a vast collection of merit and keeping our mind free from delusions that undermine or obstruct our training. By engaging in the first, we are practising the force of white seed, and by engaging in the second we are practising the force of destruction. Finally, to ensure that our practices produce the desired results, we should dedicate all our merit and make heartfelt prayers to realize the two bodhichittas.

In *Commentary to Valid Cognition* Dharmakirti says that if all the causes for something are assembled nothing can stop it occurring, but if just one of the causes is missing nothing can make it happen. To ensure that we attain the result of the two bodhichittas we need to assemble all five forces. The force of familiarity – listening, contemplating, and meditating on the two bodhichittas – is the substantial cause, and the remaining forces are contributory causes. Therefore, the force of familiarity is like the seed, the force of white seed is like the soil, the force of destruction is like clearing and preparing the soil, the force of motivation is like sowing the seeds, and the force of aspirational prayer is like the moisture and sunlight that nourish the growth of the crop. When all these causes and conditions come together we will definitely harvest the fruit of the two bodhichittas.

When we go shopping we look for the best things to buy. Similarly, if we look among the Mahayana teachings for the best practice we will see that it is the practice of the five forces. As the sadhana says, it is the 'essence of all Dharmas'. To practise the five forces we mainly need mindfulness. If our mind is always busy and distracted we will find any practice difficult, but if we have strong mindfulness we will be able to practise Dharma regardless of what we are doing. If we are walking along a road that we know to be frequented by muggers we concentrate mainly on where we are going, but occasionally we look round to make sure that we are safe. In the same way, if we want to practise the two bodhichittas continuously we should concentrate principally on the five forces and only occasionally check to see that the affairs of this life are in order. In this way our mind will stay calm and peaceful and our practice will be successful.

The measurement of success in training the mind is indicated by the last line of the second verse, which echoes the words of Bodhisattva Chekawa in the root text on training the mind:

Always rely upon a happy mind alone.

If through training our mind we find that we can keep a peaceful and happy mind at all times, even in difficult circumstances, this indicates that we have been successful in our training. Therefore we should request Lama Losang Tubwang Dorjechang to bless us so that we are successful in training our mind, and so that we will succeed in transforming all situations into our spiritual practice by means of the four preparations.

If we train our mind in this way, everything we encounter will increase our Dharma realizations. There are three types of object: attractive, unattractive, and neutral. Normally, when we encounter the first we develop attachment, when we encounter the second we develop hatred, and when we encounter the third we develop ignorance. For a successful practitioner of training the mind, however, these objects have the opposite effect. Instead of giving rise to the three poisons – attachment, hatred, and ignorance – they give rise to the three virtuous roots – non-attachment, non-hatred, and non-ignorance.

The three virtuous roots are included within the eleven virtuous mental factors. They are not simply the absence of the three poisons, but are their direct opposites. Thus non-attachment is a virtuous mind that is the direct opposite of attachment. Renunciation is a type of non-attachment. We can generate non-attachment through wisdom, and also through other minds such as faith or concentration. Whenever we contemplate the faults of attachment and generate a distaste for ordinary objects of desire, seeing them as harmful and deceptive, we are practising non-attachment. Skilful practitioners of training the mind try to generate this mind whenever they see attractive objects.

Non-hatred is a virtuous mind that is the direct opposite of hatred. We generate this mind by contemplating the faults of anger and hatred. Non-ignorance is a virtuous mind that is the direct opposite of ignorance. It is a type of wisdom. We generate this mind by resisting the ordinary appearance of objects and contemplating their empty nature.

Since we encounter attractive, unattractive, and neutral objects all the time, if we learn to generate the three virtuous roots rather than the three poisons we can make every second of our life meaningful. For practitioners of training the mind, this is the most important practice during the meditation break. As Bodhisattva Chekawa says:

> The three objects, three poisons, and three virtuous roots
> Are the brief instruction for the subsequent attainment.

Some meditators, seeing the dangers of generating the three poisons whenever they encounter the three objects, try to prevent their mind from apprehending these objects by withdrawing their gross feelings and discriminations and meditating on nothingness. While this technique can be effective in temporarily overcoming delusions, it cannot actually abandon them. The methods taught in training the mind are much more powerful and effective.

If we find it difficult to prevent a particular delusion by transforming it into its opposite, we can try to overcome it by practising taking and giving. For example, if we are having difficulty in preventing attachment towards a particular object or person, we should think how there are countless beings afflicted by attachment, which is often much stronger than our own, and out of compassion decide to take all their attachment upon ourself. We imagine that we draw all their attachment towards us in the form of black smoke. As it enters us, it completely destroys our own attachment, and then we meditate on emptiness for a while. We can use the same technique to overcome hatred and ignorance. In this way, we use our delusions to cultivate pure minds, rather as a farmer uses manure to grow crops. Seeing the great advantages of this practice, we should request our Spiritual Guide to bless us to be able to engage in it successfully.

To make our human life completely meaningful, we should practise training the mind purely by observing the eighteen commitments and the twenty-two precepts of training the mind. These are explained fully in *Universal Compassion*. Once again, we request blessings to be able to observe these purely.

HOW TO MEDITATE ON SUPERIOR INTENTION AND GENERATE BODHICHITTA

Through love, compassion, and superior intention,
And the magical practice of mounting taking and
giving upon the breath,
I seek your blessings to generate the actual
bodhichitta,
To free all migrators from this great ocean of samsara.

If we train in taking and giving for a long time, our love and compassion will become very powerful and our wish to free others from suffering will be as strong as a thirsty man's wish for water. Once we have generated great compassion we need to transform it into superior intention. The difference between these two can be understood by considering the following example. If we see a child fall into a river we will naturally want the child to be saved, but the child's mother will wish so strongly that she will decide to act to save her child herself. Great compassion is like the mind of the onlookers – a wish for all sentient beings to be freed from suffering – but superior intention is like the mind of the mother – a strong determination actually to free them.

Having generated superior intention, we then need to think how we can carry it out and actually free all migrators from the ocean of samsara. We shall see that at the moment we do not have the skills and resources to do this. To fulfil our wish to help all sentient beings, we need four special qualities: complete freedom from the fears and sufferings of samsara and from obstructions to omniscience, great compassion for all living beings, a mind completely free from bias or prejudice, and great skill in providing the most appropriate kind of help at the right time. If we examine who has such qualities, we will see that only Buddhas do. Contemplating in this way we will come to a firm conclusion:

I must become a Buddha to free all sentient beings from samsara.

This thought is bodhichitta. When, through training, it arises naturally without effort we have attained a spontaneous realization of bodhichitta, which is actual bodhichitta. When this is attained we enter Mahayana paths and become a Bodhisattva.

HOW TO TAKE THE VOWS OF ASPIRING AND ENGAGING BODHICHITTA

I seek your blessings to strive sincerely on the sole path
Traversed by all the Conquerors of the three times –
To bind my mind with pure Bodhisattva vows
And practise the three moral disciplines of the Mahayana.

There are two types of bodhichitta: aspiring bodhichitta and engaging bodhichitta. The first merely wishes to attain enlightenment and the second actually engages in the practices that lead to enlightenment. It is like the difference between wishing to go on a journey and actually setting out.

When we first generate bodhichitta, we generate aspiring bodhichitta. Although this is a very pure mind it is not completely stable, and it is possible to lose it. To stabilize this bodhichitta we take the eight precepts of the aspiring mind, which prevent it from degenerating in this and future lives.

When we take the actual Bodhisattva vows, we generate engaging bodhichitta and engage in the practice of the six perfections. All the Buddhas of the three times have attained enlightenment by first generating bodhichitta and then completing the six perfections, so we should pray for blessings to be able to do the same.

All the trainings of a Bodhisattva are included within the three moral disciplines of the Mahayana: the moral discipline of restraint, the moral discipline of gathering virtuous

Dharmas, and the moral discipline of benefiting other sentient beings. The first entails avoiding the eighteen root and forty-six secondary downfalls, the second entails practising the six perfections, and the third entails helping sentient beings in accordance with their wishes.

HOW TO PRACTISE THE PERFECTION OF GIVING

I seek your blessings to complete the perfection of giving
Through the instructions on improving the mind
of giving without attachment,
And thus to transform my body, my enjoyments, and
my virtues amassed throughout the three times
Into whatever each sentient being desires.

The perfection of giving is any giving that is motivated by bodhichitta. It can be practised only by those who have taken Bodhisattva vows. To develop the perfection of giving we have to train in the mind of giving without attachment. This means we have to train in the thought to give without any trace of miserliness or possessiveness.

To complete the perfection of giving it is not necessary to part with everything, nor is it necessary to alleviate all the poverty in the world. Poverty is the karmic effect of miserliness and it cannot be eradicated until all sentient beings abandon miserliness and create the causes to acquire wealth. As Shantideva explains in *Guide to the Bodhisattva's Way of Life*, like all the other perfections the perfection of giving is a mind, and so we complete the perfection of giving when, with bodhichitta motivation, we develop a perfect mind of giving unstained by attachment.

We train in the mind of giving primarily by contemplating the disadvantages of miserliness and possessiveness and the advantages of giving; and then practising giving during the meditation break. We should contemplate how all the poverty in the world arises from possessiveness and all the wealth from giving; and especially how the major signs and minor indications of a Buddha's holy form are accomplished principally as a result of giving. Then we should train in giving. If we do not have much to give, we can at least offer water and flowers to the Buddhas.

The sadhana explains a practice of giving that entails mentally transforming our body, enjoyments, and roots of virtue into whatever each sentient being desires. To do this, we begin by contemplating the faults of miserliness and possessiveness and the benefits of giving, and then with an intention to give we imagine that our body transforms into a wishfulfilling jewel. This jewel radiates countless rays of light throughout the universe, reaching all the beings of the six realms. To beings in the hot hells it brings cool, refreshing rain; to beings in the cold hells it brings warmth; to hungry ghosts it brings food and drink; to animals it brings protection from the sufferings of heat, cold, hunger, and thirst; to humans it brings whatever they desire such as clothes, money, medicine, and friends; to demi-gods it brings an end to jealousy and conflict; and to gods it brings freedom from lower rebirths. We imagine that all the environments throughout the six realms are completely purified and that all sentient beings experience pure happiness.

According to Lamrim, there are three types of giving: giving material things, giving fearlessness, and giving Dharma. When we transform our body into a wishfulfilling jewel as explained here we are practising all three types of giving. By imagining that we are giving all sentient beings what they want we are giving material things, by imagining that we are dispelling all their fear and suffering we are giving fearlessness, and by imagining that all sentient beings have found pure happiness we are giving Dharma.

In *Six Session Guru Yoga* it says:

From this moment on without any sense of loss,
I shall give away my body and likewise my wealth,
And my virtues amassed throughout the three times
In order to help all beings, my mothers.

Although we may not be able to practise this fully at the moment, we can rejoice in the great Bodhisattvas who can, and generate a wish to become like them in the future. This places very powerful imprints on our mind to be able to practise giving purely in the future. To keep our Bodhisattva vows we must train in the thought to give everything, including our body, but we should not actually give away our body until we can do so with a pure motivation and without obstructing our Dharma practice. There is no point in giving away our precious body if the sacrifice serves no great purpose. In the meantime, we can train in the thought of giving away our body by imagining that we are so doing. We can also practise the kusali tsog offering explained in *Guide to Dakini Land*. As far as actual giving is concerned, we should start by giving away small things and gradually increase our practice until we can happily give away those things that are precious to us. The most important thing is to train in giving without any sense of loss. We should request Lama Losang Tubwang Dorjechang for his blessings to be able to complete the perfection of giving.

HOW TO PRACTISE THE PERFECTION OF MORAL DISCIPLINE

I seek your blessings to complete the perfection of
moral discipline
By not transgressing even at the cost of my life
The discipline of the Pratimoksha, Bodhisattva,
and Secret Mantra vows,
And by gathering virtuous Dharmas, and
accomplishing the welfare of sentient beings.

As mentioned above, there are three types of moral discipline: the moral discipline of restraint, the moral discipline of gathering virtuous Dharmas, and the moral discipline of benefiting other sentient beings. The first entails avoiding all negative actions, especially transgressions of the three types of vow; the second entails striving to practise virtuous actions such as making offerings and prostrations; and the third entails helping sentient beings whenever possible in the most appropriate way. When any of these

Khädrub Tendzin Tsöndru

types of moral discipline is practised with pure bodhi-chitta motivation it is a perfection of moral discipline.

It is particularly important to keep our vows and com-mitments purely. If we have taken Pratimoksha, Bodhi-sattva, or Secret Mantra vows, we should try to learn them and keep them to the best of our ability. For example, to avoid incurring the root and secondary downfalls of the Bodhisattva vows, it is essential to know what they are; therefore as soon as we have taken the vows we should make a determined effort to learn them and commit them to memory. We should try to understand each downfall, think about how we might come to incur it, and make plans to avoid such situations.

It is important to be skilful in our approach to the vows. We should not have unrealistic expectations or make promises that we cannot keep. Instead, we should adopt the Bodhisattva's way of life gradually. Each of the vows can be kept on many levels. For example, we have a vow to abandon the obstacles to developing concentration, but it is impossible to abandon all these obstacles at once. First we should try to avoid gross distractions, and then gradu-ally strive to abandon the subtle interferences. All the Bodhisattva vows are aspects of the practice of the six perfections. Until we attain enlightenment we need con-tinually to improve our practice of the six perfections and in this way gradually deepen the level at which we are able to keep the vows.

When a Teacher gives Bodhisattva vows, he or she should explain them well. He should not encourage his disciples to promise to keep all the vows perfectly from the start. Moreover, from their side, the disciples should not make over-enthusiastic promises, pledging to keep all the vows faultlessly without even knowing what they are. Such disciples will break their vows the very next day. After taking Bodhisattva vows an intelligent disciple will first learn what they involve. Then he will resolve to keep each one to the best of his ability and gradually improve his practice of the Bodhisattva moral discipline.

The advice to keep the vows gradually does not mean that we can temporarily put to one side the vows that we do not like. We have to work with all the vows, gradually improving the way we observe them. For example, as our miserliness decreases we will be able to keep the vows relating to giving more purely, and as our anger decreases we will be able to keep those concerned with patience more purely. Thus, we should begin to practise all the vows as soon as we have taken them, practise them to the best of our ability, and never lose the determination to keep them perfectly in the future.

If a Spiritual Guide gives us vows of any kind it is not within his power to take them back or to tell us to forget about them. Therefore we should be extremely conscientious and skilful in the way we take vows. If we take vows too readily, without a proper intention to keep them purely, there is a great fault. At one time Drugpa Kunleg came upon a Sakya Lama who was granting empowerments. The Lama jeered 'Here comes Drugpa Kunleg, filthy and covered in lice. Wherever he goes he spreads infinite lice.' Drugpa Kunleg replied 'Here comes the Sakya Lama granting many empowerments. Wherever he goes he opens the gates to hell.' Although both were highly realized Yogis, and their remarks were just playful teasing, they were making a serious point. If a Spiritual Guide grants empowerments too freely and disciples take them too freely, uninterested in keeping the commitments, both the Spiritual Guide and the disciples incur serious downfalls.

Bearing all this in mind, we should request Lama Losang Tubwang Dorjechang's blessings to be able to complete the perfection of moral discipline and keep all our vows and commitments purely.

HOW TO PRACTISE THE PERFECTION OF PATIENCE

**I seek your blessings to complete the perfection of
    patience
So that even if every single being in the three realms,**

Out of anger were to abuse me, criticize me,
threaten me, or even take my life,
Undisturbed, I would repay their harm by helping
them.

There are three types of patience: the patience of not retaliating, the patience of voluntarily enduring suffering, and the patience of definitely thinking about Dharma. When any of these is practised with bodhichitta motivation it is a perfection of patience.

The first type of patience, referred to in the verse, entails not retaliating when others harm or offend us. The second type of patience entails patiently forbearing difficulties and suffering without getting angry. We have many opportunities to practise this type of patience. For example, we may experience difficulties in obtaining food, clothing, or accommodation, or we may wish to meditate but find our body is tired or our mind sluggish, or we may wish to go out and enjoy ourself but be restricted by illness. At times like these, instead of getting angry or blaming others for our misfortunes, we should patiently forbear our difficulties.

When we begin to practise Dharma, we sometimes encounter new difficulties related to maintaining pure discipline. Whereas previously we did not have to exercise restraint with respect to actions such as drinking and smoking, we now find that we have to forsake these activities. If we find these new disciplines difficult at first, we need to practise the patience of voluntarily enduring suffering. Dharma rules are not restrictions imposed from outside, but are restraints that we voluntarily take on because we see their benefits. Forsaking indulgence in objects of the senses, for example, greatly reduces our distractions and enhances our training in concentration. To attain tranquil abiding we have to overcome two types of distraction: gross and subtle. It is not possible to overcome the latter until we have overcome the former, and the way to do this is to maintain constant mindfulness in all our actions of body, speech, and mind, and practise restraint whenever we are tempted to indulge in objects of distraction. Methods for doing this are taught by Shantideva in the chapter on conscientiousness in *Guide to the Bodhisattva's Way of Life*. If we cultivate this kind of self-discipline in our everyday actions we will find it easy to discipline the mind in meditation; but if we cannot restrain our actions of body, speech, and mind, we shall never attain tranquil abiding. This is why the observance of pure moral discipline is one of the six causes of tranquil abiding.

There is no point in becoming depressed or blaming others when we experience suffering or difficulties. We are responsible for our samsaric rebirth, not others; and it is the nature of samsara to be unpleasant and frustrating. We should not be surprised or disappointed when things go wrong because this is only to be expected in samsara. It would be far more surprising not to experience problems and difficulties in samsara! We should remember Geshe Potawa's remark:

It is not sickness and death I fear so much as samsaric rebirth.

His point is that we should not use our time trying to prevent suffering in this life or feeling unhappy when it occurs, but strive to eradicate the source of suffering – rebirth in samsara – by developing renunciation and practising the three higher trainings. If we are depressed by our problems we have no inclination or energy to practise Dharma; but if we patiently accept our problems, our mind remains happy and we are encouraged to put more effort into our practice.

We should not be like those people who practise Dharma when the sun is shining and everything is going well, but give up as soon as they encounter a slight difficulty. Rather we should follow the example of the great Kadampa Geshes who were renowned for the strength and constancy of their practice. They used to say that our mind should be like a blacksmith's anvil; no matter how hard it is struck, it does not break. Thus, even if we are very sick and outwardly our appearance deteriorates, inside our mind should remain happy and calm.

The most important thing is not to blame others for our difficulties because not only is this misguided, it also makes the situation worse. The main cause of all our problems and difficulties is our own negative karma. Sometimes others create the conditions for our karma to ripen, but they do so without any choice, impelled by our karma. We have only ourself to blame for our difficulties, and we alone can prevent them from arising in the future by practising patience now.

We need to practise the third type of patience, the patience of definitely thinking about Dharma, when we are studying difficult topics such as emptiness, karma, reliance upon the Spiritual Guide, and the nature of the Three Jewels; in other words, whenever there is a danger of our generating doubts or misunderstandings. The sign that we are practising this type of patience is that we can listen to any Dharma teaching with joy, faith, and conviction.

There are three types of patience with respect to emptiness. To begin with we need to practise patience when we are listening to teachings and studying texts that establish emptiness through logical reasons. Then, on the third stage of the path of preparation we develop a special patience that prepares us for a direct realization of emptiness when our mind and emptiness mix like water mixing with water. Finally, on the eighth ground we develop a special patience that is known as the 'patience of unborn phenomena'. Whereas Bodhisattvas on the first ground who have just attained a direct realization of emptiness experience some difficulty in rising from meditation because their minds are so thoroughly absorbed, Bodhisattvas on the eighth ground have a special quick wisdom that enables them to enter into profound meditation on emptiness and rise again in a split second. This is because they have developed the patience of unborn phenomena.

Shantideva says that just as there is no evil like anger, so there is no virtue like patience. Through patience we develop a calm mind and a pleasant disposition that endears us to others. Patience also causes beauty and radiance. The beauty of a Buddha's form is the result of practising patience. Contemplating the disadvantages of anger and the benefits of patience, we should make a firm decision to practise patience purely. To begin with we can decide not to get angry for a week, or a month, and then see what happens. We will soon want to extend the period until we can practise patience for our whole life. Eventually we will be able to forbear harm and abuse without any anger arising, just as it is explained in the sadhana. Therefore we should make requests to Lama Losang Tubwang Dorjechang for his blessings to be able to complete the perfection of patience.

HOW TO PRACTISE THE PERFECTION OF EFFORT

**I seek your blessings to complete the perfection of effort
By striving for supreme enlightenment with unwavering compassion;
Even if I must remain in the fires of the deepest hell
For many aeons for the sake of each being.**

Effort is a mind that delights in virtue. Any practice of effort that is motivated by bodhichitta is a perfection of effort. There are three types of effort: armour-like effort, the effort of gathering virtuous Dharmas, and the effort of benefiting others.

Armour-like effort is described in the verse from the sadhana. It is the willingness to endure whatever hardship is necessary to complete our Dharma practice, even if it means remaining in the deepest hell for many aeons to help each living being. If we have been practising Dharma for a few years and still have no great results to show, rather than becoming discouraged we should develop armour-like effort and resolve to practise for as long as is necessary to accomplish pure results. The attainment of enlightenment is a very great objective, and we cannot expect to see results immediately. Still, we should remain joyful in our practice and apply steady and sustained effort, confident in the knowledge that when all the causes are gathered, the results will definitely come.

The effort of gathering virtuous Dharmas is an effort that strives to complete the collections of merit and wisdom, and other Dharma realizations. The effort of benefiting others is an effort that strives to do whatever needs to be done to help other sentient beings.

Effort is a happy, joyful mind that is the source of all the energy and impetus in our practice. It is the opposite of laziness, which is a mind that does not enjoy practising virtue. Seeing the benefits of effort, we should request Lama Losang Tubwang Dorjechang to bless us to be able to complete the perfection of effort.

HOW TO PRACTISE THE PERFECTION OF
MENTAL STABILIZATION

**I seek your blessings to complete the perfection of
mental stabilization
By abandoning the faults of mental sinking, mental
excitement, and mental wandering,
And concentrating in single-pointed absorption
On the state that is the lack of true existence of all
phenomena.**

Mental stabilization, or concentration, is a mind whose nature is to be single-pointedly placed on a virtuous object, and whose function is to prevent distraction. Any concentration practised with bodhichitta is a perfection of mental stabilization. There are two types of concentration: concentration focusing on conventional truths and concentration focusing on ultimate truths. The verse from the sadhana describes the second of these, and shows how to meditate single-pointedly on emptiness – free from mental sinking, mental excitement, and mental wandering. When we recite this verse, we should remember the benefits and results of concentration, as well as the stages by which it is developed, and then make heartfelt requests for blessings to be able to complete the perfection of mental stabilization. More information on training in concentration can be found in *Joyful Path of Good Fortune, Meaningful to Behold,* and *Clear Light of Bliss.*

HOW TO PRACTISE THE PERFECTION OF WISDOM BY SUSTAINING SPACE-LIKE MEDITATIVE EQUIPOISE

I seek your blessings to complete the perfection of wisdom
Through the yoga of the space-like meditative equipoise on the ultimate,
With the great bliss of the suppleness
Induced by the wisdom of individual analysis of thatness.

Wisdom is a virtuous mind that functions mainly to dispel doubt and confusion by understanding its object thoroughly. Wisdom that is practised with bodhichitta is a perfection of wisdom. *Offering to the Spiritual Guide* explains the perfection of wisdom over three verses. The present verse explains how to train in wisdom during meditation, the next verse explains how to train in wisdom out of meditation, and the third verse explains how to train in the essential point of the middle way – the union of the two truths.

The way to attain the realization of meditative equipoise on emptiness is as follows. Having developed tranquil abiding, we meditate on emptiness single-pointedly. After a while, we develop the ability to investigate the object emptiness without disturbing our concentration, rather as a small fish can swim in a pond without causing ripples in the water. With this ability we acquire a special mental suppleness, which is superior to the suppleness induced by tranquil abiding. This is the indication of having attained the wisdom of superior seeing. With this wisdom of superior seeing we continue to meditate on emptiness, striving to identify and overcome whatever subtle dualistic appearance remains in the mind. Eventually all conventional appearances cease and our mind mixes with emptiness like water mixing with water. All these realizations are realizations of the space-like meditative equipoise on emptiness.

Emptiness is similar to space in that both are mere absences. Space is the mere absence of obstructive contact, and emptiness is the mere absence of inherent existence. Both are non-affirming negatives that do not imply any other positive phenomenon. Thus, when the mind is absorbed in emptiness and remains on it single-pointedly, it is said to be in 'space-like' equipoise. Understanding this, we make requests to Lama Losang Tubwang Dorjechang to be able to attain this realization.

HOW TO PRACTISE THE PERFECTION OF WISDOM BY SUSTAINING ILLUSION-LIKE SUBSEQUENT ATTAINMENT

Outer and inner phenomena are like illusions, like dreams,
And like reflections of the moon in a clear lake,
For though they appear they do not truly exist;
Realizing this, I seek your blessings to complete the illusion-like concentration.

The yoga of illusion practised during the period of subsequent attainment, that is, during the meditation break, depends upon the yoga of space-like meditative equipoise. If we have some experience of conventional phenomena subsiding into emptiness during meditation, we will easily come to see all phenomena as illusory during the meditation break. To say that phenomena are illusory is not to say that they do not exist; it simply means that they do not exist in the way that they appear. For example, a conjurer can create an illusion of a horse that appears to his audience to be a real horse. Even though it appears to be real, in reality it is just an illusion. In the same way, until we attain enlightenment, when we rise from meditation on emptiness phenomena will continue to appear to us to be inherently existent. Even though phenomena appear in this way, they

Dorjechang Phabongkha Trinlay Gyatso

are in fact empty of inherent existence. Just as the conjurer sees a horse but does not believe it to be real, so, when we rise from meditation on emptiness, phenomena appear to be inherently existent but we do not assent to this appearance. Even so, we do not say that phenomena do not exist just because they are illusory. The illusion of a horse exists, and functions to delight the audience, and in the same way conventional phenomena also exist and function, even though they are like illusions.

The yoga of illusion is more important than the yoga of space-like meditative equipoise because we spend more of our time out of meditation than in meditation. If we can train ourself to see all phenomena as illusory during the meditation break, all our daily actions will become a collection of wisdom.

Buddha used many analogies to help us to train in wisdom during the meditation break. Often he compared phenomena to dreams. In a dream, things appear vividly to us, as if they existed from their own side, but when we wake we understand that they were simply projected by the mind. In the same way, when we are awake phenomena appear vividly to us, as if they existed from their own side, but in reality they are merely imputed by conception. Previously it was explained how dream objects, such as an attractive woman that appears to a man in a dream, exist and function despite the fact that they are merely projections of mind, and in the same way dream-like conventional phenomena exist and function, even though they are mere imputations.

Buddha also compared phenomena to reflections of the moon in a clear lake. When we see a reflection of the moon it looks like the actual moon, but in reality it is just a reflection that has no existence from its own side. Even so it functions, showing up in photographs for example. In the same way, phenomena appear to us to be real and substantial, but in reality they have no existence at all from their own side. However, these reflection-like phenomena do exist and perform functions.

When we recite the present verse we should make heart-felt requests to Lama Losang Tubwang Dorjechang for his blessings to accumulate wisdom and to abandon the mind that perceives and grasps at things as inherently existent by practising the yoga of illusion-like subsequent attainment.

HOW TO TRAIN THE MIND IN THE PROFOUND VIEW OF THE MIDDLE WAY

I seek your blessings to realize the meaning of
  Nagarjuna's intention,
That there is no contradiction but only harmony
Between the absence of even an atom of inherent
  existence in samsara and nirvana
And the non-deceptive dependent relationship of
  cause and effect.

Even though there is not an atom of inherent existence in samsara or nirvana, nevertheless the relationship between cause and effect is infallible. Thus, we need to realize that although we cannot find a cause or an effect that exists from its own side, nevertheless causes definitely produce their effects and effects definitely arise from their causes. If we realize both emptiness and the non-deceptive relationship of cause and effect, this indicates that we have understood emptiness correctly.

For as long as the two truths appear to be contradictory, we still have not realized the union of the two truths. For example, at present the fact that phenomena do not exist from their own side seems to contradict the fact that they exist and function. Thus, when we think about emptiness, cause and effect seem impossible; and when we think about cause and effect, emptiness seems impossible. By relying upon the view of the middle way revealed in the *Perfection of Wisdom Sutras* we will eventually come to see that there is no contradiction between dependent-related appearances and emptiness. Indeed, just seeing or contemplating dependent-related phenomena will improve our understanding of emptiness, and contemplating emptiness will improve our understanding of dependent-related phenomena. For example, if we apply gentle pressure to our eyeball and look at the moon we will see two moons, but that very appearance of two moons reminds us that in reality there is only one moon. In the same way, when we have realized the union of the two truths, conventional phenomena appear to our mind, but their very appearance reminds us that in reality they are empty. Only a Buddha has a complete realization of the union of the two truths. For a Buddha, conventional truths and ultimate truths appear simultaneously.

In the *Manjushri Root Tantra* Buddha predicted that after he passed away there would appear a monk called Nagarjuna who would elucidate the profound meaning of the middle way as taught in the *Perfection of Wisdom Sutras*, and he advised us to rely upon Nagarjuna's view as the only authentic path to liberation. In *Guide to the Middle Way*, Chandrakirti says that any view that strays from Nagarjuna's cannot lead to liberation from samsara. Realizing this, we should request Lama Losang Tubwang Dorjechang for his blessings to be able to realize the view of the middle way revealed by Protector Nagarjuna. More detail on this view can be found in *Ocean of Nectar* and *Meaningful to Behold*.

BECOMING A SUITABLE VESSEL FOR THE PROFOUND PATH OF SECRET MANTRA, AND KEEPING THE VOWS AND COMMITMENTS PURELY

**And then the swirling ocean of the Tantras is crossed
Through the kindness of the navigator, the Vajra
   Holder.
I seek your blessings to cherish more than my life
The vows and commitments, the root of attainments.**

So far, we have requested blessings to realize the stages of the path of Sutra. The present verse briefly introduces the stages of the path of Secret Mantra. To practise Secret Mantra we must first receive the kindness of an empowerment from a qualified Vajra Master. He is like a navigator

who guides us across the swirling ocean of the Tantric
scriptures and practices. When we take an empowerment,
we receive a number of vows and commitments. Keeping
these purely is the basis of all attainments; therefore we
request our Spiritual Guide for his blessings to cherish our
vows and commitments more dearly than our life.

HOW TO MEDITATE ON GENERATION STAGE

**Through the yoga of the first stage that transforms
birth, death, and bardo
Into the three bodies of the Conquerors,
I seek your blessings to purify all stains of
ordinary appearance and conception,
And to see whatever appears as the form of the Deity.**

Generation stage meditations are paths that lead to completion stage and cause the realizations of completion stage
to ripen. Completion stage meditations actually liberate us
from samsara and lead us to Buddhahood. Thus, generation
stage meditations are sometimes called the 'ripening paths'
and completion stage meditations the 'liberating paths'.

To understand how Tantric practices lead to Buddhahood
it is necessary to understand the basis, path, and result. The
basis is the object to be purified, the path is the means of
purifying, and the result is the pure effect. The basis to be
purified is samsara – that is, ordinary death, intermediate
state, and rebirth. Usually, these follow one upon the other,
condemning us to one samsaric rebirth after another. By
practising the yogas of generation stage and completion
stage we can purify these and transform them into the three
bodies of a Buddha: the Truth Body, the Enjoyment Body,
and the Emanation Body. Thus the yogas of generation
stage and completion stage are the path that is the means
of purifying, and the three bodies of a Buddha are the pure
effect. The yogas of generation stage indirectly purify ordinary death, intermediate state, and rebirth, and the yogas
of completion stage directly purify them.

To attain realizations of generation stage, we need to do generation stage meditation. This has the following three features:

1 Bringing the three bodies of a Buddha into the path
2 Meditating on clear appearance and divine pride
3 Overcoming ordinary appearances and ordinary conceptions in dependence upon clear appearance and divine pride.

The first of these consists of three yogas: bringing ordinary death into the path of the Truth Body, bringing the ordinary intermediate state into the path of the Enjoyment Body, and bringing ordinary rebirth into the path of the Emanation Body. With these yogas we generate ourself as the Deity and then, with concentration, train in clear appearance and divine pride. Through training in clear appearance we overcome ordinary appearances, and through training in divine pride we overcome ordinary conceptions.

Highest Yoga Tantra sadhanas include these three practices as well as other secondary practices such as mantra recitation. All three features must be present for a practice to be actual generation stage. Generating ourself as a Deity alone is not a yoga of generation stage, because even some non-Buddhists perform similar practices, generating themselves as gods such as Ishvara for example. A more extensive explanation of the yogas of generation stage can be found in *Guide to Dakini Land*.

Understanding the nature and function of the generation stage of Secret Mantra, we make requests to Lama Losang Tubwang Dorjechang for blessings to be able to train in it successfully.

HOW TO PRACTISE COMPLETION STAGE

**I seek your blessings, O Protector, that you may place your feet
On the centre of the eight-petalled lotus at my heart,**

**So that I may manifest within this life
The paths of illusory body, clear light, and union.**

In Secret Mantra, ordinary death, intermediate state, and rebirth are called the 'three basic bodies'. Ordinary death is known as the 'basic truth body'. It is not the actual Truth Body, but is the basis for accomplishing it. Similarly, ordinary intermediate state is called the 'basic enjoyment body' because it is the basis for accomplishing the actual Enjoyment Body, and ordinary rebirth is called the 'basic emanation body' because it is the basis for accomplishing the actual Emanation Body.

These three basic bodies are purified by the three path bodies, which are the completion stage practices of clear light, illusory body, and emanations of the illusory body. The yoga of clear light is called the 'path truth body' because it purifies the basic truth body, ordinary death, and transforms it into the resultant Truth Body of a Buddha; the yoga of illusory body is called the 'path enjoyment body' because it purifies the basic enjoyment body, ordinary intermediate state, and transforms it into the resultant Enjoyment Body of a Buddha; and the yoga of emanations of the illusory body is called the 'path emanation body' because it purifies the basic emanation body, ordinary rebirth, and transforms it into the resultant Emanation Body of a Buddha. Thus the essence of Secret Mantra is to use the three path bodies to purify the three basic bodies and transform them into the three resultant bodies of a Buddha. There is no way to attain enlightenment other than by practising these yogas of completion stage.

Altogether, there are five stages of completion stage: isolated speech, isolated mind, illusory body, clear light, and union. The verse from the sadhana mentions only the last three, but the first two are implied. We request our Spiritual Guide to descend into our heart and bless our subtle mental continuum so that we can attain the realizations of isolated speech and isolated mind, and then go on to accomplish the remaining three stages. More detail on the five stages of completion stage can be found in *Clear Light of Bliss*.

An authentic Tantra is one that has been taught by Buddha. All the authoritative Tantras were practised by the Buddhist Mahasiddhas such as Saraha, Nagarjuna, and Tilopa, who explained the two Tantric stages in their writings and revealed what they themselves had experienced. Furthermore, in *Great Exposition of Secret Mantra*, Je Tsongkhapa gives extensive explanations of the four classes of Tantra. Everything he writes was expressed in the Tantras by Buddha. Je Tsongkhapa quotes the words of Buddha and gives scriptural authority for everything he writes in his commentary. If we were to study Je Tsongkhapa's works we would be astounded by their clarity and beauty, and we would understand that they are the works of a realized Master who has written honestly and sincerely about his own experiences.

THE WAY TO PRACTISE THE RITUAL OF THE TRANSFERENCE OF CONSCIOUSNESS IF, HAVING MEDITATED, WE HAVE RECEIVED NO SIGNS

If by the time of my death I have not completed the path,
I seek your blessings to go to the Pure Land
Through the instruction on correctly applying the five forces,
The supremely powerful method of transference to Buddhahood.

A practitioner who has attained the isolated mind of ultimate example clear light will definitely attain enlightenment in that life. When he rises from meditation he will attain the illusory body. Eventually this will transform into the resultant Enjoyment Body and his mind of clear light will transform into the resultant Truth Body. However, if by the time of our death we have not attained the realization of ultimate example clear light, we need to practise transference of consciousness to ensure that we pass into a Pure Land, or at least into a rebirth in which we can continue our practice.

Transference of consciousness was taught by Buddha in both the Sutras and the Tantras. According to the Sutras, transference is accomplished primarily through the power of aspiration, while according to the Tantras it is accomplished primarily through the power of controlling the winds. Tantric practitioners who can dissolve their winds into the central channel through meditation can eject their consciousness and take rebirth in a Pure Land through their own power. Those who cannot yet centralize their winds can eject their consciousness by mixing it with the mind of the Deity, and then take rebirth in a Pure Land through the power of the Buddhas.

In *Offering to the Spiritual Guide* the Sutra and Tantra practices are combined. If we practise them properly at the time of death, we will definitely take rebirth in a Pure Land, and we will never fall from this state into an ordinary rebirth. However to practise transference successfully at the time of death we need to train in it now.

The practice of transference entails practising the five forces as explained in the Sutra teachings on training the mind. Suppose a practitioner is practising *Vajrayogini Tantra* and strongly wishes to be born in Pure Dakini Land. For him or her the force of motivation will be practised by maintaining a constant wish and a strong determination to be reborn in Pure Dakini Land. The force of familiarity will entail repeatedly practising the yogas of generation stage and completion stage of Vajrayogini so that at death the clear light of death can be mixed with the Truth Body. The force of white seed will involve accumulating merit. As death approaches, we should give away all our possessions to the poor and to the Sangha. This accumulates merit and prevents us from being attached to our possessions when the time comes to depart from this world. Just as a bird with stones tied to its legs cannot fly, so a mind attached to worldly possessions cannot transfer easily to a Pure Land. The force of destruction will involve purifying and restoring broken or degenerated vows. It is very important to die with pure vows on our mental continuum. Finally, the force of aspirational prayer will entail dedicating all our merit to taking rebirth in Pure Dakini Land, and making constant prayers to our Spiritual Guide and to Vajrayogini to lead us there. The most important factors ensuring rebirth in a Pure Land are pure moral discipline, many prayers, and great merit.

We should receive instructions on transference from a qualified Spiritual Guide and then train in this practice in retreat until we receive signs of accomplishment. When the signs of death occur, we should first try to extend our life by appropriate methods such as propitiating the Deities of long life; but if the signs still persist and we are certain that death is imminent, we should practise transference and go to the Pure Land.

There is one method of transference that we can practise if we are familiar with the yoga of bringing death into the path of the Truth Body. According to this method there is a special practice to perform at each stage of the dissolution of the elements, finishing with mixing the clear light of death with the Truth Body. If we practise this method at death we will definitely take rebirth in a Pure Land.

At this point, I shall explain a special method of transference in conjunction with *Offering to the Spiritual Guide* that can be practised for the benefit of others who have died, in which we act as the representative of the deceased. By way of preparation, on a table in front of the person presiding over the puja, we need to arrange an article of clothing that belonged to the deceased. Then, on a piece of paper we draw a lotus and on this we write the initial letter of the dead person's first name. If we are doing the puja for many dead people together, for example if many people have died as a result of an accident, a natural disaster, or a war, we write the Tibetan letter NI. The piece of paper is then attached to a stick, which is arranged so that it stands in the centre of the article of clothing with the letter facing us. Beside this we place a small bowl containing black grains of sand or black sesame seeds, and a candle standing on a tray or large plate. We set out offerings as usual,

Yongdzin Dorjechang Losang Yeshe

including a tsog offering. The offerings should be as extensive as possible and sponsored by the relatives of the deceased, if possible using money that he or she has left behind. If the family is poor the Dharma Centre where the puja is to be held can help with the offerings.

We then begin the actual puja following the sadhana in the usual manner. For the purposes of this ritual, we can divide the puja into four distinct stages:

1 Accumulating merit for the deceased
2 Purifying negative karma that may result in lower rebirth
3 Pacifying obstacles to taking rebirth in a Pure Land
4 The actual method for transferring the consciousness of the deceased to the Pure Land

We recite the first part of the puja, up to the end of the offering verses in the seven limb prayer as usual. During this part of the puja we are mainly emphasizing accumulating merit by making offerings and prostrations. We dedicate all this merit to the deceased. Without a great accumulation of merit it is not possible to take rebirth in a Pure Land, and so we are accumulating merit to help the dead person.

If we have strong compassion for the dead person, we can definitely increase their merit through these practices. Also, if the relatives make extensive offerings on behalf of the deceased, this will definitely help them. If possible they should use some of the money the dead person left behind and make the offerings described above, as well as tea offerings, food offerings, and general offerings to Dharma Centres. The more extensive the offerings, the more powerful the puja. We cannot take our money with us when we die, so it is better that it is used as offerings to create merit rather than for ordinary purposes. If we leave our money to just a few people there will not be much benefit. They may even use it for unwholesome purposes. However, if we leave money to a Dharma Centre there will be great meaning, and the merit will increase for as long as the Centre exists. As the Centre grows and flourishes, bringing happiness to more and more people, the power of our offering will increase. If we have a small quantity of water and we try to preserve it on its own, eventually it will evaporate; but if we pour it into an ocean it will remain for as long as the ocean remains. Therefore, it is a Buddhist tradition to bequeath our possessions to Dharma Centres; and it is a tradition in Dharma Centres to make prayers for the deceased for forty-nine days after they have died.

When we reach the point just before the verse for confession, the third of the seven limbs, we make the tsog offering. As explained before, the purpose of making the tsog offering at this point is to purify negativities. In this case we are purifying the negative karma of the deceased, particularly any broken or degenerated commitments they may have incurred. Once again, if we have compassion for the deceased it is definite that we can purify the negativities within their continuum through this practice.

After making the tsog offering we recite once, three times, seven times, or more, the *Mahayana Sutra of the Three Superior Heaps* to purify any negative karma that the deceased may have accumulated. If this is not purified there is a great danger that they will take rebirth in the lower realms. To protect them from this we now perform a special purification practice. As the assembled practitioners, together with the relatives of the deceased, recite the names of the Thirty-five Confession Buddhas, one of the relatives makes prostrations. This person is acting as a representative of the dead person, and we strongly imagine that the deceased himself or herself is actually prostrating to the Thirty-five Confession Buddhas and reciting their names. At the end of this practice we firmly believe that all their negative karma has been completely purified.

We then continue with the puja up to the point where the mantras are recited. After reciting all the mantras with strong concentration and faith, the principal practitioners blow on to the black sesame seeds that were set out previously. One person picks up the seeds and carries them along the row, and each practitioner in turn blows gently on to them. The reason for doing this is that, due to reciting these blessed mantras purely, the practitioners' breath is now very blessed and powerful. By blowing on the seeds, they make the seeds into a very pure and powerful substance with which to dispel obstacles.

The next stage is to pacify obstacles that may prevent the deceased from taking rebirth in a Pure Land. Most sentient beings have spirits and other non-humans who are continually trying to obstruct and harm them. Very often these spirits will follow a person through the death process and continue to obstruct them in their next life. If the deceased has such obstacles and they are not pacified, it will be very difficult for them to take rebirth in a Pure Land. Therefore we now perform a special ritual to dispel these obstacles, using mantras and the pure substance of the seeds.

We begin by strongly imagining that the deceased's consciousness enters into the initial letter on the paper in front of the person presiding over the puja. Then we recite the name mantra of Je Tsongkhapa seven times while the person presiding over the puja throws the seeds at the letter, driving away obstacles and hindrances. The same procedure is then repeated while reciting the mantra of Buddha Shakyamuni, the mantra of Conqueror Vajradhara, and the mantra of all Buddhas. When all the mantras have been recited, and the seeds have been used up, the dish in which they were held is turned upside down and we strongly imagine that the deceased's mental continuum is now completely free from all obstacles and hindrances.

We then continue with the puja until we reach the point just before the present verse on transference of consciousness. At this point, out of strong compassion, we make prayers and requests· for the deceased's consciousness to be transferred without obstruction to the Pure Land. The person presiding over the puja lights the candle and recites OM AH HUM three times. We contemplate that due to reciting this mantra the candle flame is transformed into the wisdom of all the Buddhas, and we prevent ordinary appearance of the flame. Then, while we recite the present verse three times, slowly and melodiously, requesting the Spiritual Guide to transfer the deceased's consciousness to the Pure Land, the person presiding over the puja burns the paper bearing the deceased's initial in the flame of wisdom. We strongly imagine that the paper is the ordinary name and contaminated consciousness of the deceased, and that these are completely destroyed in the fire of exalted wisdom. We think that because the deceased no longer has an ordinary, contaminated basis of imputation, he or she is no longer an ordinary being. Their consciousness has definitely been transferred to the Pure Land and they have taken on a completely new identity. When the paper is completely burned, the ashes are gathered up. After the puja these can either be put into a river or mixed with clay and made into a stupa or a statue.

We then make special dedication prayers. For example, if the deceased was a Vajrayogini practitioner we can recite the long prayers from the Vajrayogini sadhana. We can also use special prayers such as the *Prayer of Excellent Deeds*. Then we finish the puja in the usual way, making especially strong dedication prayers giving all the virtue to the deceased, and we pray that he or she will definitely take rebirth in a Pure Land with a special body, speech, and mind.

With this practice of transference it looks like we 'force' the deceased to take rebirth in a Pure Land without any choice. Even if the deceased has led a non-virtuous life, through the power of our faith and compassion combined with the blessings of our Spiritual Guide and all the Buddhas and Bodhisattvas, we can force them into a pure rebirth. Once someone has been born in a Buddha's Pure Land, they will never again take an ordinary birth. From then on, they will meet pure Spiritual Guides, listen to teachings, and train in all the spiritual paths in perfect conditions until they finally attain enlightenment; and all the time they will live in a body that never causes any suffering or problems.

In a Pure Land there is no sickness, ageing, or death, no conflicts or wars, no worries or problems. Everyone we meet is a pure being, a Hero or a Heroine whose very presence bestows bliss and mental peace. If we want to help beings in other realms such as the human realm, we can send our emanations there to guide them and lead them to the same state of happiness.

We can also use this practice to transfer our own consciousness at the time of death. The method is exactly the same, except that we do not burn our initials. When we reach this present verse in *Offering to the Spiritual Guide*, we recite it sincerely as many times as possible and then meditate on transference. If the time of our death has come, we should try to die at this point in the puja. We decide very strongly that it is time to die, stop reciting the puja, and through meditation transfer our consciousness to the Pure Land. If we do this, we will definitely take rebirth in the Pure Land. There are many practitioners of this tradition who have died in this way.

HOW TO OFFER PRAYERS TO BE CARED FOR BY OUR SPIRITUAL GUIDE IN ALL FUTURE LIVES

In short, O Protector, I seek your blessings so that
    throughout all my lives
I shall never be separated from you, but always
    come under your care;
And as the foremost of your disciples,
Maintain all the secrets of your body, speech, and
    mind.

O Protector, wherever you manifest as a Buddha,
May I be the very first in your retinue;
And may everything be auspicious for me to
    accomplish without effort
All temporary and ultimate needs and wishes.

Dorjechang Kelsang Gyatso Rinpoche

Finally, we make requests to our Spiritual Guide to grant us his blessings and protection so that we will never be separated from him in all our future lives. We pray that we will always be a special disciple who will maintain all his hidden qualities that are not observed by others.

Although our Spiritual Guide is already enlightened, for the sake of sentient beings he will continue to demonstrate the manner of attaining enlightenment in different worlds in the future. Therefore we pray that we will always be the first in his retinue, and through the power of his blessings be able to accomplish effortlessly all temporary and ultimate needs and wishes.

GATHERING AND DISSOLVING THE FIELD OF MERIT

Due to my making requests in this way, O Supreme Spiritual Guide,
With delight, please come to my crown to bestow your blessings;
And once again firmly place your radiant feet On the anthers of the lotus at my heart.

We imagine that as a result of our making offerings and requests with strong faith, Lama Losang Tubwang Dorjechang and all the other Buddhas and Bodhisattvas in the Field of Merit are delighted with us. Light rays radiate from the heart of Lama Losang Tubwang Dorjechang reaching all the beings in the Field of Merit. First the tree melts into light and dissolves, then the lower layer of the lotus with the Dharma Protectors, then the next layer with the Heroes and Heroines, and so on until all the holy beings have dissolved into Lama Losang Tubwang Dorjechang, the principal Field of Merit. Then the outer aspect, Je Tsongkhapa, dissolves into the inner aspect, Buddha Shakyamuni; and he in turn dissolves into the secret aspect, Conqueror Vajradhara. We then develop very strong faith that Guru Vajradhara is the synthesis of all objects of refuge.

At this point, we develop a strong wish to dissolve into Guru Vajradhara's heart, and we imagine that Guru Vajradhara also strongly wishes for this to happen. Just as when a son returns home to his mother after a long absence and both yearn to be reunited, so we should imagine that we long to dissolve into our Guru's heart and that he also longs to unite with us. With delight, he comes to the crown of our head and, entering through our crown channel wheel, descends through our central channel to our heart. We feel that our Guru's mind of spontaneous great bliss mixes with our subtle mind, and as a result our mind is transformed into spontaneous great bliss. With this mind of bliss we then meditate on emptiness, and feel as if our blissful mind and emptiness have mixed indistinguishably. We should try strongly to imagine that everything has dissolved into emptiness, and that our mind has mixed with this in a space-like equipoise. We remain in single-pointed concentration on this experience for as long as possible. This is definitive Guru yoga. Through this practice we receive very special blessings from our Spiritual Guide and we sow the seeds to attain the actual realizations of the Mahamudra. This meditation is very similar to the first union of the Mahamudra, the union of bliss and emptiness.

At this point we can train in the practice of Vajrayana Mahamudra, which is the actual completion stage meditation. Previously, after generating bodhichitta, we trained in generation stage; now we train in completion stage. The main purpose of completion stage is to generate a mind of spontaneous great bliss and then to meditate on emptiness with that mind. Training in a meditation that establishes an experience of great bliss associated with emptiness is the actual training in Vajrayana Mahamudra. With the special blessings that we receive by dissolving our Spiritual Guide into our heart, this is the ideal place to engage in this training.

If we are a Vajrayogini practitioner, at this point we should contemplate that Guru Vajradharma, who is inseparable from our mind at our heart, is in the aspect of a red letter BAM. This expands to the ends of space and then contracts and dissolves from the bottom upwards until even the nada dissolves into the emptiness of the Truth Body. We then meditate on this emptiness mixed with great bliss.

If we are a Heruka practitioner, we begin training in Vajrayana Mahamudra by meditating on the indestructible drop inside the central channel at the heart. We visualize this drop as very clear, the nature of radiant light, and inside this, standing on a moon cushion, we visualize our very subtle mind in the aspect of a letter HUM, which is white with a slight tint of red. We strongly imagine that our subtle mind and our Guru's mind are indistinguishably one, appearing as a white letter HUM. It is important that this is visualized within the drop inside the central channel at the heart, and that the precise location is identified, if this meditation is to be effective in bringing the winds into the central channel. We meditate on the HUM single-pointedly, not by observing it from a distance but by absorbing our mind into it so that there is no gap between our mind and the HUM.

This meditation is the first of the five stages of completion stage of Heruka according to the system of Ghantapa. Whereas for the Yamantaka and Vajrayogini practices, completion stage begins at the navel, for the Guhyasamaja and Heruka practices it begins at the heart. Thus, Ghantapa said:

> You should always abide within the indestructible drop at your heart and meditate on it single-pointedly.

If we become familiar with this meditation, we will definitely attain the wisdom of great bliss and emptiness, the union of the Mahamudra. When we have some experience of this stage, we can go on to accomplish the other four stages of Heruka. Even if we cannot do actual completion stage meditation at present, we can simulate it, and thus sow the seeds to gain actual realizations in the future.

At the end of the meditation, the HUM transforms into a white Heruka. This is the illusory body, the vajra body of the Deity. It is the same aspect as the Deity, except that it is white. When we first attain the illusory body, it is white because the substance of the subtle winds out of which it is formed are naturally white in colour. We always maintain this illusory body at our heart without ever forgetting it, even when we rise from meditation to engage in the yogas of daily actions.

If we prefer, we can practise completion stage meditation according to the Six Yogas of Naropa. This is explained in *Clear Light of Bliss*, which is based on Je Tsongkhapa's commentary to that practice. This practice is more extensive, and the object is slightly different, but the aim and meaning are the same.

If we rely upon Je Tsongkhapa, our practice of Mahamudra will be very clear and pure. First we meditate on the Mahamudra that is the union of bliss and emptiness. We begin by studying *Guide to the Middle Way* by Chandrakirti to gain a clear understanding of emptiness. A commentary to this text is given in *Ocean of Nectar*. Then we try to generate the mind of spontaneous great bliss and mix it with the emptiness we have realized. We then proceed to the second union of the Mahamudra, the union of the two truths: conventional truth and ultimate truth. In this context, conventional truth is the pure illusory body and ultimate truth is meaning clear light. First we realize illusory body, then we realize meaning clear light. When we gain the union of these two, we attain the union of the two truths. This is called the 'union that needs learning' because we are not yet enlightened and must meditate further to remove the obstructions to omniscience. Eventually, our illusory body transforms into the resultant Enjoyment Body, and simultaneously our mind of clear light transforms into the resultant Truth Body. This is the resultant Union of the Mahamudra – the union of mind and body – the state of enlightenment possessing the seven pre-eminent qualities of embrace.

These practices are exactly the same as those practised by the great Master Saraha, Nagarjuna's root Guru, who wrote three texts on Mahamudra. Many of the eighty-four Mahasiddhas relied upon Saraha, and both Je Tsongkhapa and the first Panchen Lama quote from him a great deal. Also Marpa and Milarepa practised exactly the same methods.

Prior to Je Tsongkhapa, many Tibetans misunderstood the instructions on Mahamudra. Some Tibetans criticized these instructions and some actually rejected them. Many Tibetans claimed to be practising Mahamudra, without any experience of renunciation, bodhichitta, wisdom realizing emptiness, generation stage, or completion stage. Without any understanding of the practice, they immediately engaged in union with a partner, and before long had children and found themselves engaged in business to support their families! These actions brought the Mahamudra into disrepute, and it was a time of great degeneration for the Buddhadharma. When Je Tsongkhapa appeared, however, he gave clear and precise instructions on the Mahamudra, exactly as it had been practised in the past by great Yogis such as Master Saraha, and cleared up all the misunderstandings. Thus if we follow Je Tsongkhapa's instructions there is no danger of our engaging in wrong practices, and it is definite that we will accomplish pure results.

THE CONCLUDING STAGES

We conclude the practice of the meditation session by dedicating and reciting auspicious prayers. The dedication prayers from the sadhana are as follows:

I dedicate all the pure white virtues I have gathered here
So that I may accomplish all the prayers
Made by the Sugatas and Bodhisattvas of the three times,
And maintain the holy Dharma of scripture and insight.

Through the force of this, throughout all my lives,
May I never be separated from the four wheels of the Supreme Vehicle,
And thus may I complete the paths of renunciation,
Bodhichitta, correct view, and the two Tantric stages.

We pray that, through the force of all the merit we have accumulated by making offerings and requests to our Spiritual Guide and training in the stages of the path of Sutra and Tantra, we may fulfil all the prayers of the Buddhas and Bodhisattvas and practise purely the Dharma of scripture and insight. In particular we pray that in all our future lives we will never be separated from the four wheels of the Mahayana. These are:

1 Birth in a religious country, ideally in a place that possesses the five qualities of a retreat place described by Maitreya in *Ornament for Mahayana Sutras*.
2 Meeting with a fully-qualified Mahayana Spiritual Guide.
3 Having a strong inclination to practise Dharma and being able easily to engage in virtue with our body, speech, and mind.
4 Being endowed with the eight special attributes: long life, beauty, high status, wealth and resources, persuasive speech, power and influence, freedom and independence, a strong mind, and a strong body. These are explained fully in *Joyful Path of Good Fortune*.

If we possess these four wheels in future lives, we will be able to practise Dharma easily and thereby benefit many people. Since it is quite possible that we may not finish our training in this life, it is very important to pray to attain these qualities in the future. Then we can go on to complete all the realizations of renunciation, bodhichitta, wisdom realizing emptiness, generation stage, and completion stage.

HOW TO PRACTISE DURING THE MEDITATION BREAK

During the meditation break, we should always remember Lama Losang Tubwang Dorjechang at our heart and think of him as inseparable from the vajra body of the Deity. Whenever we eat or drink, we should bless the food or drink and offer it to our Spiritual Guide at our heart. By remembering him at all times and making constant prayers and requests we will receive uninterrupted blessings, our mind will become calm and peaceful, we will have fewer problems and obstacles, and our experience of essential Dharma realizations such as bodhichitta and wisdom will naturally improve.

Throughout our daily actions we should always remember that phenomena are empty of inherent existence and that they have arisen from the indivisible union of bliss and emptiness. We should regard all forms as manifestations of bliss and emptiness, inseparable from the Guru-Deity, all sounds as mantra, and all mental activity as manifestations of the bliss and emptiness of the Truth Body. In this way we will prevent ordinary appearances and develop pure appearance. Then we will quickly attain the realizations of the Mahamudra and accomplish the enlightened state of the Guru-Deity, the resultant Union possessing the seven pre-eminent qualities of embrace.

Dedication

We should pray:

To accomplish all the purposes of sentient beings,
By this virtue may I quickly attain
The seven pre-eminent qualities of embrace:
A Form Body endowed with the signs and
     indications
Embracing a wisdom knowledge woman,
A mind abiding in a state of great bliss,
This bliss realizing lack of inherent existence,
A compassion that has abandoned the extreme of
     peace,
An uninterrupted continuum of body,
And unceasing enlightened deeds.

May everything be auspicious.

Appendix I
The Condensed Meaning of the Text

The Condensed Meaning of the Text

The commentary Great Treasury of Merit *is presented in three parts:*

1 Introduction
2 The actual commentary
3 Dedication

The actual commentary has two parts:

1 The pre-eminent qualities of Je Tsongkhapa and his doctrine
2 The Guru yoga of Je Tsongkhapa

The Guru yoga of Je Tsongkhapa has three parts:

1 Why we need to practise the Guru yoga of Je Tsongkhapa
2 The origin and lineage of these instructions
3 The actual instructions

The actual instructions has two parts:

1 How to practise during the meditation session
2 How to practise during the meditation break

How to practise during the meditation session has three parts:

1 The preliminary practices
2 The actual practice
3 The concluding stages

The preliminary practices has four parts:

1 Going for refuge and generating bodhichitta
2 Self-generation as the Deity
3 Purifying the environment and its inhabitants
4 Blessing the offerings

Going for refuge and generating bodhichitta has two parts:

1 Going for refuge
2 Generating bodhichitta

Generating bodhichitta has two parts:

1 Generating aspiring bodhichitta
2 Generating engaging bodhichitta

The actual practice has five parts:

1 Visualizing the Field of Merit and inviting and
absorbing the wisdom beings
2 Offering the practice of the seven limbs and the
mandala
3 Making praises and requests
4 Receiving blessings
5 Gathering and dissolving the Field of Merit

*Visualizing the Field of Merit and inviting and absorbing
the wisdom beings has two parts:*

1 Visualizing the Field of Merit
2 Inviting and absorbing the wisdom beings

*Offering the practice of the seven limbs and the mandala
has seven parts:*

1 Prostration
2 Offering
3 Confession
4 Rejoicing

5 Requesting the turning of the Wheel of Dharma
6 Beseeching the Spiritual Guide not to pass away
7 Dedication

Prostration has five parts:

1 Prostrating to the Spiritual Guide as the Enjoyment Body
2 Prostrating to the Spiritual Guide as the Emanation Body
3 Prostrating to the Spiritual Guide as the Truth Body
4 Prostrating to the Spiritual Guides as the synthesis of all Three Jewels
5 Prostrating to the lineage Gurus and Three Jewels

Offering has seven parts:

1 Offering the outer offerings and the five objects of desire
2 Offering the mandala
3 Offering our spiritual practice
4 Inner offering
5 Secret offering
6 Suchness offering
7 Offering medicines, and ourself as a servant

Offering the outer offerings and the five objects of desire has two parts:

1 Offering the outer offerings
2 Offering the five objects of desire

Making praises and requests has four parts:

1 Requesting by reciting the name mantra
2 Requesting by remembering his good qualities and his kindness
3 Requesting by expressing his good qualities
4 Single-pointed request

Requesting by remembering his good qualities and his kindness has six parts:

1 Requesting by remembering his good qualities as explained in the Vinaya scriptures
2 Requesting by remembering his good qualities as a Mahayana Spiritual Guide
3 Requesting by remembering his good qualities as a Vajrayana Spiritual Guide
4 Requesting by remembering that he is kinder than all the Buddhas
5 Requesting by remembering that he is kinder even than Buddha Shakyamuni
6 Requesting by remembering that he is a supreme Field of Merit

Requesting by expressing his good qualities has four parts:

1 Requesting by expressing his outer qualities
2 Requesting by expressing his inner qualities
3 Requesting by expressing his secret qualities
4 Requesting by expressing his suchness qualities

Receiving blessings has two parts:

1 Receiving the blessings of the four empowerments and reciting the mantras
2 Receiving the blessings of all the stages of the path

Receiving the blessings of the four empowerments and reciting the mantras has two parts:

1 Receiving the blessings of the four empowerments
2 Reciting the mantras

Receiving the blessings of all the stages of the path has twenty-seven parts:

1 How to rely upon our Spiritual Guide, the root of spiritual paths
2 Developing the aspiration to take the essence of our human life

Appendix II
Sadhanas

CONTENTS

Offering to the Spiritual Guide

compiled by
Losang Chökyi Gyaltsän

Offering to the Spiritual Guide

Going for refuge

With a perfectly pure mind of great virtue,
I and all mother sentient beings as extensive as space,
From now until we reach the essence of enlightenment,
Go for refuge to the Guru and Three Precious Jewels.

Namo Gurubhä
Namo Buddhaya
Namo Dharmaya
Namo Sanghaya   (3x)

Generating aspiring bodhichitta

For the sake of all mother sentient beings,
I shall become the Guru-Deity,
And then lead every sentient being
To the Guru-Deity's supreme state.   (3x)

Generating engaging bodhichitta

For the sake of all mother sentient beings I shall attain
as quickly as possible in this very life the state of the
Guru-Deity, the primordial Buddha.

I shall free all mother sentient beings from their
suffering and lead them to the great bliss of the Buddha
grounds. Therefore I shall practise the profound path of
the yoga of the Guru-Deity.

*At this point we can perform brief self-generation as our
personal Deity.*

Self-generation as the Deity

From the state of great bliss I arise as the Guru-Deity.

Purifying the environment and its inhabitants

Light rays radiate from my body,
Blessing all worlds and beings in the ten directions.
Everything becomes an exquisite array
Of immaculately pure good qualities.

Blessing the offerings

OM AH HUM   (3x)

By nature exalted wisdom, having the aspect of the inner
offering and the individual offering substances, and
functioning as objects of enjoyment of the six senses to
generate a special exalted wisdom of bliss and emptiness,
inconceivable clouds of outer, inner, and secret offerings,
commitment substances, and attractive offerings cover all
the ground and fill the whole of space.

Visualizing the Field of Merit

Within the vast space of indivisible bliss and emptiness,
amidst billowing clouds of Samantabhadra's offerings,
fully adorned with leaves, flowers, and fruits, is a
wishfulfilling tree that grants whatever is wished for. At
its crest, on a lion throne ablaze with jewels, on a lotus,
moon, and sun seat, sits my root Guru who is kind in
three ways, the very essence of all the Buddhas. He is in
the aspect of a fully-ordained monk, with one face, two
hands, and a radiant smile. His right hand is in the
mudra of expounding Dharma, and his left hand, in the
mudra of meditative equipoise, holds a bowl filled with
nectar. He wears three robes of resplendent saffron, and
his head is graced with a golden Pandit's hat. At his
heart are Buddha Shakyamuni and Vajradhara, who has
a blue-coloured body, one face, and two hands. Holding
vajra and bell, he embraces Yingchugma and delights in

289

the play of spontaneous bliss and emptiness. He is adorned with many different types of jewelled ornament and wears garments of heavenly silk. Endowed with the major signs and minor indications, and ablaze with a thousand rays of light, my Guru sits in the centre of an aura of five-coloured rainbows. Sitting in the vajra posture, his completely pure aggregates are the five Sugatas, his four elements are the four Mothers, and his sources, veins, and joints are in reality Bodhisattvas. His pores are the twenty-one thousand Foe Destroyers, and his limbs are the wrathful Deities. His light rays are directional guardians such as givers of harm and smell-eaters, and beneath his throne are the worldly beings. Surrounding him in sequence is a vast assembly of lineage Gurus, Yidams, hosts of mandala Deities, Buddhas, Bodhisattvas, Heroes, Dakinis, and Dharma Protectors. Their three doors are marked by the three vajras. Hooking light rays radiate from the letter HUM and invite the wisdom beings from their natural abodes to remain inseparable.

Inviting the wisdom beings

You who are the source of all happiness and goodness,
The root and lineage Gurus of the three times, the
    Yidams, and Three Precious Jewels,
Together with the assembly of Heroes, Dakinis,
    Dharmapalas, and Protectors,
Out of your great compassion please come to this place
    and remain firm.

Even though phenomena are by nature completely free
    from coming and going,
You appear in accordance with the dispositions of
    various disciples
And perform enlightened deeds out of wisdom and
    compassion;
O Holy Refuge and Protector, please come to this place
    together with your retinue.

OM GURU BUDDHA BODHISATTÖ DHARMAPALA
SAPARIWARA EH HAYE HI: DZA HUM BAM HO
The wisdom beings become inseparable from
the commitment beings.

Prostrating to the Spiritual Guide as the Enjoyment Body

Spiritual Guide with a jewel-like form,
Who out of compassion bestow in an instant
Even the supreme state of the three bodies, the sphere of
    great bliss,
O Vajra Holder I prostrate at your lotus feet.

Prostrating to the Spiritual Guide as the Emanation Body

Exalted wisdom of all the infinite Conquerors
Out of supremely skilful means appearing to suit disciples,
Now assuming the form of a saffron-robed monk,
O Holy Refuge and Protector I prostrate at your lotus feet.

Prostrating to the Spiritual Guide as the Truth Body

Abandonment of all faults together with their imprints,
Precious treasury of countless good qualities,
And sole gateway to all benefit and happiness,
O Venerable Spiritual Guide I prostrate at your lotus feet.

Prostrating to the Spiritual Guides as the synthesis of
all Three Jewels

Essence of all Guru-Buddhas and Deities,
Source of all eighty-four thousand classes of holy Dharma,
Foremost amongst the entire Superior Assembly,
O Kind Spiritual Guides I prostrate at your lotus feet.

Prostrating to the lineage Gurus and Three Jewels

To the Gurus who abide in the three times and the ten
 directions,
The Three Supreme Jewels, and all other objects of
 prostration,
I prostrate with faith and respect, a melodious chorus of
 praise,
And emanated bodies as numerous as atoms in the world.

Offering the outer offerings and the five objects of desire

O Guru, Refuge, and Protector, together with your retinue,
I offer you these vast clouds of various offerings:

The purifying nectars of the four waters gently flowing
From expansive and radiant jewelled vessels perfectly
 arrayed;

Beautiful flowers, petals, and garlands finely arranged,
Covering the ground and filling the sky;

The lapis-coloured smoke of fragrant incense
Billowing in the heavens like blue summer clouds;

The playful light of the sun and the moon, glittering
 jewels, and a vast array of lamps
Dispelling the darkness of the three thousand worlds;

Exquisite perfume scented with camphor, sandalwood,
 and saffron,
In a vast swirling ocean stretching as far as the eye can see;

Nutritious food and drink endowed with a hundred flavours
And delicacies of gods and men heaped as high as a
 mountain;

From an endless variety of musical instruments,
Melodious tunes filling all three worlds;

Delightful bearers of forms, sounds, smells, tastes, and
 objects of touch –
Goddesses of outer and inner enjoyments filling all directions.

Offering the mandala

O Treasure of Compassion, my Refuge and Protector,
  supremely perfect Field of Merit,
With a mind of devotion I offer to you
A thousand million of the Great Mountain, the four
  continents,
The seven major and minor royal possessions, and so forth,
A collection of perfect worlds and beings that give rise
  to all joys,
A great treasury of the desired enjoyments of gods and men.

Offering our spiritual practice

O Venerable Guru, I offer these pleasure gardens,
Both actually arranged and emanated by mind, on the
  shores of a wish-granting sea,
In which, from the pure white virtues of samsara and nirvana,
There arise offering substances of broad, thousand-
  petalled lotuses that delight the minds of all;
Where my own and others' mundane and supramundane
  virtues of the three doors
Are flowers that bring colour to every part
And emit a multitude of scents like Samantabhadra's
  offerings;
And where the three trainings, the five paths, and the
  two stages are the fruit.

Inner offering

I offer this ocean of nectar with the five hooks, the five
  lamps, and so forth,
Purified, transformed, and increased,
Together with a drink of excellent tea
Endowed with a hundred flavours, the radiance of saffron,
  and a delicate aroma.

*If we wish to make a tsog offering to emphasize the accumu-
lation of great merit, such as in a long life puja, we should
do so at this point. The tsog offering is on page 307.*

Secret offering

And I offer most attractive illusory mudras,
A host of messengers born from places, born from
    mantra, and spontaneously-born,
With slender bodies, skilled in the sixty-four arts of love,
And possessing the splendour of youthful beauty.

Suchness offering

I offer you the supreme, ultimate bodhichitta,
A great, exalted wisdom of spontaneous bliss free from
    obstructions,
Inseparable from the nature of all phenomena, the
    sphere of freedom from elaboration,
Effortless, and beyond words, thoughts, and expressions.

Offering medicines, and ourself as a servant

I offer many different types of excellent medicine
That destroy the four hundred and four diseases of the
    delusions,
And to please you I offer myself as a servant;
Please keep me in your service for as long as space exists.

If we wish, we may recite the Mahayana Sutra of the
Three Superior Heaps *or the* General Confession *at this
point.*

*If we wish to make a tsog offering to emphasize purifi-
cation, we should do so at this point. The tsog offering
is on page 307.*

Confession

In the presence of the great Compassionate Ones
    I confess with a mind of great regret
All the non-virtues and negative actions that, since
    beginningless time,
I have done, ordered to be done, or rejoiced in;
And I promise that from now on I shall not commit
    them again.

Rejoicing

Though phenomena have no sign of inherent existence,
From the depths of our hearts we rejoice
In all the dream-like happiness and pure white virtue
That arise for ordinary and Superior beings.

Requesting the turning of the Wheel of Dharma

From the myriads of billowing clouds of your sublime
  wisdom and compassion,
Please send down a rain of vast and profound Dharma,
So that in the jasmine garden of benefit and happiness
There may be growth, sustenance, and increase for all
  these living beings.

Requesting the Spiritual Guide not to pass away

Though your vajra body has no birth or death,
We request the vessel of the great King of Union
To remain unchanging according to our wishes,
Without passing away until samsara ends.

Dedication

I dedicate all the pure white virtues I have gathered here,
  so that in all my lives
I shall never be separated from the venerable Guru who
  is kind in three ways;
May I always come under his loving care,
And attain the Union of Vajradhara.

It is customary to recite the nine-line Migtsema *prayer
at this point. This is on page 317.*

*If we wish to make a mandala offering together with
the three great requests we may do so at this point. The
mandala offering is on page 315.*

*Also, if we wish to receive blessings so as to gain the
realizations of the Mahamudra, we may recite the* Prayers
of Request to the Mahamudra Lineage Gurus *and/or*
The Condensed Meaning of the Swift Vajrayana Path
at this point. These are on pages 333 and 325.

Requesting by remembering his good qualities as explained in the Vinaya scriptures

Great ocean of moral discipline, source of all good
    qualities,
Replete with a collection of jewels of extensive learning,
Second Buddha, venerable saffron-robed monk,
O Elder and Holder of the Vinaya, to you I make
    requests.

Requesting by remembering his good qualities as a Mahayana Spiritual Guide

You who possess the ten qualities
Of an authentic Teacher of the path of the Sugatas,
Lord of the Dharma, representative of all the Conquerors,
O Mahayana Spiritual Guide, to you I make requests.

Requesting by remembering his good qualities as a Vajrayana Spiritual Guide

Your three doors are perfectly controlled, you have great
    wisdom and patience,
You are without pretension or deceit, you are well-versed
    in mantras and Tantra,
You possess the two sets of ten qualities, and you are
    skilled in drawing and explaining,
O Principal Holder of the Vajra, to you I make requests.

Requesting by remembering that he is kinder than all the Buddhas

To the coarse beings of these impure times who, being
    so hard to tame,
Were not subdued by the countless Buddhas of old,
You correctly reveal the excellent path of the Sugatas;
O Compassionate Refuge and Protector, to you I make
    requests.

Requesting by remembering that he is kinder even than Buddha Shakyamuni

Now, when the sun of Buddha has set,
For the countless migrators without protection or refuge
You perform exactly the same deeds as the Conqueror;
O Compassionate Refuge and Protector, to you I make
requests.

Requesting by remembering that he is a supreme Field of Merit

Even just one of your hair pores is praised for us
As a Field of Merit that is superior to all the Conquerors
Of the three times and the ten directions;
O Compassionate Refuge and Protector, to you I make
requests.

Requesting by expressing his outer qualities

From the play of your miracle powers and skilful means
The ornament wheels of your three Sugata bodies
Appear in an ordinary form to guide migrators;
O Compassionate Refuge and Protector, to you I make
requests.

Requesting by expressing his inner qualities

Your aggregates, elements, sources, and limbs
Are by nature the Fathers and Mothers of the five
Buddha families,
The Bodhisattvas, and the Wrathful Deities;
O Supreme Spiritual Guide, the nature of the Three
Jewels, to you I make requests.

Requesting by expressing his secret qualities

You are the essence of the ten million circles of mandalas
That arise from the state of the all-knowing exalted wisdom;
Principal Holder of the Vajra, pervasive source of the
hundred families,
O Protector of the Primordial Union, to you I make requests.

297

Requesting by expressing his suchness qualities

Pervasive nature of all things stable and moving,
Inseparable from the experience of spontaneous joy
  without obstructions;
Thoroughly good, from the beginning free from extremes,
O Actual, ultimate bodhichitta, to you I make requests.

Single-pointed request

You are the Guru, you are the Yidam, you are the Daka
  and Dharma Protector;
From now until I attain enlightenment I shall seek no
  refuge other than you.
In this life, in the bardo, and until the end of my lives,
  please hold me with the hook of your compassion,
Liberate me from the fears of samsara and peace, bestow
  all the attainments, be my constant companion, and
  protect me from all obstacles.   (3x)

Receiving the blessings of the four empowerments

Through the force of requesting three times in this way,
white, red, and blue light rays and nectars, serially and
together, arise from the places of my Guru's body, speech,
and mind, and dissolve into my three places, serially and
together. My four obstructions are purified and I receive
the four empowerments. I attain the four bodies and, out
of delight, an emanation of my Guru dissolves into me
and bestows his blessings.

*At this point we meditate briefly on receiving the bless-
ings of the four empowerments according to the commentary. Then we imagine that an emanation of Lama Losang
Tubwang Dorjechang comes to the crown of our head and,
entering into our central channel, descends to our heart.
We imagine that our subtle body, speech, and mind
become of one taste with our Spiritual Guide's body,
speech, and mind, and meditate on this special feeling of
bliss for a while. After this we recite the mantras according to the commentary (see pages 198–200).*

If we wish to make a tsog offering to emphasize the swift attainment of the realizations of the stages of the path, we should do so after reciting the mantras. The tsog offering is on page 307.

If we wish to offer a long mandala to request the realizations of the stages of the path, we should do so here. The mandala offering is on page 315.

How to rely upon our Spiritual Guide, the root of spiritual paths

Through the force of my making offerings and respectful requests
To the venerable Spiritual Guide, the holy, supreme Field of Merit,
I seek your blessings, O Protector, the root of all goodness and joy,
So that you will gladly take me into your loving care.

Developing the aspiration to take the essence of our human life

Realizing that this freedom and endowment, found only once,
Are difficult to attain, and yet decay so quickly,
I seek your blessings to seize their essential meaning,
Undistracted by the meaningless activities of this life.

The actual method for gaining the happiness of higher states in future lives

Fearing the blazing fires of the sufferings of bad migrations,
From the depths of my heart I go for refuge to the Three Jewels,
And seek your blessings to strive sincerely
To abandon non-virtue and practise the entire collection of virtue.

Developing the wish to gain liberation

Being violently tossed by the waves of delusion and karma
And tormented by the sea-monsters of the three sufferings,
I seek your blessings to develop a strong wish for liberation
From the boundless and fearful great ocean of samsara.

How to practise the path that leads to liberation

Forsaking the mind that views as a pleasure garden
This unbearable prison of samsara,
I seek your blessings to take up the victory banner of
  liberation
By maintaining the three higher trainings and the
  wealths of Superiors.

How to generate great compassion, the foundation of the Mahayana

Contemplating how all these pitiful migrators are my
  mothers,
Who out of kindness have cherished me again and again,
I seek your blessings to generate a spontaneous
  compassion
Like that of a loving mother for her dearest child.

Equalizing self and others

In that no one wishes for even the slightest suffering,
Or is ever content with the happiness they have,
There is no difference between myself and others;
Realizing this, I seek your blessings joyfully to make
  others happy.

The dangers of self-cherishing

Seeing that this chronic disease of cherishing myself
Is the cause that gives rise to unwanted suffering,
I seek your blessings to destroy this great demon of
  selfishness
By resenting it as the object of blame.

The benefits of cherishing others

Seeing that the mind that cherishes mother beings and
    would secure their happiness
Is the gateway that leads to infinite good qualities,
I seek your blessings to cherish these beings more than
    my life,
Even if they rise up against me as my enemies.

Exchanging self with others

In short, since the childish are concerned for themselves
    alone,
Whereas Buddhas work solely for the sake of others,
I seek your blessings to distinguish the faults and benefits,
And thus be able to exchange myself with others.

Since cherishing myself is the door to all faults
And cherishing mother beings is the foundation of all
    good qualities,
I seek your blessings to take as my essential practice
The yoga of exchanging self with others.

Taking and giving

Therefore, O Compassionate, Venerable Guru, I seek
    your blessings
So that all the suffering, negativities, and obstructions of
    mother sentient beings
Will ripen upon me right now;
And through my giving my happiness and virtue to others,
May all migrating beings be happy.   (3x)

The third to the seventh points of training the mind

Though the world and its beings, filled with the effects
    of evil,
Pour down unwanted suffering like rain,
This is a chance to exhaust the effects of negative actions;
Seeing this, I seek your blessings to transform adverse
    conditions into the path.

In short, whether favourable or unfavourable conditions
arise,
I seek your blessings to transform them into the path of
improving the two bodhichittas
Through practising the five forces, the essence of all
Dharmas,
And thereby maintain a happy mind alone.

I seek your blessings to make this freedom and
endowment extremely meaningful
By immediately applying meditation to whatever I meet
Through the skilful means of the four preparations,
And by practising the commitments and precepts of
training the mind.

How to meditate on superior intention and generate bodhichitta

Through love, compassion, and superior intention,
And the magical practice of mounting taking and giving
upon the breath,
I seek your blessings to generate the actual bodhichitta,
To free all migrators from this great ocean of samsara.

How to take the vows of aspiring and engaging bodhichitta

I seek your blessings to strive sincerely on the sole path
Traversed by all the Conquerors of the three times –
To bind my mind with pure Bodhisattva vows
And practise the three moral disciplines of the
Mahayana.

*At this point we can send out the left-over substances to
the spirits. See page 312.*

How to practise the perfection of giving

I seek your blessings to complete the perfection of giving
Through the instructions on improving the mind of
giving without attachment,

And thus to transform my body, my enjoyments, and
   my virtues amassed throughout the three times
Into whatever each sentient being desires.

How to practise the perfection of moral discipline

I seek your blessings to complete the perfection of moral
   discipline
By not transgressing even at the cost of my life
The discipline of the Pratimoksha, Bodhisattva, and
   Secret Mantra vows,
And by gathering virtuous Dharmas, and accomplishing
   the welfare of sentient beings.

How to practise the perfection of patience

I seek your blessings to complete the perfection of patience
So that even if every single being in the three realms,
Out of anger were to abuse me, criticize me, threaten
   me, or even take my life,
Undisturbed, I would repay their harm by helping them.

How to practise the perfection of effort

I seek your blessings to complete the perfection of effort
By striving for supreme enlightenment with unwavering
   compassion;
Even if I must remain in the fires of the deepest hell
For many aeons for the sake of each being.

How to practise the perfection of mental stabilization

I seek your blessings to complete the perfection of
   mental stabilization
By abandoning the faults of mental sinking, mental
   excitement, and mental wandering,
And concentrating in single-pointed absorption
On the state that is the lack of true existence of all
   phenomena.

How to practise the perfection of wisdom by sustaining space-like meditative equipoise

I seek your blessings to complete the perfection of
    wisdom
Through the yoga of the space-like meditative equipoise
    on the ultimate,
With the great bliss of the suppleness
Induced by the wisdom of individual analysis of thatness.

How to practise the perfection of wisdom by sustaining illusion-like subsequent attainment

Outer and inner phenomena are like illusions, like dreams,
And like reflections of the moon in a clear lake,
For though they appear they do not truly exist;
Realizing this, I seek your blessings to complete the
    illusion-like concentration.

How to train the mind in the profound view of the middle way

I seek your blessings to realize the meaning of
    Nagarjuna's intention,
That there is no contradiction but only harmony
Between the absence of even an atom of inherent
    existence in samsara and nirvana
And the non-deceptive dependent relationship of cause
    and effect.

Becoming a suitable vessel for the profound path of Secret Mantra, and keeping the vows and commitments purely

And then the swirling ocean of the Tantras is crossed
Through the kindness of the navigator, the Vajra Holder.
I seek your blessings to cherish more than my life
The vows and commitments, the root of attainments.

How to meditate on generation stage

Through the yoga of the first stage that transforms birth,
    death, and bardo
Into the three bodies of the Conquerors,
I seek your blessings to purify all stains of ordinary
    appearance and conception,
And to see whatever appears as the form of the Deity.

How to practise completion stage

I seek your blessings, O Protector, that you may place
    your feet
On the centre of the eight-petalled lotus at my heart,
So that I may manifest within this life
The paths of illusory body, clear light, and union.

The way to practise the ritual of the transference of consciousness if, having meditated, we have received no signs

If by the time of my death I have not completed the path,
I seek your blessings to go to the Pure Land
Through the instruction on correctly applying the five
    forces,
The supremely powerful method of transference to
    Buddhahood.

How to offer prayers to be cared for by our Spiritual Guide in all future lives

In short, O Protector, I seek your blessings so that
    throughout all my lives
I shall never be separated from you, but always come
    under your care;
And as the foremost of your disciples,
Maintain all the secrets of your body, speech, and mind.

O Protector, wherever you manifest as a Buddha,
May I be the very first in your retinue;
And may everything be auspicious for me to accomplish
without effort
All temporary and ultimate needs and wishes.

Gathering and dissolving the Field of Merit

Due to my making requests in this way, O Supreme
Spiritual Guide,
With delight, please come to my crown to bestow your
blessings;
And once again firmly place your radiant feet
On the anthers of the lotus at my heart.

*At this point we can train in the practice of Vajrayana
Mahamudra, the actual completion stage meditation,
according to the commentary.*

Dedication

I dedicate all the pure white virtues I have gathered here
So that I may accomplish all the prayers
Made by the Sugatas and Bodhisattvas of the three times,
And maintain the holy Dharma of scripture and insight.

Through the force of this, throughout all my lives,
May I never be separated from the four wheels of the
Supreme Vehicle,
And thus may I complete the paths of renunciation,
Bodhichitta, correct view, and the two Tantric stages.

*At this point we can recite the auspicious prayers. These
are on pages 313–4.*

The Tsog Offering

Blessing the offering substances

OM AH HUM   (3x)

By nature exalted wisdom, having the aspect of the inner offering and the individual offering substances, and functioning as objects of enjoyment of the six senses to generate a special exalted wisdom of bliss and emptiness, inconceivable clouds of outer, inner, and secret offerings, commitment substances, and attractive offerings, cover all the ground and fill the whole of space.

EH MA HO Great manifestation of exalted wisdom.
All realms are vajra realms
And all places are great vajra palaces
Endowed with vast clouds of Samantabhadra's offerings,
An abundance of all desired enjoyments.
All beings are actual Heroes and Heroines.
Everything is immaculately pure,
Without even the name of mistaken impure appearance.

HUM All elaborations are completely pacified in the state of the Truth Body. The wind blows and the fire blazes. Above, on a grate of three human heads, AH within a qualified skullcup, OM the individual substances blaze. Above these stand OM AH HUM, each ablaze with its brilliant colour. Through the wind blowing and the fire blazing, the substances melt. Boiling, they swirl in a great vapour. Masses of light rays from the three letters radiate to the ten directions and invite the three vajras together with nectars. These dissolve separately into the three

letters. Melting into nectar, they blend with the mixture.
Purified, transformed, and increased,
EH MA HO They become a blazing ocean of magnificent
delights.

OM AH HUM   (3x)

Inviting the guests of the tsog offering

O Root and lineage Gurus, whose nature is compassion,
The assembly of Yidams and objects of refuge, the Three
    Precious Jewels,
And the hosts of Heroes, Dakinis, Dharma Protectors,
    and Dharmapalas,
I invite you, please come to this place of offerings.

Amidst vast clouds of outer, inner, and secret offerings,
With light radiating even from your feet,
O Supremely Accomplished One please remain firm on
    this beautiful throne of jewels
And bestow the attainments that we long for.

Making the tsog offering

HO This ocean of tsog offering of uncontaminated nectar,
Blessed by concentration, mantra, and mudra,
I offer to please the assembly of root and lineage Gurus.
OM AH HUM
Delighted by enjoying these magnificent objects of desire,
EH MA HO
Please bestow a great rain of blessings.

HO This ocean of tsog offering of uncontaminated nectar,
Blessed by concentration, mantra, and mudra,
I offer to please the divine assembly of Yidams and their
    retinues.
OM AH HUM
Delighted by enjoying these magnificent objects of desire,
EH MA HO
Please bestow a great rain of attainments.

HO This ocean of tsog offering of uncontaminated nectar,
Blessed by concentration, mantra, and mudra,
I offer to please the assembly of Three Precious Jewels.
OM AH HUM
Delighted by enjoying these magnificent objects of desire,
EH MA HO
Please bestow a great rain of sacred Dharmas.

HO This ocean of tsog offering of uncontaminated nectar,
Blessed by concentration, mantra, and mudra,
I offer to please the assembly of Dakinis and Dharma
    Protectors.
OM AH HUM
Delighted by enjoying these magnificent objects of desire,
EH MA HO
Please bestow a great rain of virtuous deeds.

HO This ocean of tsog offering of uncontaminated nectar,
Blessed by concentration, mantra, and mudra,
I offer to please the assembly of mother sentient beings.
OM AH HUM
Delighted by enjoying these magnificent objects of desire,
EH MA HO
May suffering and mistaken appearance be pacified.

Making the tsog offering to the Vajra Master

EH MA HO Great circle of tsog!
O Great Hero we understand
That, following in the path of the Sugatas of the three
    times,
You are the source of all attainments.
Forsaking all minds of conceptualization
Please continuously enjoy this circle of tsog.
AH LA LA HO

The Master's reply

OM With a nature inseparable from the three vajras
I generate as the Guru-Deity.
AH This nectar of uncontaminated exalted wisdom and
  bliss,
HUM Without stirring from bodhichitta
I partake to delight the Deities dwelling in my body.
AH HO MAHA SUKHA

Song of the Spring Queen

HUM All you Tathagatas,
Heroes, Yoginis,
Dakas, and Dakinis,
To all of you I make this request:
O Heruka who delight in great bliss,
You engage in the Union of spontaneous bliss,
By attending the Lady intoxicated with bliss
And enjoying in accordance with the rituals.
AH LA LA, LA LA HO, AH I AH, AH RA LI HO
May the assembly of stainless Dakinis
Look with loving affection and accomplish all deeds.

HUM All you Tathagatas,
Heroes, Yoginis,
Dakas, and Dakinis,
To all of you I make this request:
With a mind completely aroused by great bliss
And a body in a dance of constant motion,
I offer to the hosts of Dakinis
The great bliss from enjoying the lotus of the mudra.
AH LA LA, LA LA HO, AH I AH, AH RA LI HO
May the assembly of stainless Dakinis
Look with loving affection and accomplish all deeds.

HUM All you Tathagatas,
Heroes, Yoginis,
Dakas, and Dakinis,
To all of you I make this request:
You who dance with a beautiful and peaceful manner,
O Blissful Protector and the hosts of Dakinis,
Please come here before me and grant me your blessings,
And bestow upon me spontaneous great bliss.
AH LA LA, LA LA HO, AH I AH, AH RA LI HO
May the assembly of stainless Dakinis
Look with loving affection and accomplish all deeds.

HUM All you Tathagatas,
Heroes, Yoginis,
Dakas, and Dakinis,
To all of you I make this request:
You who have the characteristic of the liberation of great
    bliss,
Do not say that deliverance can be gained in one lifetime
Through various ascetic practices having abandoned
    great bliss,
But that great bliss resides in the centre of the supreme
    lotus.
AH LA LA, LA LA HO, AH I AH, AH RA LI HO
May the assembly of stainless Dakinis
Look with loving affection and accomplish all deeds.

HUM All you Tathagatas,
Heroes, Yoginis,
Dakas, and Dakinis,
To all of you I make this request:
Like a lotus born from the centre of a swamp,
This method, though born from attachment, is unstained
    by the faults of attachment.
O Supreme Dakini, through the bliss of your lotus,
Please quickly bring liberation from the bonds of samsara.
AH LA LA, LA LA HO, AH I AH, AH RA LI HO
May the assembly of stainless Dakinis
Look with loving affection and accomplish all deeds.

311

HUM All you Tathagatas,
Heroes, Yoginis,
Dakas, and Dakinis,
To all of you I make this request:
Just as the essence of honey in the honey source
Is drunk by swarms of bees from all directions,
So through your broad lotus with six characteristics
Please bring satisfaction with the taste of great bliss.
AH LA LA, LA LA HO, AH I AH, AH RA LI HO
May the assembly of stainless Dakinis
Look with loving affection and accomplish all deeds.

Blessing the offerings to the spirits

HUM Impure mistaken appearances are purified in
    emptiness,
AH Great nectar accomplished from exalted wisdom,
OM It becomes a vast ocean of desired enjoyment.

OM AH HUM   (3x)

Actual offering to the spirits

HO This ocean of remaining tsog offering of
    uncontaminated nectar,
Blessed by concentration, mantra, and mudra,
I offer to please the assembly of oath-bound guardians.
OM AH HUM
Delighted by enjoying these magnificent objects of desire,
EH MA HO
Please perform perfect actions to help practitioners.

Send out the offering to the spirits.

HO
O Guests of the remainder together with your retinues
Please enjoy this ocean of remaining tsog offering.
May those who spread the precious doctrine,
The holders of the doctrine, their benefactors, and others,
And especially I and other practitioners

Have good health, long life, power,
Glory, fame, fortune,
And extensive enjoyments.
Please grant me the attainments
Of pacifying, increasing, controlling, and wrathful actions.
You who are bound by oaths please protect me
And help me to accomplish all the attainments.
Eradicate all untimely death, sicknesses,
Harm from spirits, and hindrances.
Eliminate bad dreams,
Ill omens, and bad actions.

May there be happiness in the world, may the years be
    good,
May crops increase, and may the Dharma flourish.
May all goodness and happiness come about,
And may all wishes be accomplished.

By the force of this bountiful giving,
May I become a Buddha for the sake of migrators
And through my generosity may I liberate
All those not liberated by previous Buddhas.

Return to page 302.

Auspicious prayers

Through the force of all the pure white virtue in
    samsara and nirvana,
Henceforth may there be a celestial treasury of
    temporary and ultimate goodness and joy,
Free from all stains of inauspiciousness;
And thus may there be the auspiciousness of enjoying
    magnificent delight.

May the Dharma Centres of all-knowing Losang Dragpa
Be filled with hosts of Sangha and Yogis
Striving to practise single-pointedly the three pure
    trainings;
And thus may there be the auspiciousness of Buddha's
    doctrine remaining for a very long time.

313

Abiding in the blessings of Losang Dragpa,
Who from the time of his youth made requests to the
supreme Guru-Deity,
May we effortlessly accomplish the welfare of others;
And thus may there be the auspiciousness of Losang
Dorjechang.

May desired endowments increase like a summer lake,
May we find uninterrupted birth with freedom in
stainless families,
May we pass each day and night with Losang's holy
Dharma;
And thus may there be the auspiciousness of enjoying
magnificent delight.

From now until I and others attain enlightenment,
Through the virtues we have already created and will
create,
May there be the auspiciousness of the Venerable Guru's
holy form
Remaining like an immutable vajra in this world.

Colophon: This translation has been prepared under
the compassionate guidance of Venerable
Geshe Kelsang Gyatso Rinpoche.

Offering the Mandala

OM VAJRA BHUMI AH HUM
Great and powerful golden ground,
OM VAJRA REKHE AH HUM
At the edge the iron fence stands around the outer circle.
In the centre Mount Meru the king of mountains,
Around which are four continents:
In the east, Purvavideha, in the south, Jambudipa,
In the west, Aparagodaniya, in the north, Uttarakuru.
Each has two sub-continents:
Deha and Videha, Tsamara and Abatsamara,
Satha and Uttaramantrina, Kurava and Kaurava.
The mountain of jewels, the wish-granting tree,
The wish-granting cow, and the harvest unsown.
The precious wheel, the precious jewel,
The precious queen, the precious minister,
The precious elephant, the precious supreme horse,
The precious general, and the great treasure vase.
The goddess of beauty, the goddess of garlands,
The goddess of music, the goddess of dance,
The goddess of flowers, the goddess of incense,
The goddess of light, and the goddess of scent.
The sun and the moon, the precious umbrella,
The banner of victory in every direction.
In the centre all treasures of both gods and men,
An excellent collection with nothing left out.
I offer this to you my kind root Guru and lineage Gurus,
To all of you sacred and glorious Gurus;
And especially to you, great Lama Losang Tubwang
    Dorjechang together with your retinues.
Please accept with compassion for migrating beings,
And having accepted, out of your great compassion,

Please bestow your blessings on all sentient beings
   pervading space.

The ground sprinkled with perfume and spread with
   flowers,
The Great Mountain, four lands, sun and moon,
Seen as a Buddha Land and offered thus,
May all beings enjoy such Pure Lands.

I offer without any sense of loss
The objects that give rise to my attachment, hatred, and
   confusion,
My friends, enemies, and strangers, our bodies and
   enjoyments;
Please accept these and bless me to be released directly
   from the three poisons.

IDAM GURU RATNA MANDALAKAM NIRYATAYAMI

The Nine-line Migtsema Prayer

Tsongkhapa, crown ornament of the scholars of the Land
    of the Snows,
You are Buddha Shakyamuni and Vajradhara, the source
    of all attainments,
Avalokiteshvara, the treasury of unobservable compassion,
Manjushri, the supreme stainless wisdom,
And Vajrapani, the destroyer of the hosts of maras.
O Venerable Guru-Buddha, synthesis of all Three Jewels
With my body, speech, and mind, respectfully
    I make requests:
Please grant your blessings to ripen and liberate myself
    and others,
And bestow the common and supreme attainments.

ngö drub kün jung tub wang dor je chang
mig me tse wai ter chen chän rä zig
dri me khyen pai wang po jam päl yang
dü pung ma lü jom dzä sang wai dag
gang chän khä pai tsug gyän lo zang drag
kyab sum kün dü la ma sang gyä la
go sum gü pai go nä söl wa deb
rang zhän min ching dröl war jin gyi lob
chog dang tün mong ngö drub tsäl du söl

The Quick Path

A CONDENSED PRACTICE OF
HERUKA FIVE DEITIES ACCORDING TO
MASTER GHANTAPA'S TRADITION

The Quick Path

Requests to the lineage Gurus

Fortunate beings are led to the state of Union in one life
Through depending upon great secret Deity yoga;
O Glorious Guide, Father Mother Heruka,
I request you, please bestow Union in this life.

O Ghantapa, Rubälshab,
Dzalandara, Krishnapada,
And all the other lineage Gurus of this path,
I request you, please bestow Union in this life.

And especially my kind root Guru,
The compassion of all the Conquerors
Arisen in a perfect form,
I request you, please bestow Union in this life.

Please grant me your blessings so that I may quickly
   attain
A stable and spontaneous experience
Of renunciation, bodhichitta, correct view,
And all the stages of the two-fold path.

In short, venerable Guru Father and Mother,
May I never be parted from you, but always come under
   your care.
Through the power of your blessings may I swiftly
   complete the grounds and paths
And quickly attain the state of Heruka.

Going for refuge and generating bodhichitta

Eternally I shall go for refuge
To Buddha, Dharma, and Sangha.
For the sake of all living beings
I shall become Heruka.   (3x)

Bringing death into the path of the Truth Body

Light rays from the HUM at my heart melt all worlds
and beings into light. This dissolves into me, and I, in
turn, gradually melt into light from below and above
and dissolve into the HUM at my heart. The letter HUM
dissolves in stages from the bottom up into the nada.
The nada too becomes smaller and smaller and dissolves
into clear light emptiness.

Bringing the intermediate state into the path of the Enjoyment Body

From the state of emptiness my mind appears in the
form of a nada.

Bringing rebirth into the path of the Emanation Body

Upon the four elements stands Mount Meru crowned by
a lotus. In the centre of this, from vowels and consonants,
there arises a moon which is white with a shade of red.
I, the nada, enter the centre of the moon and gradually
transform into a HUM.

Five-coloured lights radiate from the HUM and lead all
migrators to the state of Chakrasamvara. At the same
time all the Heroes and Heroines are invited from the
Buddha Lands of the ten directions. They all melt into
light and dissolve into the HUM, and the letter HUM
becomes the nature of spontaneous joy. The moon,
vowels, consonants, and HUM completely transform
and the supported Deities and supporting mandala
arise fully and all at once.

Checking meditation on the mandala and the beings within it

Now I am the Blessed One Heruka, with a blue-coloured body, one face and two hands, holding vajra and bell and embracing Vajravarahi. I stand on a lotus and sun and tread on Bhairawa and Kalarati.

On the petals of the four directions, counter-clockwise from the east, stand Dakini, Lama, Khandarohi, and Rupini. Together with the square celestial mansion, protection circle, and charnel grounds, everything is complete.

Inviting the wisdom beings and empowering Deities

PHAIM
My three places are marked by the three letters. Light rays radiate from the letter HUM and invite all at once all the Buddhas of the ten directions in the aspect of the visualized mandala, together with the empowering Deities.

DZA HUM BAM HO
The wisdom beings and commitment beings become inseparable.

Granting empowerment and adorning the crown

The empowering Deities grant empowerment. The Father's crown is adorned with Vajrasattva and the Mother's with Vairochana.

Offerings and praises

Offering and praising goddesses emanate from my heart and perform the offerings and praises.

Outer offerings

OM CHAKRASAMVARA SAPARIWARA AHRGHAM PARTITZA
SÖHA
OM CHAKRASAMVARA SAPARIWARA PADÄM PARTITZA
SÖHA
OM CHAKRASAMVARA SAPARIWARA PUPE PARTITZA
SÖHA
OM CHAKRASAMVARA SAPARIWARA DHUPE PARTITZA
SÖHA
OM CHAKRASAMVARA SAPARIWARA DIWE PARTITZA
SÖHA
OM CHAKRASAMVARA SAPARIWARA GÄNDHE PARTITZA
SÖHA
OM CHAKRASAMVARA SAPARIWARA NEWIDE PARTITZA
SÖHA
OM CHAKRASAMVARA SAPARIWARA SHAPTA PARTITZA
SÖHA

Inner offering

OM CHAKRASAMVARA SAPARIWARA OM AH HUM

Secret offering

Father and Mother engage in union and generate
spontaneous bliss and emptiness.

Praise

To Glorious Heruka Father and Mother,
Synthesis of all objects of knowledge in the supreme
    sphere of spontaneous bliss,
To the beautiful Goddesses in the four directions,
And to the entire supported and supporting mandala,
    respectfully I prostrate.

Blessing the rosary

The rosary becomes vajra speech, the nature of
Pämanarteshvara.

Mantra recitation

On a sun seat at the heart of Father and Mother is a letter HUM surrounded by a mantra rosary. These radiate and gather light.

The essence mantra of the Father

OM SHRI VAJRA HE HE RU RU KAM HUM HUM PHAT DAKINI
 DZALA SHAMBARAM SÖHA

The essence mantra of the Mother

OM VAJRA BEROTZANIYE HUM HUM PHAT SÖHA

Absorption

The celestial mansion and Mother dissolve into me.

Dedication

For the sake of all living beings,
May I become Heruka,
And then lead every living being
To Heruka's supreme state.

Auspicious prayer

Through the force of the blessings of Guru Heruka,
The truth of non-deceptive actions and their effects,
And through the power of my pure, superior intention,
May everything be auspicious for the spontaneous
 accomplishment of my wishes.

Colophon: This sadhana was composed by Venerable Geshe
Kelsang Gyatso Rinpoche and translated
under his compassionate guidance.

The Condensed Meaning of the Swift Vajrayana Path

THE MAHAMUDRA OF THE ORAL LINEAGE OF THE UNEQUALLED VIRTUOUS TRADITION

This condensed meaning, or outlines, of *Clear Light of Bliss*, a commentary to the practice of Mahamudra in Vajrayana Buddhism by the same author, was composed by Geshe Kelsang Gyatso Rinpoche.

The Condensed Meaning of the Swift Vajrayana Path

The explanation of the stages of how to practise the swift Vajrayana path of the Mahamudra of the oral lineage of the unequalled Virtuous Tradition is in three parts:

1 An introduction to the general paths
2 The source of the lineage from which these instructions are derived
3 The actual explanation of the instructions possessing this lineage

The actual explanation of the instructions possessing this lineage has three parts:

1 The preliminary practices
2 The actual practice
3 The concluding stages

The preliminary practices has two parts:

1 The common preliminary practices
2 The uncommon preliminary practices

The common preliminary practices has four parts:

1 The guide of going for refuge and generating bodhichitta, the gateway to the Buddhadharma and the Mahayana
2 The guide of mandala offerings, the gateway to accumulating a collection of merit
3 The guide of meditation and recitation of Vajrasattva, the gateway to purifying negativities and downfalls
4 The guide of Guru yoga, the gateway to receiving blessings

The actual practice has three parts:

1 How to practise the Mahamudra that is the union of bliss and emptiness
2 How to practise the Mahamudra that is the union of the two truths
3 How to accomplish the Mahamudra that is the resultant Union of No More Learning, the state possessing the seven pre-eminent qualities of embrace

How to practise the Mahamudra that is the union of bliss and emptiness has two parts:

1 An explanation of the method for generating the object-possessor, spontaneous great bliss
2 An explanation of the method for correctly realizing the object, emptiness

An explanation of the method for generating the object-possessor, spontaneous great bliss, has two parts:

1 Penetrating the precise points of one's own body
2 Penetrating the precise points of another's body

Penetrating the precise points of one's own body has four parts:

1 Identifying the ten doors through which the winds can enter the central channel
2 The reason why the winds can enter the central channel by penetrating the precise points through these doors
3 An explanation of their different functions
4 An explanation of the stages of meditation on inner fire (tummo) in particular

An explanation of the stages of meditation on inner fire (tummo) in particular has two parts:

1 How to meditate on inner fire (tummo) in eight stages
2 Based on these, an explanation of the practice of the four joys and the nine mixings

How to meditate on inner fire (tummo) in eight stages has eight parts:

1 An explanation of dispelling impure winds and meditating on a hollow body
2 Visualizing and meditating on the channels
3 Training in the paths of the channels
4 Visualizing and meditating on the letters
5 Igniting the inner fire (tummo)
6 Causing the fire to blaze
7 Mere blazing and dripping
8 An explanation of extraordinary blazing and dripping

Based on these, an explanation of the practice of the four joys and the nine mixings has two parts:

1 An explanation of the four joys
2 An explanation of the nine mixings

An explanation of the nine mixings has three parts:

1 An explanation of the mixings during waking
2 An explanation of the mixings during sleep
3 An explanation of the mixings during death

An explanation of the mixings during waking has three parts:

1 Mixing with the Truth Body during waking
2 Mixing with the Enjoyment Body during waking
3 Mixing with the Emanation Body during waking

An explanation of the mixings during sleep has three parts:

1 Mixing with the Truth Body during sleep
2 Mixing with the Enjoyment Body during sleep
3 Mixing with the Emanation Body during sleep

An explanation of the mixings during death has three parts:

1 Mixing with the Truth Body during death
2 Mixing with the Enjoyment Body during death
3 Mixing with the Emanation Body during death

Penetrating the precise points of another's body has two parts:

1 Relying upon an action mudra
2 Relying upon a wisdom mudra

An explanation of the method for correctly realizing the object, emptiness, has three parts:

1 How a direct realization of emptiness depends upon tranquil abiding
2 The uncommon explanation of how to meditate on tranquil abiding
3 How to seek the view of emptiness with meditation

The uncommon explanation of how to meditate on tranquil abiding has two parts:

1 An introduction to the object of meditation, the mind itself
2 The actual explanation of how to train

An introduction to the object of meditation, the mind itself, has three parts:

1 An introduction to the general mind
2 An introduction to the individual minds
3 Avoiding mistaking the introduction to the conventional nature of the mind for an introduction to the ultimate nature of the mind

An introduction to the individual minds has three parts:

1 An introduction to gross minds
2 An introduction to subtle minds
3 An introduction to the very subtle mind

The actual explanation of how to train has three parts:

1 How to train by means of general mindfulness
2 How to train by means of specific mindfulnesses
3 How to train by means of the six methods for settling the mind

How to train by means of specific mindfulnesses has five parts:

1 How to train by means of new mindfulness
2 How to train by means of old mindfulness
3 How to train by means of appropriate methods
4 How to train by means of labels known to others
5 How to train by means of the natural cessation of conceptual thoughts

How to train by means of the six methods for settling the mind has six parts:

1 Settling like the sun unobscured by clouds
2 Settling like a garuda circling in the sky
3 Settling like a still ocean
4 Settling like a small child staring at a temple
5 Settling like the trail of a bird flying in the sky
6 Settling like fine cotton thread

How to seek the view of emptiness with meditation has three parts:

1 How to meditate on selflessness of persons
2 How to meditate on selflessness of phenomena
3 Advising those who desire an unmistaken understanding of the ultimate view of both Sutra and Tantra of the necessity of listening to, contemplating, and meditating on Nagarjuna's root text on the Middle Way and its commentaries

How to meditate on selflessness of persons has three parts:

1 Identifying the object of negation
2 The way to refute the object of negation
3 How to train in emptiness during meditative equipoise and subsequent attainment

The way to refute the object of negation has three parts:

1 The essential point of ascertaining the pervasion
2 The essential point of ascertaining the absence of oneness

3 The essential point of ascertaining the absence of difference

How to train in emptiness during meditative equipoise and subsequent attainment has two parts:

1 The yoga of space-like meditative equipoise
2 The yoga of illusion-like subsequent attainment

How to meditate on selflessness of phenomena has three parts:

1 Meditation on the lack of inherent existence of the body
2 Meditation on the lack of inherent existence of the mind
3 Meditation on the lack of inherent existence of other phenomena

Each of these three has the three parts, identifying the object of negation and so forth.

How to practise the Mahamudra that is the union of the two truths has three parts:

1 An explanation of the stages of attaining the illusory body with respect to conventional truth
2 An explanation of the stages of attaining meaning clear light with respect to ultimate truth
3 The actual explanation of the Mahamudra that is the union of the two truths

An explanation of the stages of attaining the illusory body with respect to conventional truth has four parts:

1 How disciples possessing four attributes request the meaning of the illusory body from a qualified Spiritual Guide
2 How a correct understanding of the illusory body depends upon the Spiritual Guide's instructions
3 Recognizing the basis for attaining the illusory body
4 The actual way of attaining the illusory body on this basis

An explanation of the stages of attaining meaning clear light with respect to ultimate truth has three parts:

1 An explanation of the method for cultivating it
2 The way of cultivating it by relying upon this method
3 The reason why this clear light alone acts as the direct antidote to both the intellectually-formed and the innate delusions

The actual explanation of the Mahamudra that is the union of the two truths has two parts:

1 An introduction to the union
2 Showing the stages by which it is gradually accomplished

How to accomplish the Mahamudra that is the resultant Union of No More Learning, the state possessing the seven pre-eminent qualities of embrace, has five parts:

1 The place where Buddhahood is attained
2 The basis upon which Buddhahood is attained
3 The way in which Buddhahood is attained
4 The good qualities of a Buddha
5 An explanation of the relationships of serial and reverse order

Dedication

To accomplish all the purposes of sentient beings,
By this virtue may I quickly attain
The seven pre-eminent qualities of embrace:
A Form Body endowed with the signs and indications
Embracing a wisdom knowledge woman,
A mind abiding in a state of great bliss,
This bliss realizing lack of inherent existence,
A compassion that has abandoned the extreme of peace,
An uninterrupted continuum of body,
And unceasing enlightened deeds.

May everything be auspicious.

Prayers of Request to the Mahamudra Lineage Gurus

Prayers of Request to the Mahamudra Lineage Gurus

Homage to the Mahamudra

O Great Vajradhara, pervading all natures,
Glorious first Buddha, Principal of all Buddha families,
Within the celestial mansion of the spontaneous three
    bodies,
I request you please to grant me your blessings
So that I may cut the creeping vine of self-grasping within
    my mental continuum,
Train in love, compassion, and bodhichitta,
And swiftly accomplish the Mahamudra of the Path of Union.

O Omniscient Superior Manjushri,
Father of all the Conquerors of the three times
In the Buddha Lands throughout the worlds of the ten
    directions,
I request you please to grant me your blessings
So that I may cut the creeping vine of self-grasping within
    my mental continuum,
Train in love, compassion, and bodhichitta,
And swiftly accomplish the Mahamudra of the Path of Union.

O Venerable Losang Dragpa,
Second Able One of Buddha's doctrine
Appearing in the northern Land of the Snows,
I request you please to grant me your blessings
So that I may cut the creeping vine of self-grasping within
    my mental continuum,
Train in love, compassion, and bodhichitta,
And swiftly accomplish the Mahamudra of the Path of Union.

O Togdän Jampäl Gyatso,
Principal holder of the doctrine of the lineage of
accomplishment
Of Je Tsongkhapa, the Son of Manjushri,
I request you please to grant me your blessings
So that I may cut the creeping vine of self-grasping within
my mental continuum,
Train in love, compassion, and bodhichitta,
And swiftly accomplish the Mahamudra of the Path of Union.

O Baso Chökyi Gyaltsän,
Who opened the treasury of instructions of the Whispered
Lineage
And ripened fortunate disciples,
I request you please to grant me your blessings
So that I may cut the creeping vine of self-grasping within
my mental continuum,
Train in love, compassion, and bodhichitta,
And swiftly accomplish the Mahamudra of the Path of Union.

O Supreme Yogi Dharmavajra,
Who completed the yogas of the two stages
And attained the deathless body of a Knowledge-holder,
I request you please to grant me your blessings
So that I may cut the creeping vine of self-grasping within
my mental continuum,
Train in love, compassion, and bodhichitta,
And swiftly accomplish the Mahamudra of the Path of Union.

O Losang Dönyö Drubpa (Gyalwa Ensäpa),
Who upheld the victory banner of the definitive doctrine,
Unfettered by the chains of the eight worldly dharmas,
I request you please to grant me your blessings
So that I may cut the creeping vine of self-grasping within
my mental continuum,
Train in love, compassion, and bodhichitta,
And swiftly accomplish the Mahamudra of the Path of Union.

O Khädrub Sangye Yeshe,
Who guide all migrators with your ordained aspect
In the enchanting palace of the three bodies,
I request you please to grant me your blessings
So that I may cut the creeping vine of self-grasping within
    my mental continuum,
Train in love, compassion, and bodhichitta,
And swiftly accomplish the Mahamudra of the Path of Union.

O Venerable Losang Chögyän (First Panchen Lama),
All-knowing one inseparable from the Protector of the
    doctrine
Of the Conqueror, Venerable Losang Dragpa,
I request you please to grant me your blessings
So that I may cut the creeping vine of self-grasping within
    my mental continuum,
Train in love, compassion, and bodhichitta,
And swiftly accomplish the Mahamudra of the Path of Union.

O Great Yogi Gendun Gyaltsän (Nächu Rabjampa),
Who completed all practices, integrating into one meaning
The words of the Sutras, Tantras, and commentaries,
I request you please to grant me your blessings
So that I may cut the creeping vine of self-grasping within
    my mental continuum,
Train in love, compassion, and bodhichitta,
And swiftly accomplish the Mahamudra of the Path of Union.

O Accomplished One Gyaltsän Dzinpa (Drungpa Tsöndru
    Gyaltsän),
Who through great effort attained the supreme state
By experiencing the essence of the doctrine of the
    Conqueror, Venerable Losang,
I request you please to grant me your blessings
So that I may cut the creeping vine of self-grasping within
    my mental continuum,
Train in love, compassion, and bodhichitta,
And swiftly accomplish the Mahamudra of the Path of Union.

O Holder of the great lineage Könchog Gyaltsän,
Who are skilled at expounding to fortunate disciples
The essential nectar of the holy vast and profound Dharma,
I request you please to grant me your blessings
So that I may cut the creeping vine of self-grasping within
    my mental continuum,
Train in love, compassion, and bodhichitta,
And swiftly accomplish the Mahamudra of the Path of Union.

O Venerable Losang Yeshe (Second Panchen Lama),
Who are Venerable Losang Chökyi Gyaltsän himself,
Returning for the glory of migrators and the doctrine,
I request you please to grant me your blessings
So that I may cut the creeping vine of self-grasping within
    my mental continuum,
Train in love, compassion, and bodhichitta,
And swiftly accomplish the Mahamudra of the Path of Union.

O Venerable Losang Trinlay (Lhapa Tulku),
Who accomplished the profound path of the Whispered
    Lineage,
Blessed directly by the venerable Buddhas,
I request you please to grant me your blessings
So that I may cut the creeping vine of self-grasping within
    my mental continuum,
Train in love, compassion, and bodhichitta,
And swiftly accomplish the Mahamudra of the Path of Union.

O Supremely Accomplished One Drubwang Losang Namgyal,
Who completed the practice of the essential meaning
Of the Conqueror, Venerable Losang's Whispered Lineage,
I request you please to grant me your blessings
So that I may cut the creeping vine of self-grasping within
    my mental continuum,
Train in love, compassion, and bodhichitta,
And swiftly accomplish the Mahamudra of the Path of Union.

O Kind Kachen Yeshe Gyaltsän,
Who out of compassion elucidate without error
The instructions of the Venerable Lama's Whispered Lineage,
I request you please to grant me your blessings
So that I may cut the creeping vine of self-grasping within
    my mental continuum,
Train in love, compassion, and bodhichitta,
And swiftly accomplish the Mahamudra of the Path of Union.

O Venerable Phurchog Ngawang Jampa,
Who spread throughout all the central lands and the
    border regions
The essence of the unmistaken doctrine of the entire path
I request you please to grant me your blessings
So that I may cut the creeping vine of self-grasping within
    my mental continuum,
Train in love, compassion, and bodhichitta,
And swiftly accomplish the Mahamudra of the Path of Union.

O Panchen Palden Yeshe,
Who as a glorious first Buddha in an ordained aspect
Ripened the whole of China and Tibet with the Dharma,
I request you please to grant me your blessings
So that I may cut the creeping vine of self-grasping within
    my mental continuum,
Train in love, compassion, and bodhichitta,
And swiftly accomplish the Mahamudra of the Path of Union.

O Khädrub Ngawang Dorje,
Who single-pointedly accomplished all the attainments,
The completion of the excellent paths of Sutra and Tantra,
I request you please to grant me your blessings
So that I may cut the creeping vine of self-grasping within
    my mental continuum,
Train in love, compassion, and bodhichitta,
And swiftly accomplish the Mahamudra of the Path of Union.

O Venerable Ngulchu Dharmabhadra,
Protector who clarified the Conqueror's doctrine through
    explanation and composition,
With skill and steadfastness, like a second Buddha,
I request you please to grant me your blessings
So that I may cut the creeping vine of self-grasping within
    my mental continuum,
Train in love, compassion, and bodhichitta,
And swiftly accomplish the Mahamudra of the Path of Union.

O Yangchän Drubpay Dorje,
Whose eyes of great, unobservable compassion are never
    closed,
And whose profound and extensive wisdom is like that of
    Manjushri,
I request you please to grant me your blessings
So that I may cut the creeping vine of self-grasping within
    my mental continuum,
Train in love, compassion, and bodhichitta,
And swiftly accomplish the Mahamudra of the Path of Union.

O Khädrub Tendzin Tsöndru,
Who completed the yogas of bliss and emptiness
And went directly to the capital city of Union,
I request you please to grant me your blessings
So that I may cut the creeping vine of self-grasping within
    my mental continuum,
Train in love, compassion, and bodhichitta,
And swiftly accomplish the Mahamudra of the Path of Union.

O Venerable Phabongkha Trinlay Gyatso,
Who through the power of your love for all migrators,
Upheld the victory banner of the doctrines of Sutra and
    Tantra,
I request you please to grant me your blessings
So that I may cut the creeping vine of self-grasping within
    my mental continuum,
Train in love, compassion, and bodhichitta,
And swiftly accomplish the Mahamudra of the Path of Union.

O Kind Losang Yeshe (Trijang Rinpoche),
Spiritual Guide who, for fortunate disciples,
Promoted the heart-essence of the Venerable Second
    Conqueror,
I request you please to grant me your blessings
So that I may cut the creeping vine of self-grasping within
    my mental continuum,
Train in love, compassion, and bodhichitta,
And swiftly accomplish the Mahamudra of the Path of Union.

O Venerable Kelsang Gyatso Rinpoche,
Who through your compassion and with your great skill
Explain to fortunate disciples
The instructions of your Guru and the profound lineage,
I request you please to grant me your blessings
So that I may cut the creeping vine of self-grasping within
    my mental continuum,
Train in love, compassion, and bodhichitta,
And swiftly accomplish the Mahamudra of the Path of Union.

Please grant me your blessings
So that I may see the venerable Guru as a Buddha,
Overcome attachment for the abodes of samsara,
And having assumed the burden of liberating all migrators,
Accomplish the common and uncommon paths,
And swiftly attain the Union of the Mahamudra.

This body of mine and your body, O Father,
This speech of mine and your speech, O Father,
This mind of mine and your mind, O Father,
Through your blessings may they become inseparably one.

Colophon: This traditional prayer of requests to the Mahamudra
    lineage Gurus was translated by disciples of Geshe Kelsang
  Gyatso Rinpoche under his compassionate guidance. The verse
    of request to Geshe Kelsang Gyatso Rinpoche was composed
      by the glorious Dharma Protector, Duldzin Dorje Shugdän,
        at the request of Geshe Kelsang's faithful disciples.

Glossary

Action mudra A Highest Yoga Tantra consort who assists in developing great bliss. See *Clear Light of Bliss*.

Aggregate In general, all functioning things are aggregates because they are an aggregation of their parts. In particular, a person of the desire or form realm has five aggregates: the aggregates of form, feeling, discrimination, compositional factors, and consciousness. A being of the formless realm lacks the aggregate of form but has the other four. A person's form aggregate is their body. The remaining four aggregates are aspects of their mind. See *Heart of Wisdom*.

Akshobya The manifestation of the aggregate of consciousness of all Buddhas. He has a blue-coloured body.

Amitabha The manifestation of the aggregate of discrimination of all Buddhas. He has a red-coloured body.

Amoghasiddhi The manifestation of the aggregate of compositional factors of all Buddhas. He has a green-coloured body.

Analytical meditation The mental process of investigating a virtuous object, analyzing its nature, function, characteristics, and other aspects. See *Joyful Path* and *A Meditation Handbook*.

Arya See *Superior being*.

Atisha (AD 982-1054) A famous Indian Buddhist scholar and meditation master. He was Abbot of the great Buddhist monastery of Vikramashila at a time when Mahayana Buddhism was flourishing in India. He was later invited to Tibet and his arrival there led to the re-establishment of Buddhism in Tibet. He is the author of the first text on the stages of the path, *Lamp for the Path*. His tradition later became known as the 'Kadampa Tradition'. See *Joyful Path*.

Attainment 'Siddhi' in Sanskrit. These are of two types: common attainments and supreme attainments. Common attainments are of four principal types: pacifying attainments (the ability to purify negativity, overcome obstacles, and cure sickness), increasing attainments (the ability to increase Dharma realizations, merit, life span, and wealth), controlling attainments (the ability to control one's own and others' minds and actions), and wrathful attainments (the ability to use wrathful actions where appropriate to benefit others). Supreme attainments are the special realizations of a Buddha.

Bardo See *Intermediate state*.

Blessing 'Jin gyi lab' in Tibetan. The transformation of our mind from a negative state to a positive state, from an unhappy state to a happy state, or from a state of weakness to a state of strength through the inspiration of holy beings such as our Spiritual Guide, Buddhas, and Bodhisattvas.

Bodhichitta Sanskrit word for 'mind of enlightenment'. 'Bodhi' means enlightenment, and 'chitta' means mind. There are two types of bodhichitta: conventional bodhichitta and ultimate bodhichitta. Generally speaking, the term 'bodhichitta' refers to conventional bodhichitta, which is a primary mind motivated by great compassion that spontaneously seeks enlightenment to benefit all sentient beings. Conventional bodhichitta is of two types: aspiring bodhichitta and engaging bodhichitta. Ultimate bodhichitta is a wisdom motivated by conventional bodhichitta that directly realizes emptiness, the ultimate nature of phenomena. See *Joyful Path*, *Meaningful to Behold*, and *Universal Compassion*.

Bodhisattva A person who has generated spontaneous bodhichitta but who has not yet become a Buddha. From the moment a practitioner generates a non-artificial, or spontaneous, bodhichitta he or she becomes a Bodhisattva and enters the first Mahayana path, the path of accumulation. An ordinary Bodhisattva is one who has not realized emptiness directly, and a Superior Bodhisattva is one who has achieved a direct realization of emptiness. See *Joyful Path* and *Meaningful to Behold*.

Body mandala The transformation into a Deity of any part of the body of oneself generated as a Deity. See *Guide to Dakini Land*.

Buddha A being who has completely abandoned all delusions and their imprints. There are many beings who have become Buddhas in the past, and there are many who will become Buddhas in the future. See *Joyful Path*.

Buddha lineage The root mind of a sentient being and its ultimate nature. Buddha lineage, Buddha nature, and Buddha seed are synonymous. All sentient beings have Buddha lineage and therefore have the potential to attain Buddhahood.

Buddha Shakyamuni The fourth of one thousand Buddhas who are to appear in this world during this Fortunate Aeon. The first three were Krakuchchhanda, Kanakamuni, and Kashyapa. The fifth Buddha will be Maitreya.

Buddha's bodies A Buddha has four bodies – the Wisdom Truth Body, the Nature Truth Body, the Enjoyment Body, and the Emanation Body. The first is Buddha's omniscient mind; the second is the emptiness or ultimate nature of his mind; the third is his actual Form Body, which is very subtle; and the fourth, of which each Buddha manifests a countless number, are gross Form Bodies that are visible to ordinary beings. The Wisdom Truth Body and the Nature Truth Body are both included within the Truth Body, and the Enjoyment Body and the Emanation Body are both included within the Form Body. See *Joyful Path* and *Ocean of Nectar*.

Buddhadharma Buddha's teachings and the inner realizations attained by practising them.

Central channel The principal channel at the very centre of the body where the channel wheels are located. See *Clear Light of Bliss*.

Chakra See *Channel wheel*.

Chandrakirti A great Indian Buddhist scholar and meditation Master who composed, among many other books, *Guide to the Middle Way*, in which he clearly elucidates the view of the Madhyamika-Prasangika school according to Buddha's teachings given in the *Perfection of Wisdom Sutras*. See *Ocean of Nectar*.

Channel wheel 'Chakra' in Sanskrit. A focal centre where secondary channels branch out from the central channel. Meditating on these points can cause the inner winds to enter the central channel. See *Clear Light of Bliss*.

Channels Subtle inner passageways of the body through which flow subtle drops moved by inner winds. See *Clear Light of Bliss*.

Clairvoyance Abilities that arise from special concentration. There are five principal types of clairvoyance: the clairvoyance of the divine eye (the ability to see subtle and distant forms), the clairvoyance of the divine ear (the ability to hear subtle and distant sounds), the clairvoyance of miracle powers (the ability to emanate various forms by mind), the clairvoyance of remembering former lives, and the clairvoyance of knowing others' minds. Some beings such as bardo beings and some humans and ghosts have contaminated clairvoyance that develops due to karma, but these are not actual clairvoyance.

Clear appearance Generally, any clear appearance of an object of meditation to the concentration focused on it. More specifically, a Secret Mantra practice whereby the practitioner, having generated himself or herself as a Deity and the environment as the Deity's mandala, tries to attain clear appearance of the whole object to his or her concentration. It is the antidote to ordinary appearance. See *Guide to Dakini Land* and *Heart Jewel*.

Collection of merit Any virtuous action motivated by bodhichitta that is the main cause of attaining the Form Body of a Buddha. Examples are: making offerings and prostrations to holy beings with bodhichitta motivation, and the practice of the perfections of giving, moral discipline, and patience. See also *Buddha's bodies.*

Collection of wisdom A virtuous mental action motivated by bodhichitta that is the main cause for attaining the Truth Body of a Buddha. Examples are: hearing, contemplating, and meditating on emptiness with bodhichitta motivation. See also *Buddha's bodies.*

Commitment being A visualized Buddha or ourself visualized as a Buddha. A commitment being is so called because in general it is the commitment of all Buddhists to visualize or remember Buddha, and in particular it is a commitment of those who have received an empowerment into Highest Yoga Tantra to generate themselves as a Deity.

Commitments Promises and pledges taken when engaging in certain spiritual practices. See *Guide to Dakini Land.*

Completion stage Highest Yoga Tantra realizations that are attained through completing a special method that causes the winds to enter, abide, and dissolve within the central channel. See *Clear Light of Bliss* and *Guide to Dakini Land.*

Concentration being A symbol of Buddha's Truth Body, usually visualized as a seed-letter at the heart of a commitment being or a wisdom being. It is so called because it is generated through concentration.

Contaminated aggregates Any of the aggregates of form, feeling, discrimination, compositional factors, or consciousness of a samsaric being. See *Heart of Wisdom* and *Joyful Path.*

Contaminated phenomenon Any phenomenon that gives rise to delusions or that causes them to increase. Examples are the environments, beings, and enjoyments of samsara. See *Joyful Path.*

Conventional truth Any phenomenon other than emptiness. Conventional truths are true with respect to the minds of ordinary beings, but in reality they are false. See *Heart of Wisdom, Meaningful to Behold,* and *Ocean of Nectar.*

Cyclic existence See *Samsara.*

Dakas See *Dakinis.*

Dakini Land The Pure Land of Vajrayogini. In Sanskrit it is called 'Keajra' and in Tibetan 'Dagpa Khachö'. See *Guide to Dakini Land.*

Dakinis Female Tantric Buddhas and those women who have attained the realization of meaning clear light. Dakas are the male equivalent. See *Guide to Dakini Land.*

Degenerate times A period when spiritual activity degenerates.

Deity 'Yidam' in Sanskrit. A Tantric enlightened being.

Delusion A mental factor that arises from inappropriate attention and functions to make the mind unpeaceful and uncontrolled. There are three main delusions: ignorance, attachment, and hatred. From these all other delusions such as jealousy, pride, and deluded doubt arise. See *Joyful Path* and *Understanding the Mind.*

Delusion-obstructions See *Obstructions to liberation.*

Demon 'Mara' in Sanskrit. Anything that obstructs the attainment of liberation or enlightenment. There are four principal types of demon: the demon of the delusions, the demon of the contaminated aggregates, the demon of death, and the Devaputra demons. Of these, only the last are actual sentient beings. The principal Devaputra demon is wrathful Ishvara, the highest of the desire realm gods who inhabits the Land Controlling Others' Emanations. Buddha is called a 'Conqueror' because he has conquered all four types of demon. See *Heart of Wisdom* and *Ocean of Nectar.*

Desire realm The environment of humans, animals, hungry ghosts, hell beings, and the gods who enjoy the five objects of desire.

Dharma Buddha's teachings and the realizations that are attained in dependence upon them. See *Joyful Path.*

Dharma Protectors Manifestations of Buddhas or Bodhisattvas whose main function is to eliminate obstacles and to gather all necessary conditions for pure Dharma practitioners. See *Heart Jewel.*

Divine pride A non-deluded pride that regards oneself as a Deity and one's environments and enjoyments as those of the Deity. It is the antidote to ordinary conceptions. See *Clear Light of Bliss, Guide to Dakini Land,* and *Heart Jewel.*

Dorje Shugdän A Dharma Protector who is an emanation of the Wisdom Buddha Manjushri. See *Heart Jewel.*

Drops The essence of blood and sperm. When the drops melt and flow through the inner channels they give rise to an experience of bliss. See *Clear Light of Bliss.*

Dualistic appearance The appearance to mind of an object together with the inherent existence of that object. See *Heart of Wisdom* and *Ocean of Nectar.*

Eight freedoms and ten endowments Eight freedoms from impediment to spiritual practice and ten special conditions for practice, that characterize a precious human life. See *Joyful Path.*

345

Element The nature of any phenomenon. All phenomena hold their own natures, which are all included within the eighteen elements. See *Heart of Wisdom* and *Ocean of Nectar*.

Emptiness Lack of inherent existence, the ultimate nature of all phenomena. See *Heart of Wisdom* and *Ocean of Nectar*.

Enlightenment Usually the full enlightenment of Buddhahood. There are three levels of enlightenment: small enlightenment, or the enlightenment of a Hearer; middling enlightenment, or the enlightenment of a Solitary Conqueror; and great enlightenment, or the enlightenment of a Buddha. An enlightenment is a liberation and a true cessation. See *Clear Light of Bliss*, *Joyful Path*, and *Ocean of Nectar*.

Ensa Whispered Lineage Another name for the Uncommon Whispered Lineage of the Virtuous Tradition. See also *Kadam Emanation Scripture*.

Exalted wisdom Any Dharma realization maintained by renunciation or bodhichitta. Generally, exalted wisdom, ground, and path are synonyms. See also *Ground*.

Five omniscient wisdoms The five exalted wisdoms of a Buddha: the exalted mirror-like wisdom, the exalted wisdom of equality, the exalted wisdom of individual analysis, the exalted wisdom of accomplishing activities, and the exalted wisdom of the Dharmadhatu.

Foe Destroyer 'Arhat' in Sanskrit. A practitioner who has abandoned all delusions and their seeds by training on the spiritual paths, and who will never again be born in samsara. In this context, the term 'foe' refers to the delusions.

Form Body See *Buddha's bodies*.

Form realm The environment of the gods who possess form.

Formless realm The environment of the gods who do not possess form.

Fortunate Aeon The name given to this world age. It is so called because one thousand Buddhas will appear during this aeon. Buddha Shakyamuni was the fourth and Buddha Maitreya will be the fifth.

Four noble truths True sufferings, true origins, true cessations, and true paths. They are called 'noble' truths because they are supreme objects of meditation. Through meditation on these four objects we can realize ultimate truth directly and thus become a noble, or Superior being. Sometimes referred to as the 'Four truths of Superiors'. See *Heart of Wisdom* and *Joyful Path*.

Generation stage A realization of a creative yoga achieved as a result of the pure concentration on bringing the three bodies into the path in which one mentally generates oneself as a Tantric Deity and one's surroundings as the Deity's mandala. Meditation on generation stage is called a 'creative yoga' because its object is created by correct imagination. See *Guide to Dakini Land*.

Generic image That which is the appearing object of a conceptual mind. See *Heart of Wisdom* and *Understanding the Mind*.

Geshe A title given by the Kadampa Monasteries to accomplished Buddhist scholars.

Geshe Langri Tangpa (AD 1054-1123) A great Kadampa Geshe who was famous for his realization of exchanging self with others. He composed *Eight Verses of Training the Mind*.

God A being of the god realm, the highest of the six realms of samsara. There are many different types of god. Some belong to the desire realm and others to the form and formless realms.

Golden age A time when sentient beings have abundant merit and when Dharma activities flourish. It is contrasted with a degenerate time.

Great compassion A mind wishing to protect all sentient beings from suffering. See *Joyful Path, Universal Compassion*, and *Ocean of Nectar*.

Ground In general, ground and path are synonyms, a ground being any realization maintained by a spontaneous realization of renunciation or bodhichitta. The ten grounds are the realizations of Superior Bodhisattvas. They are: Very Joyful, Stainless, Luminous, Radiant, Difficult to Overcome, Approaching, Gone Afar, Immovable, Good Intelligence, and Cloud of Dharma. See *Ocean of Nectar*.

Hell realm The lowest of the three lower realms. See *Joyful Path*.

Heroes and Heroines A Hero is a male Tantric Deity embodying method. A Heroine is a female Tantric Deity embodying wisdom. See *Guide to Dakini Land*.

Hinayana Sanskrit term for 'Lesser Vehicle'. The Hinayana goal is to attain merely one's own liberation from suffering by completely abandoning delusions. See *Joyful Path*.

Ignorance A mental factor that is confused about the ultimate nature of phenomena. See also *Self-grasping*. See *Heart of Wisdom, Joyful Path*, and *Understanding the Mind*.

Illusory body When a practitioner of Highest Yoga Tantra rises from the meditation of the isolated mind of ultimate example clear light he or she attains a body that is not the same as his or her ordinary physical body. This new body is the illusory body. It has the same appearance as the body of the personal Deity of generation stage, except that it is white in colour. It can be perceived only by those who have already attained an illusory body. See *Clear Light of Bliss*.

Inherent existence An imagined mode of existence whereby phenomena are held to exist from their own side, independent of other phenomena. In reality all phenomena are empty of inherent existence because they depend upon their parts. See *Heart of Wisdom*, *Joyful Path*, and *Ocean of Nectar*.

Innate delusions Delusions that are not the product of intellectual speculation, but arise naturally. See *Joyful Path* and *Understanding the Mind*.

Inner Dakini Land A mind of clear light that realizes emptiness directly. Synonymous with meaning clear light. See *Guide to Dakini Land*.

Inner fire 'Tummo' in Tibetan. An inner heat located at the centre of the navel channel wheel. See *Clear Light of Bliss* and *Guide to Dakini Land*.

Inner offering A Highest Yoga Tantra offering that is produced by transforming ten inner substances into nectar. See *Guide to Dakini Land*.

Inner winds Special winds related to the mind that flow through the channels of our body. Our mind cannot function without these winds. See *Clear Light of Bliss*.

Intellectually-formed delusions Delusions that arise as a result of relying upon incorrect reasoning or mistaken tenets. See *Joyful Path* and *Understanding the Mind*.

Intermediate state 'Bardo' in Tibetan. The state between death and rebirth. It begins the moment the consciousness leaves the body and ceases the moment the consciousness enters the body of the next life. See *Joyful Path*.

Je Phabongkhapa (AD 1878-1941) A great Tibetan Lama who was an emanation of Heruka. Phabongkha Rinpoche was the holder of many lineages of Sutra and Secret Mantra.

Kadampa A follower of the Kadampa Tradition passed down from Atisha and his disciple Dromtönpa. Up to the time of Je Tsongkhapa the tradition is known as the 'Old Kadampa Tradition' and after the time of Je Tsongkhapa it is known as the 'New Kadampa Tradition.'

Karma Sanskrit term referring to actions and their effects. Through the force of intention we perform actions with our body, speech, and mind, and all of these actions produce effects. The effect of virtuous actions is happiness and the effect of negative actions is suffering. See *Joyful Path*.

Lamrim See *Stages of the path*.

Liberation Complete freedom from samsara and its cause, the delusions. See *Joyful Path*.

Lojong See *Training the mind*.

Madhyamika One of the two main schools of Mahayana tenets. The Madhyamika view was taught by Buddha in the *Perfection of Wisdom Sutras* during the Second Turning of the Wheel of Dharma and was subsequently elucidated by Nagarjuna and his followers. There are two divisions of this school, Madhyamika-Svatantrika and Madhyamika-Prasangika, of which the latter is Buddha's final view. See *Meaningful to Behold* and *Ocean of Nectar*.

Mahasiddha Sanskrit term for 'greatly accomplished one'. Used to refer to Yogis with high attainments.

Mahayana Sanskrit term for 'Great Vehicle', the spiritual path to great enlightenment. See *Joyful Path* and *Meaningful to Behold*.

Maitreya The embodiment of the loving-kindness of all the Buddhas. At the time of Buddha Shakyamuni he manifested as a Bodhisattva disciple. In the future he will manifest as the fifth universal Buddha.

Mandala A celestial mansion in which a Tantric Deity abides.

Manjushri The embodiment of the wisdom of all the Buddhas. At the time of Buddha Shakyamuni he manifested as a Bodhisattva disciple. See *Heart Jewel*.

Mantra Literally, 'mind protection'. Mantra protects the mind from ordinary appearances and conceptions. See *Guide to Dakini Land*.

Mara See *Demon*.

Meditation Constant acquaintance of the mind with a virtuous object. See *Joyful Path* and *A Meditation Handbook*.

Meditative equipoise Single-pointed concentration on a virtuous object such as emptiness.

Mental factor A cognizer that principally apprehends a particular attribute of an object. There are fifty-one specific mental factors. See *Understanding the Mind*.

Merit The good fortune created by virtuous actions. It is the potential power to increase our good qualities and produce happiness.

Method Any spiritual path that functions to ripen our Buddha lineage. Training in renunciation, compassion, and bodhichitta are examples of method practices.

Middle way See *Madhyamika*.

Migrators Beings within samsara who migrate from one uncontrolled birth to another.

Mind That which is clarity and cognizes. See *Clear Light of Bliss* and *Understanding the Mind*.

Miracle powers See *Clairvoyance*.

Mother Tantra A Tantra that principally emphasizes the attainment of clear light.

Mount Meru According to Buddhist cosmology, a large mountain that stands at the centre of the universe.

Mudra Generally, the Sanskrit word for 'seal', as in Mahamudra, the 'Great seal'. More specifically, 'mudra' is used to refer to a consort, as in 'action mudra' or 'wisdom mudra', and to hand gestures used in Tantric rituals. See *Clear Light of Bliss* and *Guide to Dakini Land*.

Naga A non-human being not normally visible to humans. Nagas usually live in the oceans of the world but they sometimes inhabit land in the region of rocks and trees. They are very powerful, some being benevolent and some malevolent.

Nagarjuna A great Indian Buddhist scholar and meditation master who revived the Mahayana in the first century AD by bringing to light the teachings on the *Perfection of Wisdom*. See *Ocean of Nectar*.

Naropa An Indian Buddhist Mahasiddha. See *Guide to Dakini Land*.

Non-virtuous actions The ten non-virtuous actions are: killing, stealing, sexual misconduct, lying, divisive speech, hurtful speech, idle gossip, covetousness, malice, and holding wrong view. See *Joyful Path* and *Meaningful to Behold*.

Obstructions to liberation Obstructions that prevent the attainment of liberation. All delusions, such as ignorance, attachment, and anger, together with their seeds are obstructions to liberation. Also called 'delusion-obstructions'. See *Joyful Path*.

Obstructions to omniscience The imprints of delusions that prevent simultaneous direct realization of all phenomena. Only Buddhas have overcome these obstructions. See *Joyful Path*.

Ordinary being A being who has not realized emptiness directly.

Path According to Dharma a path is an internal path. There are two types: correct paths and incorrect paths. Examples of the first are those stages of the path that lead to liberation and enlightenment and examples of the second are contaminated actions and concentrations that lead to cyclic rebirth. See also *Ground*.

Perfection of wisdom Any wisdom maintained by bodhichitta motivation. See *Heart of Wisdom*, *Joyful Path*, and *Ocean of Nectar*.

Perfection of Wisdom Sutras Sutras of the Second Turning of the Wheel of Dharma in which Buddha revealed his final view of the ultimate nature of all phenomena – lack of inherent existence. See *Heart of Wisdom* and *Ocean of Nectar*.

Prasangika See *Madhyamika*.

Pratimoksha A Sanskrit word meaning 'individual liberation'. See *The Bodhisattva Vow*.

Primary mind A cognizer that principally apprehends the mere entity of an object. There are six primary minds: the eye awareness, the ear awareness, the nose awareness, the tongue awareness, the body awareness, and the mental awareness. See *Understanding the Mind*.

Profound path The profound path includes all the wisdom practices that lead to a direct realization of emptiness and ultimately to the Truth Body of a Buddha. See *Joyful Path* and *Ocean of Nectar*.

Puja A ceremony in which offerings and other acts of devotion are performed in front of holy beings.

Ratnasambhava The manifestation of the feeling aggregate of all Buddhas. He has a yellow-coloured body.

Retreat A period of time during which we impose various restrictions on our actions of body, speech, and mind so as to be able to concentrate more fully on a particular spiritual practice. See *Guide to Dakini Land* and *Heart Jewel*.

Sadhana A method for attainment associated with a Tantric Deity.

Samkhya A non-Buddhist school. See *Meaningful to Behold*.

Samsara Also known as 'cyclic existence'. It can be understood in two ways: as uninterrupted rebirth without freedom or control, or as the aggregates of a being who has taken such a rebirth. There are six realms of samsara. Listed in ascending order according to the type of karma that causes rebirth in them, they are the realms of the hell-beings, hungry ghosts, animals, humans, demi-gods, and gods. The first three are lower realms or unhappy migrations and the second three are higher realms or happy migrations. Although, from the point of view of the karma that causes rebirth there, the god realm is the highest realm in samsara, the human realm is said to be the most fortunate realm because it provides the best conditions for attaining liberation and enlightenment. See *Joyful Path*.

Sangha According to the Vinaya tradition, any community of four or more fully ordained monks. In general, ordained or lay people who take Bodhisattva vows or Tantric vows can also be said to be Sangha.

Secret Mantra Synonymous with Tantra. Secret Mantra teachings are distinguished from Sutra teachings in that they reveal methods for training the mind by bringing the future result, or Buddhahood, into the present path. Secret Mantra is the supreme path to full enlightenment. The term 'mantra' indicates that it is Buddha's special instruction for protecting our mind from ordinary appearances and conceptions. Practitioners of Secret Mantra overcome ordinary appearances and conceptions by visualizing their environment, body, enjoyments, and deeds as those of a Buddha. The term 'secret' indicates that the practices are to be done in private, and that they can be practised only by those who have received a Tantric empowerment. See *Guide to Dakini Land* and *Clear Light of Bliss*.

Seed-letter The sacred letter from which a Deity is generated. Each Deity has a particular seed-letter. For example, the seed-letter of Manjushri is DHI, of Tara is TAM, of Vajrayogini is BAM, and of Heruka is HUM.

Self-cherishing A mental attitude that considers oneself to be precious or important. It is regarded as a principal object to be abandoned by Bodhisattvas. See *Universal Compassion, Joyful Path*, and *Meaningful to Behold*.

Self-grasping A conceptual mind that holds any phenomenon to be inherently existent. The mind of self-grasping gives rise to all other delusions such as anger and attachment. It is the root cause of all suffering and dissatisfaction. See *Joyful Path, Heart of Wisdom*, and *Ocean of Nectar*.

Sentient being Any being who possesses a mind that is contaminated by delusions or their imprints. Both 'sentient being' and 'living being' are terms used to distinguish beings whose minds are contaminated by any of the two obstructions from Buddhas, whose minds are completely free from these obstructions.

Seven-point posture of Vairochana A special posture for meditation in which parts of our body adopt a particular position: sitting on a comfortable cushion with the legs crossed in the vajra position, the back straight, the head inclined slightly forward, the eyes remaining open slightly gazing down the nose, the shoulders level, the mouth gently closed, and the right hand placed upon the left, palms up, four finger widths below the navel with the two thumbs touching just above the navel. See *Meaningful to Behold*.

Shantideva (AD 687-763) A great Indian Buddhist scholar and meditation master. He composed *Guide to the Bodhisattva's Way of Life*. See *Meaningful to Behold*.

Siddhi See *Attainment*.

Six perfections The perfections of giving, moral discipline, patience, effort, mental stabilization, and wisdom. They are called perfections because they are motivated by bodhichitta. See *Joyful Path, Meaningful to Behold*, and *Ocean of Nectar*.

Solitary Conqueror A type of Hinayana practitioner. Also known as 'Solitary Realizer'.

Stages of the path A systematic presentation of all the stages of the path to enlightenment. See *Joyful Path* and *A Meditation Handbook*.

Sugata Another term for a Buddha. It indicates that Buddhas have attained a state of immaculate and indestructible bliss.

Sukhavati Blissful Land – Pure Land of Amitabha.

Superior being 'Arya' in Sanskrit. A being who has a direct realization of emptiness. There are Hinayana Superiors and Mahayana Superiors.

Superior seeing A special wisdom that sees its object clearly and that is maintained by tranquil abiding and the special suppleness that is induced by investigation. See *Joyful Path*.

Supreme attainments See *Attainment*.

Sutra The teachings of Buddha that are open to everyone to practise. These include Buddha's teachings of the three Turnings of the Wheel of Dharma.

Tantra See *Secret Mantra*.

Tara A female Buddha who is the manifestation of the wind element of all Buddhas.

Tathagata Another name for Buddha.

Ten directions The four cardinal directions, the four intermediate directions, and the directions above and below.

Thangka A traditional painting of a Buddha.

Thirty-five Confession Buddhas Thirty-five Buddhas who have special powers to purify negativities and downfalls in those who recite their names with faith. See *The Bodhisattva Vow*.

Three Jewels The three objects of refuge: Buddha Jewel, Dharma Jewel, and Sangha Jewel. They are called 'Jewels' because they are both rare and precious. See *Joyful Path*.

Three realms The three levels within samsara: the desire realm, the form realm, and the formless realm.

Three times Past, present, and future.

Torma offering A special food offering made according to either Sutric or Tantric rituals.

Training the mind A special lineage of instructions deriving from Manjushri and passed down through Shantideva, Atisha, and the Kadampa Geshes, that emphasizes the generation of bodhichitta through the practices of equalizing and exchanging self with others combined with taking and giving. See *Universal Compassion*, *Joyful Path*, and *Meaningful to Behold*.

Tranquil abiding A concentration that possesses the special bliss of suppleness of body and mind that is attained in dependence upon completing the nine mental abidings. See *Clear Light of Bliss, Joyful Path,* and *Meaningful to Behold.*

Trijang Rinpoche A precious Tibetan Lama of the twentieth century who was an emanation of Buddha Shakyamuni, Heruka, Atisha, Amitabha, and Je Tsongkhapa. Also known as 'Trijang Dorjechang' and 'Losang Yeshe'.

True cessation The ultimate nature of a mind freed from any obstruction by means of a true path. See *Joyful Path* and *Heart of Wisdom.*

True origin An action or a delusion that is the main cause of a true suffering. See *Joyful Path* and *Heart of Wisdom.*

True path A spiritual path held by a wisdom directly realizing emptiness. See *Joyful Path* and *Heart of Wisdom.*

True suffering A contaminated object produced by delusions and karma. See *Joyful Path* and *Heart of Wisdom.*

Truth Body See *Buddha's bodies.*

Twelve sources The six powers (the eye sense power and so forth) and the six objects of those powers (visual forms and so forth). See *Heart of Wisdom* and *Ocean of Nectar.*

Twenty-four Holy Places Twenty-four special places in this world where the mandalas of Heruka and Vajrayogini still remain. They are: Puliramalaya, Dzalandhara, Odiyana, Arbuta, Godawari, Rameshöri, Dewikoti, Malawa, Kamarupa, Ote, Trishakune, Kosala, Kalinga, Lampaka, Kanchra, Himalaya, Pretapuri, Grihadewata, Shaurashtra, Suwanadvipa, Nagara, Sindhura, Maru, and Kuluta. See *Guide to Dakini Land.*

Two truths Conventional truth and ultimate truth.

Ultimate truth Synonymous with emptiness, lack of inherent existence. See *Ocean of Nectar* and *Joyful Path.*

Ushnisha A Buddha's crown protruberance. One of the thirty-two major signs.

Vairochana The manifestation of the form aggregate of all Buddhas. He has a white-coloured body.

Vajra Generally the Sanskrit word 'vajra' means indestructible like a diamond and powerful like a thunderbolt. In the context of Secret Mantra it means the indivisibility of method and wisdom.

Vajra and bell A ritual sceptre symbolizing great bliss and a ritual hand-bell symbolizing emptiness. See *Guide to Dakini Land.*

Vajra body Generally, the channels, inner winds, and drops. More specifically, the pure illusory body. The body of a Buddha is known as the 'resultant vajra body'. See *Clear Light of Bliss*.

Vajra brothers/sisters Practitioners who have received any Highest Yoga Tantra empowerment from the same Vajra Master, either at the same time or at different times. See *Guide to Dakini Land*.

Vajra posture The perfect cross-legged posture. See *Seven-point posture of Vairochana*.

Vajrayana The Secret Mantra vehicle.

Vajrayogini A Highest Yoga Tantra Deity who is the embodiment of indivisible bliss and emptiness. She is the same nature as Heruka. See *Guide to Dakini Land*.

Vast path The vast path includes all the method practices from the initial cultivation of compassion through to the final attainment of the Form Body of a Buddha. See *Joyful Path* and *Ocean of Nectar*.

Vasubhandu A great Buddhist scholar who was converted to the Mahayana by his brother, Asanga.

Vinaya Sutras Sutras in which Buddha principally explained the practice of moral discipline, and in particular the Pratimoksha moral discipline.

Vows Promises to refrain from certain actions. The three sets of vows are the Pratimoksha vows of individual liberation, the Bodhisattva vows, and the Secret Mantra vows. See *The Bodhisattva Vow* and *Guide to Dakini Land*.

Winds See *Inner winds*.

Wisdom being An actual Buddha, especially one who is invited to unite with a visualized commitment being.

Wishfulfilling jewel A legendary jewel that grants whatever is wished for.

Yamantaka A Highest Yoga Tantra Deity who is a wrathful manifestation of Manjushri.

Yidam See *Deity*.

Yoga A term used for various spiritual practices that entail maintaining a special view, such as Guru yoga and the yogas of eating, sleeping, dreaming, and waking. 'Yoga' also refers to union, such as the union of tranquil abiding and superior seeing.

Bibliography

Geshe Kelsang Gyatso is a highly respected meditation master and scholar of the Mahayana Buddhist tradition founded by Je Tsong-khapa. Since arriving in the UK in 1977, Geshe Kelsang has worked tirelessly to establish pure Buddhadharma in the West. Over this period he has given extensive teachings on the major scriptures of the Mahayana. These teachings are currently being published and provide a comprehensive presentation of the essential Sutra and Tantra practices of Mahayana Buddhism.

Books in print

The Bodhisattva Vow. The essential practices of Mahayana Buddhism. (Tharpa, 1991.)

Buddhism in the Tibetan Tradition. A guide to Tibetan Buddhism. (2nd. edn. Penguin, 1990.)

Clear Light of Bliss. A commentary to the practice of Mahamudra in Vajrayana Buddhism. (2nd. edn. Tharpa, 1992.)

Guide to Dakini Land. A commentary to the Highest Yoga Tantra practice of Venerable Vajrayogini. (Tharpa, 1991.)

Heart Jewel. A commentary to the essential practice of the New Kadampa Tradition of Mahayana Buddhism. (Tharpa, 1991.)

Heart of Wisdom. A commentary to the *Heart Sutra.* (3rd. edn. Tharpa, 1990.)

Joyful Path of Good Fortune. The stages of the path to enlightenment. (Tharpa, 1990.)

Meaningful to Behold. A commentary to Shantideva's *Guide to the Bodhisattva's Way of Life.* (3rd. edn. Tharpa, 1990.)

A Meditation Handbook. A practical guide to Buddhist meditation. (Tharpa, 1990.)

Universal Compassion. A commentary to Bodhisattva Chekhawa's *Training the Mind in Seven Points.* (2nd. edn. Tharpa, 1992.)

Forthcoming books

Essence of Vajrayana. A commentary to the Highest Yoga Tantra practice of Glorious Heruka.

Going for Refuge. An introduction to the practice of Buddhist refuge.

Great Mother of the Conquerors. A commentary to the *Perfection of Wisdom Sutras.*

Introduction to Buddhism. An explanation of the basic thought and practice of Buddhism.

Ocean of Nectar. A commentary to Chandrakirti's *Guide to the Middle Way.*

Tantric Grounds and Paths. An explanation of the grounds and paths of the four classes of Tantra.

Understanding the Mind. An explanation of the nature, types, and functions of mind.

Sadhanas

Geshe Kelsang is also supervising the translation of a collection of essential sadhanas. Those already in print include:

The Bodhisattva's Confession of Moral Downfalls. The purification practice of the *Mahayana Sutra of the Three Superior Heaps.*

Chenrezig Sadhana. Prayers and requests to the Buddha of compassion.

Dakini Yoga: Vajrayogini Six-Session Sadhana. Six-session Guru yoga combined with self-generation as Vajrayogini.

Essence of Good Fortune. Prayers for the six preparatory practices for meditation on the stages of the path to enlightenment.

Essence of Vajrayana. The condensed meaning of Vajrayana Mahamudra and prayers of request to the lineage Gurus.

Great Compassionate Mother. The sadhana of Arya Tara.

The Great Mother. A method to overcome hindrances and obstacles by reciting the *Essence of Wisdom Sutra* (the *Heart Sutra*).

Heart Jewel. The Guru yoga of Je Tsongkhapa combined with the condensed sadhana of his Dharma Protector.

The Hundreds of Deities of the Joyful Land. The Guru yoga of Je Tsongkhapa.

Medicine Guru Sadhana. The method for making requests to the Assembly of Seven Medicine Buddhas.

Offering to the Spiritual Guide. A special Guru yoga practice of Je Tsongkhapa's tradition (*Lama Chöpa Puja*).

The Quick Path. A condensed practice of Heruka Five Deities according to Master Ghantapa's tradition.

Wishfulfilling Jewel. The Guru yoga of Je Tsongkhapa combined with the sadhana of his Dharma Protector.

The Yoga of Buddha Amitayus. A special method for increasing lifespan, wisdom, and merit.

For a complete list of books and sadhanas by Geshe Kelsang Gyatso please write to:

Tharpa Publications
15 Bendemeer Road
London SW15 1JX
England

Study Programmes

Geshe Kelsang has prepared three study programmes based on his books: the General Programme, the Foundation Programme, and the Teacher Training Programme. These are designed to fulfil the wishes of those who would like to study Buddhism systematically and thereby deepen their experience of the essential practices.

The General Programme provides a basic introduction to Buddhist view, meditation, and action, and various kinds of teaching and practice from both Sutra and Tantra.

The Foundation Programme is designed for those who prefer a more structured approach to their spiritual training. Based on five of Geshe Kelsang's books, this programme lasts for approximately four years. The classes consist of readings, teachings, discussion, pujas, and meditations. Each subject concludes with an examination.

The Teacher Training Programme is designed for those who wish to train as authentic Dharma Teachers. This programme, which takes seven years to complete, is based on eleven of Geshe Kelsang's books. To qualify as Dharma Teachers, participants must complete the study of all eleven texts, pass an examination in each subject, satisfy certain criteria with regard to behaviour and life-style, and complete various meditation retreats.

These three programmes are taught at Centres of the New Kadampa Tradition in the UK, the US, and Europe. All these Centres are under the Spiritual Direction of Geshe Kelsang. The two main Centres are:

Manjushri Institute
Conishead Priory,
Ulverston,
Cumbria, LA12 9QQ, UK.
Tel 0229-54029
Founded 1975

Madhyamaka Centre
Kilnwick Percy Hall,
Pocklington,
York, YO4 2UF, UK.
Tel 0759-304832
Founded 1979

Addresses of all the other Centres are available from: James Belither, Chairman of the Education Council of the New Kadampa Tradition, Conishead Priory, Ulverston, Cumbria, LA12 9QQ, UK. Tel 0229-54029.

Index